DYSFUNCTION

Advance Praise for *Dysfunction*

Dennis McConaghy writes compellingly about the series of errors by corporate executives and politicians alike that led to the eventual rejection of the Keystone XL pipeline. Ultimately, Canada failed to achieve its economic interests because it failed to account for environmental interests. McConaghy suggests a better approach would be to implement an effective climate policy, based on a carbon tax, in exchange for an explicit commitment to market access. Many will question whether this trade-off is workable or even desirable, but as *Dysfunction* documents, the failure of the status quo is beyond doubt.

— MARK CAMERON, EXECUTIVE DIRECTOR,
CANADIANS FOR CLEAN PROSPERITY

While many will find the policy prescriptions offered by McConaghy contentious and difficult, his book presents an unparalleled opportunity to view the denouement of the Keystone XL pipeline from inside the executive suite of TransCanada.

— ANDREW LEACH, PROFESSOR, UNIVERSITY OF ALBERTA,
AND CHAIR, ALBERTA'S CLIMATE REVIEW PANEL

DYSFUNCTION

Canada after Keystone XL

DENNIS MCCONAGHY

DUNDURN
TORONTO

Cover image: istock.com/Hazlan Abdul Hakim
Printer: Webcom

Library and Archives Canada Cataloguing in Publication

McConaghy, Dennis, author

Dysfunction : Canada after Keystone XL / Dennis McConaghy.

Includes bibliographical references and index.
Issued in print and electronic formats.
ISBN 978-1-4597-3819-5 (paperback).--ISBN 978-1-4597-3820-1 (pdf).--ISBN 978-1-4597-3821-8 (epub)

1. Petroleum pipelines--Economic aspects--Canada. 2. Petroleum pipelines--Government policy--Canada. 3. Carbon dioxide mitigation--Government policy--Canada. I. Title.

TD195.P5M33 2017   665.5'44   C2016-906092-6
                                            C2016-906093-4

1 2 3 4 5   21 20 19 18 17

Conseil des Arts du Canada   Canada Council for the Arts

Canada

ONTARIO ARTS COUNCIL
CONSEIL DES ARTS DE L'ONTARIO
an Ontario government agency
un organisme du gouvernement de l'Ontario

We acknowledge the support of the **Canada Council for the Arts** and the **Ontario Arts Council** for our publishing program. We also acknowledge the financial support of the **Government of Ontario**, through the **Ontario Book Publishing Tax Credit** and the **Ontario Media Development Corporation**, and the **Government of Canada**.

Care has been taken to trace the ownership of copyright material used in this book. The author and the publisher welcome any information enabling them to rectify any references or credits in subsequent editions.

— *J. Kirk Howard, President*

The publisher is not responsible for websites or their content unless they are owned by the publisher.

Printed and bound in Canada.

VISIT US AT

dundurn.com | @dundurnpress | dundurnpress | dundurnpress

Dundurn
3 Church Street, Suite 500
Toronto, Ontario, Canada
M5E 1M2

In memory of Dr. Don Quon
Professor Emeritus
Chemical Engineering
University of Alberta

* * *

Dr. Quon did as much as anyone I ever met to help me
achieve whatever level of critical thinking and strategic
insight I was ever able to develop. Especially to understand
the real purpose of markets and their indispensability for
wealth creation. I owe him so much.

CONTENTS

INTRODUCTION

This was what retirement was meant to be: a sunny fall day in New York City, with a stunning view of the skyline from an Upper East Side high-rise. My daughter and son-in-law had gone to work, and I sat in their condo's living room, holding my extremely wide awake and chatty nine-month-old granddaughter, Isla. I'd flown in from my hometown of Calgary to babysit her for the weekend. Any time with her is precious and surprisingly inspiring.

I hadn't read or watched the news yet that day, so I didn't know anything that had happened until my Blackberry lit up with a barrage of messages. My former colleagues at the Calgary-based pipeline company TransCanada, along with other associates and friends, were all contacting me to tell me the same long-awaited news: President Barack Obama, via a formal statement from Secretary of State John Kerry, had rejected the Keystone XL (KXL) pipeline.[1]

I lowered Isla into her playpen, where she managed to amuse herself, while I tried to compose a concise op-ed piece expressing what President Obama's rejection represented.[2] I had expected Obama to deny KXL's presidential permit for well over a year. Perhaps so had the executive team at TransCanada, although a week earlier TransCanada's CEO, Russ Girling, had attempted to have the KXL decision deferred in a desperate last effort to preserve the project.[3] A reporter from Canadian Press had interviewed me the day after Girling's attempt about a proposal I had put forward that involved Canada's newly elected prime minister, Justin Trudeau, implementing a carbon-pricing regime, which would, thereby, change the dynamic of the KXL debate enough for President Obama to rationalize an approval.[4] However, Girling's request was denied.[5] Prime Minister Trudeau took office far too late to make any difference. President Obama had, apparently, decided to reject KXL as a symbolic gesture, to position himself as a climate hero before the United Nations' climate summit in Paris, only three weeks away.

Although this ultimate decision was no surprise, it dismayed me greatly. I felt a substantial sadness — one I hadn't expected. I had an immense amount invested in this pipeline project, professionally and emotionally. In 2007, as TransCanada's executive vice-president responsible for pipeline business development, I had helped lay the commercial groundwork for the 1,897-kilometre pipeline that was to extend from central Alberta, south to Nebraska, and then on to refineries in the American Gulf Coast. KXL was designed to move, via a 36-inch steel pipeline, more than 800,000 barrels per day (bbl/d) of crude oil — primarily diluted bitumen derived from Alberta's oil sands and potentially other volumes from Montana and North Dakota. The exuberance and confidence with which TransCanada's executive and board had once pursued the project was now painful to recall.

If this description of KXL evokes a mundane piece of infrastructure, unworthy of a book, unworthy of hundreds of print media articles, extensive electronic media time, and untold quantities of social media advocacy and rebuttal — it was. Or at least it should have been. But since 2011, Keystone XL had become practically a household name. Certainly, it had become an icon of resistance for the environmental movement. Furthermore, it had also become an emblem of political dysfunction for the hydrocarbon industry. By 2015, KXL was the most famous pipeline in North America, if not the only famous pipeline. On November 6, 2015, after seven years of regulatory process and political intervention, the pipeline's fate was ultimately sealed when President Obama finally made a decision. An agonizing and disingenuous charade was over.

After reading the news that day, I looked at my granddaughter, who was clearly tired of playing by herself, and clamouring for my attention. She gave me some perspective. Of course there was more to life than this one pipeline. But the world had just changed — more materially than many would acknowledge. Much of the environmental movement was already celebrating KXL's demise as a genuine step toward a decarbonized future.[6] To be clear, I believe that greenhouse gas emissions from human activity increase the risk of climate change. It is a risk that must be dealt with. However, KXL's rejection was unfair and disproportionate, a major blow to Canada's economy — and worse because in itself its cancellation was a solely symbolic act, without real consequence for seriously dealing with the risk of climate change.

|

The story of Keystone XL began back in the early part of 2007. At that time, my colleagues at TransCanada and I believed that the company would be able to simply apply to the appropriate regulatory entities for necessary permits, and then, within a reasonable time frame, proceed with constructing KXL. Operations would likely begin, we believed, as soon as late 2012.

In our estimation, KXL had no fundamentally special elements differentiating it from comparable pipelines that traversed most of North America. It was merely a logical extension of the base Keystone system, for which the company would soon receive the necessary permits from the same regulatory entities that would next adjudicate KXL. Construction of base Keystone would commence while we prepared and submitted the regulatory applications for KXL. Base Keystone was to connect the Alberta oil sands to the United States mid-continent, and KXL would extend that reach to the U.S. Gulf Coast. That market access and the overall scale of the project were enormously significant for the Alberta oil sands industry's long-term economic prospects. At TransCanada, we were genuinely excited about the project, as a private economic opportunity and also as essential infrastructure for Canada.[7]

TransCanada applied for permission to build KXL in September 2008,[8] and even in mid-2009, no one seriously imagined that this pipeline project might be rejected. Yet when I retired in mid-2014, the approval still remained unresolved, despite over five years of review. The project needed a presidential permit from Barack Obama to cross the Canadian border into the United States — a permit that was supposed to be predicated on an environmental impact assessment and a National Interest Determination (NID) process led by the U.S. Department of State (DoS). The U.S. government's vesting of the final decision with the president himself was meant to expedite the approval process, but in this case leaving the decision with the president had had the opposite effect. When I retired in late 2014, I had come to the view that the Obama administration would likely reject the project, despite the DoS's two separate, extensive environmental assessments, in 2011 and 2014, that consistently found the project environmentally acceptable, albeit with certain special operating conditions, to which TransCanada had agreed.[9] Environmentalist resistance to the project and the president's response to that resistance had, incredibly, proved decisive. It was a triumph of symbolism over substance and reasonable expectation of due process.

So, when the project I had so enthusiastically contributed to conceiving and planning, the project that had once seemed so valuable for the continent, and especially to Canada, my company, and, yes, me personally, was formally rejected, I asked myself the questions I had pondered so many times: How and why did this happen? Why did TransCanada persist so intensely? Why did we meet ultimate failure and unprecedented notoriety? These questions deserve substantial analysis and rationalization. The first part of this book sets out to provide that, directly and fairly.

II

A specific confluence of events precipitated KXL's demise — Nebraska's resistance to the company's route through the state, the breakdown of the Kyoto Treaty and subsequent failure of the 2009 Copenhagen conference to find a viable alternative, U.S. Congress's 2010 failure to enact an economy-wide cap-and-trade bill to deal with carbon emissions, a few highly publicized oil spills, the basic reality of the higher carbon intensity of oil sands–derived crude oil, a regulatory process vesting ultimately with President Obama, and failure in both countries to find an accommodation to rationalize its approval. Was this pipeline's rejection an anomalous experience or a harbinger of things to come? Has social acceptance of the oil sands resource been lost?

The Alberta oil sands resource offers Canada a great economic opportunity; more than $200 billion of investment in production and related facilities over the last twenty years is a testament to that.[10] In 2016, notwithstanding current low commodity prices, production has continued at over two million bbl/d.[11] Without KXL, is Canada prepared to go forward with alternatives such as the Northern Gateway, Energy East, and TransMountain pipeline projects? Although those projects may not represent the same value to Canada as KXL could have, the economic potential of the oil sands resource cannot be realized without them.

Of course, if Canada fully exploits this potential, Canadian carbon emissions will grow; that is an inescapable reality in the short and medium term.[12] We need to rationalize that growth to a world committed to dealing with the risk of climate change. Producing and consuming hydrocarbons cause increasing risk of climate change. Yet, those hydrocarbons still provide great economic value. Whether the world can significantly decrease its demand for hydrocarbons, especially crude oil and natural gas, over the remainder of this century is an open question.

As well, it must be conceded that the oils sands resource emits more carbon on a unit basis than most other crudes in its production processes. This carbon intensity is perhaps the fundamental reason for the unique hostility directed at this Canadian resource, culminating, even within Canada, in an implacable resistance to its exploitation.

However, Canadians should be able to support hydrocarbon development, provided the country adopts a credible and proportionate carbon policy. Unfortunately, this is not the case at present. The hydrocarbon industry and several successive governments have failed to show Canadians adequately that resource development not only serves their economic self-interest but can be managed within an acceptable climate-policy framework, comparable and proportionate to those embraced by other relevant countries, especially the United States.

Canadians remain largely misinformed about oil sands carbon emissions and the economic consequences of extreme carbon policy. Sadly, much of the animosity over the oil sands is now aimed at obstructing the regulatory processes related to hydrocarbon infrastructure, with opposition to KXL serving as the template for that larger struggle. National, non-partisan regulators adjudicate the costs and benefits of hydrocarbon infrastructure projects, but their authority is increasingly diminished if not entirely undermined by legal obstruction, outright civil disobedience, and a lack of political will. Dysfunction has become the default. How much economic opportunity is Canada prepared to lose?

The demise of KXL should force Canada to come to terms with the difficult issues created by the loss of that project. The second part of this book is dedicated to confronting those issues. What has the pipeline's demise cost Canada? What can, and must, Canada learn from the experience? Do Canadians agree with the reasons President Obama gave when he rejected KXL? Where do we stand on our other pipeline projects, such as the Northern Gateway pipeline through British Columbia and Energy East to New Brunswick, in the wake KXL's demise? Even more fundamentally, where does Canada stand on hydrocarbon development at all?

III

The environmental movement insists that Canada reduce its carbon emissions principally by limiting oil sands and natural gas development,[13] yet the increased emissions due to Canada's oils sands production are insignificant in the context of global greenhouse gas (GHG) emissions.[14] Moreover, according to credible forecasts of global crude oil demand until mid-century, world demand for crude oil continues, and will very likely exceed current levels, notwithstanding improving energy efficiency in North America.[15] Animus toward hydrocarbon development has ingrained itself into our political culture, despite its inherent economic value. Yet it is unclear whether the world can accept substantially more expensive alternatives to crude oil in order to emit less carbon, or to accept the real economic cost of dealing with the climate-change risk on the terms implicit in the current U.N. process.[16] Yet the environmental movement insists with moral certitude that current generations must now accept such costs to stabilize, if not reduce, carbon emissions in absolute terms.

Admittedly, the hydrocarbon industry exhibits hypocrisies when it comes to dealing with climate change. Industry leaders broadly acknowledge risk of climate change but rarely endorse specific policy to deal with it credibly. Why advocate for higher costs while society's capacity to accept those costs is still in doubt? That somewhat cynical but not illogical reasoning only incites an enraged environmental movement to take more extreme positions on policy, and to employ more extreme tactics to manipulate public opinion. All of this points to a pervasive dysfunction in North America. We have lost our capacity to reconcile legitimate economic self-interest with proportionate policy to deal with a valid environmental risk. Political polarization has eroded this capacity.

Yet for Canada, I see a rational path forward. The latter part of this book lays out that path. People ask me whether oil and gas executives are climate-change deniers, and I say no: I believe them to be extremely intelligent and well-informed people. They are more capable than most to appreciate that the carbon emitted by human consumption of hydrocarbons raises GHG concentrations in the atmosphere, increasing the risk of climate change. But they live in a world where they have to deliver quarterly results, and serious action to deal with this climate-change risk will cost their companies in the short and medium term. So, oil and gas executives agonize: they can't reasonably deny the science or the risk, but they have typically chosen not to advocate actual policy to address that risk credibly. They are ultimately paid for financial results, not elegant, inspired carbon policy. But the KXL experience has shown us that in today's world neither may be possible without the other.

As a retired industry executive, I can say publicly what I believe would serve the national interest. I believe that carbon pricing is the pre-eminent policy tool for dealing with the risk of climate change and the only reasonable way forward for Canada. Expectations of dealing with climate, both within Canada and internationally, require that hydrocarbons reflect economically the unaccounted-for costs related to their consumption and production. A carbon tax can best do that. For Canada, that means a tax based on genuine scientific consensus, considerations of current economic affordability, and the comparable efforts of relevant trading nations, especially the United States.

Many in the hydrocarbon industry understand the intellectual underpinnings of a tax, but they ask what they would get for it in terms of market access and improved social acceptance. For most environmental advocates, proposed carbon taxes are never high enough, nor are they sufficient without hard targets to contain actual emissions. Is there a way to find a compromise between these adversaries? This book is devoted to finding a viable compromise — a common ground that satisfies both positions. If Canada cannot find that, if we learn nothing from losing KXL, then more dysfunction and economic atrophy will follow.

My career has been devoted to hydrocarbon infrastructure development, most notably KXL, and as I write this book I still have a financial interest in TransCanada. I don't apologize for my career; it has afforded me a perspective from which I see that the risk of climate change and related carbon policy to deal with it could pose nothing less than an existential threat to hydrocarbon development, and especially to Canadian hydrocarbon development. But radical intervention would cause significant economic costs in the short and medium term. Only gradualism and genuine compromise will allow us to deal rationally with the risk.

PART ONE

MORE SINNED AGAINST THAN SINNING
— *King Lear* – Act 3, Scene 2

CHAPTER ONE

GETTING TO KEYSTONE XL

Beginnings

I believe myself to be the typical Albertan. I was born in Edmonton, Alberta, Canada, in 1952. My life has roughly spanned the same sixty-five years as Alberta's modern hydrocarbon industry. My parents were both working class, yet I never believed it beyond my reach to transcend the economic limits of my parents, or to do so relatively simply. Still, I did not have the luxury to pursue an impractical education, and so, with an aptitude for mathematics, I went to engineering school. In the late 1960s, my family could afford my university education largely because it was substantially subsidized by the revenues available from Alberta's hydrocarbon endowment, all sanctioned by the profoundly conservative provincial governments of the 1950s and 1960s. I studied chemical engineering, completed graduate school in 1975, and began a career in the hydrocarbon industry.

Before the famous oil strike at Leduc, however, Alberta was an entirely different place from the prosperous province I have known for virtually all of my life. I learned about that former Alberta from my parents, both raised in rural areas of the province in the 1920s and 1930s. My father was born outside Edmonton near the turn of the century, and my mother was born in Poland before her family immigrated to Alberta in the 1930s. Neither had any significant formal education, and they both knew humble lives in an Alberta reliant primarily on agriculture and forestry. Like many Albertans, my parents both left rural life for the city in the late 1940s, and they met in Edmonton. My father served in the Canadian Armed Forces in the Second World War, returning from Holland and Italy in 1945; two years later, in 1947, the oil discovery at Leduc validated Alberta as significant hydrocarbon production location.[1]

By the mid-1950s, the province was developing and constructing the first pipelines to move Alberta's oil across the continent. Then, as now, the provincial government owned the resources and extracted significant revenues from the industry via royalties, lease payments, and other taxes.[2] Alberta's affluence gave rise to a long-standing conservative political culture, not unlike that found in oil-producing American states such as Texas and Oklahoma — a basic symbiosis between the hydrocarbon industry and the body politic. Until the 2015 election of a left-leaning New Democratic Party (NDP) government, Alberta elected right-of-centre political leadership for roughly eighty years: first the Social Credit Party from 1935 to 1971, and then the arguably more moderate Progressive Conservative (PC) Party from 1971 until 2015. Albertans have always understood what the hydrocarbon industry means: affluence, relative to Canada's other provinces, that manifests itself in abundant public services and infrastructure, traditionally lower taxes, including no provincial sales tax, and, of course, enduring employment and investment opportunities. When I was growing up, even Albertans who didn't directly participate in the industry knew the option was there for their children. That same affluence created a distinct and often tense relationship between Alberta and central Canada, quintessentially represented by the federal Liberal party.

In the early 1970s, world oil prices rose to over $10/bbl (U.S. dollars per barrel) — the world's first "oil-price shock" — caused by the collective action of the oil cartel known as the Organization of Petroleum Exporting Countries (OPEC).[3] Throughout the 1960s and early 1970s, the price of oil had remained in the range of $2 or $3/bbl, in nominal dollars. Then OPEC, dominated by the Middle Eastern oil producers, made production cuts that caused supply and demand to rebalance at higher price levels, thereby creating a significant transfer of wealth from the world's oil consumers to producers. The price shock also created a period of perceived energy crisis that led to various initiatives for energy independence, especially in the United States. But for Canada, which had no issue with energy self-sufficiency, the price shock led to a protracted period of acrimonious struggle between Alberta's Conservative government and Canada's Liberal government over how to raise the domestic price of oil to world levels, and over what jurisdiction owned the majority of the associated economic rent (returns in excess of what would justify investment).[4] This dynamic was exacerbated by the second oil-price shock in the late 1970s, which sent world oil prices to even higher levels.[5]

Such was the political and economic environment in May 1980, when I received an offer to join Alberta Gas Trunkline. That Calgary-based natural gas pipeline company would be renamed Nova before merging with TransCanada Pipelines in the late 1990s. Just as I was settling into Calgary in 1980, Prime Minister Pierre Elliott Trudeau was, surprisingly, re-elected, defeating a brief Conservative government that had been more aligned with Alberta and industry positions on hydrocarbon pricing and export access. Trudeau imposed the National Energy Program (NEP) — infamous in Alberta still as memories of Leduc No. 1 are fondly recollected — a complicated set of initiatives designed to reallocate a higher portion of hydrocarbon revenues to the federal treasury, maintain some price subsidization within Canada, and increase Canadian ownership in the resource sector.[6] The second OPEC price shock had tripled prices to levels approaching $40/bbl. Trudeau wanted to moderate that price shock for the rest of Canada, a policy that would result in Alberta receiving less than the world price for its hydrocarbon resources. The NEP also sought to appropriate a greater share for the federal government of the economic rents from hydrocarbon production in Canada. Hydrocarbon pricing had not yet been fully deregulated, and governments controlled pricing; the evolution to market pricing across North America would take the rest of the decade. The NEP not only reallocated economic rent between Ottawa and Alberta but also increased the fiscal burden on the industry. The resulting animosity between Alberta and rest of the country arguably colours, perhaps even dominates, the province's politics up to the present. Alberta's ethos has traditionally been distinguished by comparative affluence and opportunity but also by conflict and grievance with the rest of the country.

However, through the rest of the 1980s, hydrocarbon prices were deregulated across North America. A transparent commodity market for hydrocarbons subsequently emerged. Within Canada, material constraints on hydrocarbon exports were gradually removed. And most importantly for Alberta, the advent of a federal Conservative government in 1984 resulted in an end to the acrimonious and arduous negotiations with the federal government that had stretched out over almost fifteen years. A settlement was finally reached, which culminated in an acceptable accommodation on the sharing of the economic rents from Alberta's hydrocarbon resources. Alberta reaffirmed ownership rights, and it would control resource development and derive most of the economic value from that development, with the federal government relying on federal income and corporate taxes, interprovincial transfers, and monetary policy as its principal mechanisms to deal with macroeconomic impacts of hydrocarbon commodity prices within Canada. Ottawa cancelled the various special taxes it had formulated under the National Energy Board (NEB) that tried to replicate the Alberta royalty. Importantly for the future, Alberta would control how those resources were developed within its own borders. That would become profoundly important for oil sands development.[7]

During the 1970s and 1980s, policy debates about hydrocarbons had little if anything to do with climate change. The key issues were whether or not industry could unearth enough hydrocarbons (the very essence of the "energy crisis") and how they would be priced — relying on free markets rather than regulation. Hydrocarbons were fundamental to the world's geopolitics and macroeconomic conditions, reflecting the inherent economic value hydrocarbons provided modern nation states. Adjusting to higher prices proved a difficult economic transition, but it never occurred to anyone that social acceptance of hydrocarbon use could become an issue. For the first decade of my professional career in the hydrocarbon industry, the issue of climate change was simply non-existent for me, and for the various executives, engineers, lawyers, and other professionals I worked with every day.

I clearly remember the first time carbon emissions and the risk of climate effects were raised in a business meeting. It was in 1990. That meeting took place in a boardroom on the thirty-sixth floor of then Nova building in downtown Calgary, now known as the Nexen building, named after a subsidiary of the Chinese National Offshore Oil Corporation (CNOOC). We sat right on the western edge of downtown, with the most amazing view of the mountains and city, a typically bright blue sky, snow-capped mountains on the horizon, with the west side of Calgary in the foreground blending into the southern Alberta foothills. The Canadian and Alberta governments had requested from Nova an estimate of the potential greenhouse gas emissions from our facilities, in order to measure the scale and source of Canadian carbon emissions. In gas pipelines, compressors move the product through the pipe, and we power those compressors by burning gas. That process creates the emissions we were to measure — a first sign that the federal government was responding to climate-change risk.[8]

NASA scientist James Hansen had already delivered his now historic testimony before the U.S. Congress, in which he warned about the dangers of global warming.[9] At roughly the same time in the late 1980s, the World Meteorological Organization (WMO) and the United Nations Environment Program (UNEP) established the Intergovernmental Panel on Climate Change (IPCC), the pre-eminent scientific organization to provide assessments as the scientific underpinning of future international climate negotiations. By the early 1990s, the United Nations had established its process to deal with the risk — the United Nations Framework Convention on Climate Change (UNFCCC), to which Canada was to be a signatory.[10]

But those of us assembled that morning in 1990, in the NOVA boardroom, seemingly had no sense that dealing with this climate-change risk could become antithetical to the economic interests of the hydrocarbon industry. In any event, the Canadian industry began to measure its emissions. But the world's attempts to deal with that risk continued to exert little, if any, apparent impact on hydrocarbon related investment decisions through the 1990s.

The Kyoto Protocol on climate change emerged out of the UNFCCC process,[11] and in late 1997 Liberal Prime Minister Jean Chrétien committed Canada to Kyoto's targets, leaving subsequent governments to figure out how to actually achieve the specific emission reductions implicit in such targets.[12] As I will discuss at length in chapter three, the Kyoto Protocol was intended to materially contain the risk of the Earth's temperature increasing more than 2 °C above the average throughout pre-industrial human history. Developed countries generally had to reduce their GHG emissions by about 5 percent compared with 1990 levels between 2008 and 2012. For Canada, achieving the targets imposed by the protocol would prove very difficult, if not entirely implausible. As the Liberal federal government tried between 2000 and 2006 to find commitments from key economic sectors to comply with Kyoto, industry consistently made the case that it could not or should not contract its scale or structure to comply: we either "keep the lights on or we don't," they declared, adding, "we extract value or others will." Few, if any, economic compliance mechanisms existed. Moreover, the United States rejected participating in the protocol after the election of President George W. Bush, despite having been a key driving force in Kyoto's development.

By the late 1990s, I personally began to consider how global concern over carbon emissions might affect the pipeline industry and, more broadly, the hydrocarbon industry. Were governments serious about containing the risk, and what would that mean for hydrocarbons, the demand for which was only increasing on a global basis?[13] How much short-run cost would the world be willing to assume to contain a risk that was still uncertain and contentious in terms of its impact and timing? Those concerns felt very abstract to us in our executive offices, and to most Albertans and Canadians.

Although hydrocarbon prices were modest throughout most of the 1990s, Alberta remained one of Canada's most affluent provinces. World demand for hydrocarbons continued to grow steadily into the new millennium, particularly due to demand from various emerging economies, notably China. With that came a real prospect of substantially higher prices that would improve the economic viability of Alberta's oil sands resource and natural gas potential. As TransCanada merged with NOVA in 1998, becoming one of the continent's largest pipeline companies in terms of assets and geography, those of us working for the company were not fundamentally concerned with how the U.N. process to deal with the climate-change risk could materially impact our company's, Alberta's, or Canada's economic prospects. Nevertheless, Canada's commitment to Kyoto created the same basic dilemma between climate commitments and economic potential that continues today.

Inside TransCanada: A Pipeline Company

Alberta Gas Trunkline, renamed NOVA in the early 1980s, merged with TransCanada in 1998. NOVA's primary role had been to gather gas from producers in western Canada, while TransCanada transported gas long haul to consumption markets across North America. Together they formed a single company that would substantially consolidate Canada's major gathering and long-distance infrastructure for transporting natural gas. I stayed with the merged entity and was fortunate to find myself in an exciting new phase of my career. TransCanada employs many talented and dedicated professionals, mostly engineers but also regulatory and financial specialists. I ascended to the senior leadership ranks of the company by 2001, moving into an office on the newly constructed TransCanada tower's third floor, with its gleaming maple-panelled executive offices and boardrooms. Over the years, I held various senior executive positions, primarily related to the business development of new pipeline infrastructure, corporate strategy, and business unit commercial operations. My career applied the actual engineering I had studied at university indirectly, as I typically led interdisciplinary teams to advance specific projects and business results. The focus of my work has been the planning and commercial realization of major pipeline projects.

Since Alberta has no access to tidewater, transporting its hydrocarbon production via pipelines across the continent is an integral determinant in realizing Alberta's economic potential. Pipelines offer economically efficient and environmentally responsible transport for hydrocarbons over long distances at high volumes, even across various challenging topographies such as water crossings and mountainous terrain.[14] The scale of North American hydrocarbon infrastructure is a testament to that. The basic pipelining technology of hydrocarbons has been well established for well over a century, and its efficacy is not fundamentally disputed by any knowledgeable and fair-minded analyst of transportation alternatives,[15] notwithstanding the occasional occurrence of spills and ruptures.

TransCanada's "mainline" linked western Canadian gas producers to markets in eastern Canada and the northeastern United States. Other infrastructure provided access for Canadian gas to northern California and Chicago. By 2010, my colleagues and I had established TransCanada as a major North American natural gas transmission company, with various acquisitions of transmissions systems in the United States, in addition to the significant position created from the 1998 merger of Canadian transmission assets. The company operated infrastructure in the U.S. Gulf Coast, mid-continent, and Mexico, in addition to its historic geographies. One of the core "blue-chip" holdings in the Canadian equity market, TransCanada, nevertheless, had no unique public profile among the general public within Canada, let alone the United States. Of course, that would change as the decade unfolded, with the advent of KXL.[16]

Just as my life's trajectory forms a typical Albertan narrative, reflecting typical Alberta political attitudes, I feel confident saying the same for most of my colleagues within TransCanada's senior management ranks. Most were raised and educated and began their careers in Alberta, where for six decades hydrocarbon resource development has provided a broadly shared affluence for many, if not most, of its citizens. I worked most closely with Hal Kvisle, CEO of TransCanada until Russ Girling took over in 2010.

Kvisle was a near-perfect professional colleague for me, a gifted executive with extensive operating expertise and a real capacity for strategic insight and action. Like me, he had a modest childhood in rural Alberta, and also had similar engineering and commercial education and work experience. On his watch, various transformative projects and initiatives, such as the Alaska and MacKenzie gas pipelines, the Bruce Power investment, the company's Mexican gas transmission infrastructure and, eventually, KXL, were conceived and developed.

Kvisle retired from TransCanada in 2010, before KXL evolved into a high-profile *cause célèbre*. Girling, who became the face of TransCanada during the entire Keystone XL experience, succeeded him. About ten years younger than I am, Girling studied commerce rather than engineering, and completed his schooling in the mid-1980s. I first crossed paths with him back then, when he worked at Dome and Suncor, two prominent hydrocarbon production companies of the period. He struck me even then as dedicated, studious, and self-effacing. He worked as a gas marketer, and then moved to an affiliate of TransCanada, where he built up their electric power generation business. When I joined TransCanada in 1998, he had just been appointed the company's chief financial officer.

Girling, Kvisle, and I led the organization through most of its major pipeline developments over the period of 2000 to 2010, while Don Wishart, another Albertan, was head of engineering operations and project implementation. Kristine Delkus, the company's senior regulatory lawyer, another key colleague, had the formidable task of dealing with the various regulatory processes impacting the company, both on existing assets and proposed projects.

Alex Pourbaix, a talented lawyer by education, and also a native Albertan, was more extroverted and affable than many of the TransCanada senior management team. He would become a key player in the KXL saga after mid-2010, when Girling became CEO, and Pourbaix became the senior executive responsible for TransCanada's crude oil business.

In addition to the inescapable Albertan ethos of its executive team, TransCanada's corporate culture is typical of any large North American energy company, insofar as it is dominated by engineers. Engineers expect to solve problems rationally, based on relevant facts, accepted scientific theory, reasonable extrapolation, basic decision criteria of expected benefits relative to expected costs, and due process. They strive for efficiency and robustness, all contextualized numerically. Moreover, in the energy industry, people are taken at their word. Pragmatism rules. Russ Girling, even with his commerce background, was perhaps the most pragmatic of us all within the leadership ranks of TransCanada, trying to seize reasonable opportunities to advance the company financially, consistent with its basic competencies and competitive advantages.

We expected business to unfold rationally and reasonably predictably. That was the norm for most of the roughly thirty years of my career, up to the advent of KXL. Hydrocarbon pipelines across North America received regulatory sanction according to expected due process, without undue political attention, and with reasonable operating conditions. The basic process of developing and constructing major pipeline infrastructure was the essential competence within TransCanada that had evolved over fifty years.

Before TransCanada's project and construction engineers can actually build a pipeline, the company requires regulatory sanction. And before the company applies for permits, it requires a design, environmental assessments, and contracts with counterparties, owners of the commodities that the pipelines were designed to move — in KXL's case, oil sands-derived crude oil.

The design engineers typically first provide a preliminary cost estimate to the business development team, which then strives to complete acceptable commercial terms with the appropriate counterparties. Those terms can include a myriad of considerations and commercial trade-offs, but fundamental terms typically include basic pricing structure for service. A regulatory approval team comprising lawyers, engineers, and various environmental experts strive to acquire the necessary sanctions to actually use the route. Ultimately, construction engineers build the pipeline. Acquiring approvals for a pipeline the scale of KXL now costs in the hundreds of millions of dollars. The process includes extensive field studies assessing existing marine, wildlife, terrain, and groundwater conditions, with special concern for threatened and endangered species potentially impacted by route alternatives. All of this is to determine the incremental environmental impacts of the project.

A selected route will likely pass through privately owned land, often in use for agriculture or other activities. The right to lay pipe through owners' land is typically acquired by negotiating with the owners for right-of-way easements. An easement allows the company to construct, operate, and maintain a pipeline within a landowner's property. Responsibility for its ultimate remediation and ongoing stewardship as long as the pipeline operates is also a requirement imposed on pipeline companies. TransCanada negotiates with individual landowners to find appropriate financial remuneration to gain access to their property to lay a pipeline through it; such settlements are factored into the cost of the project.

A whole system of surface rights jurisprudence has evolved and governs this process of accessing land for pipelines and to establish of value access when consensual agreement is not achievable.[17] If pipelines are ultimately deemed in the public interest, access can be obtained despite the potential resistance of certain landowners. If negotiations fail, a company can "expropriate" the land along a pipeline route — the United States uses the less appealing term "condemn" — and then an ultimate money settlement is imposed and access provided. But when selecting routes at TransCanada, the company seeks to minimize the impact of construction, and after construction, it seeks to restore the land as completely as possible. Historically, TransCanada has rarely needed to resort to expropriation or condemnation.

For its pipeline developments, the company does much more than negotiate with individual landowners to acquire land, specific access, and right-of-way. The process includes approaching directly impacted communities to provide as much information as possible about emergency response, how we deal with spills, and the whole litany of legitimate questions and concerns that a pipeline raises. TransCanada does not take route selection lightly, nor does it trivialize or dismiss out of hand legitimate stakeholder and environmental concerns. The company accounts for those concerns as reasonably as possible while maintaining an economically viable project. Ultimately, its experts make a determination that proposed mitigations can be commercially accommodated, which is in turn validated by senior management.

The Advent of Keystone

By 2005, a significant opportunity had evolved for TransCanada to branch out from gas transmission, extending its competencies to crude oil transport, specifically, developing major infrastructure for transporting crude oil derived from the northern Alberta oil sands to refineries in the United States. The oil sands were forecast to produce more crude oil than Canada's existing oil pipelines could accommodate other than by constructing a major expansion, an expectation of production levels on the order of three million barrels a day by the middle of the next decade.[18] TransCanada believed it could be competitive in providing the required new crude oil pipeline infrastructure. The resulting investment would conform to its preferred investment criteria and risk/reward preferences and potentially provide the company with another substantial strategic business platform for future sustainable growth.

I had long been acquainted with the oil sands resource. In the summer of 1973, just before entering graduate school, I had worked for Syncrude, a joint venture oil sands production company, at their research facility on the outskirts of Edmonton. The company would soon proceed with the first major commercial "unconventional" oil sands production facility.

Crude derived from the oil sands is called "unconventional" oil because producing it requires more than simply drilling wells into reservoirs and allowing the reservoir's innate pressure to propel the oil to the surface. Oil sands are, literally, deposits of sand coated with thick, black, heavy oil, otherwise known as bitumen. Oil sands deposits cover an enormous area of northeastern Alberta. Some of the resource can be accessed by surface mining, but most of the resource is too deep to mine economically. Various in situ (literally, in place) recovery technologies have been developed. For most of the twentieth century, the technological

Dusk at Suncor Millennium Mine.

challenge became how to separate the sand and bitumen, with a technology that could be both potentially economic and scalable. Even though these technologies were optimized over time (most notably with the Clark hot water and SAGD, "steam assisted gravity drainage," processes), their costs relative to the price of crude oil remained problematic for most of the twentieth century. Before oil prices rose significantly in the first decade of the new millennium, oil sands exploitation remained economically challenged.[19]

To recover the Alberta oil sands' viscous bitumen, producers either mine the bitumen before processing and refining it into synthetic crude oil, or produce the bitumen in situ by injecting steam into the reservoirs and retrieving the flowing bitumen. Strip mining requires removing the "overburden," which includes trees and shrubs, to expose the oil sands underneath. This sand is mined in chunks, hauled away on belts, and stirred in massive vessels with heated water from the nearby Athabasca River. The heat and the motion cause the oil and the sand to separate. Bitumen, viscous black oil, rises to the top, sand sinks to the bottom, and in between remain "middlings," water mixed with whatever oil and sediment failed to separate. The bitumen is skimmed off and refined into synthetic crude in a reactor; heat and catalytic metals break the long chain carbon molecules and add hydrogen to make the oil lighter. The sand is eventually moved into tailings ponds, which are lined with impermeable plastic materials to prevent groundwater contamination. The middlings undergo more processing to retrieve further bitumen. In the summer of 1973, I worked on a technology called secondary centrifuging, designed to extract more oil from the middlings and to reclaim as much water as possible.[20]

It is important to realize that the oil sands resource represents a world-scale inventory of crude oil, rivalling the reserves of even the Middle East.[21] The issue was always how much could be economically recovered.

In the late 1970s, Syncrude's private sector participants, along with the Alberta government, the Ontario government, and the federal government, invested in large-scale (for its time) oil sands development. In retrospect, we can see that this investment was enormously risky. Yet, Alberta gained the benefit of initial investment, which the price shock of the late 1970s helped justify. This initial investment contributed significantly to the eventual optimization of technology for mining oil sands. As well, leading up to 2000, in situ technology continued to advance via various pilots and smaller-scale commercial projects, despite challenging geology and economics. Considerable public sector funding helped develop in situ technology, a credit to the various provincial governments who sustained this commitment.

Environmentalists have now elevated the oil sands to a special status of climate and environmental opprobrium — infamy, really — however, until the late 1990s, oil sands production was minimal, even in North American terms, and virtually unknown outside the hydrocarbon industry. For much of the period between 1980 and 2000, the world oil price remained too low for the resource to attract significant investment attention, even as basic technology improvements were achieved. But as world crude demand increased into the new millennium, the price of oil rose in excess of $60/bbl, with the reasonable prospect of even higher sustained price levels over the longer term.

This view of the future price environment, coupled with technology improvements, became the fundamental drivers of significant commercial-scale oil sands investment. The potential economic rent from a price environment rising above $80/bbl and an anticipated cost structure in the range of $60/bbl would be sufficient to attract investment despite the still formidable risks of oil sands development. This rationalization would lead to significant oil sands investment in the 2000s, in excess of $200 billion as of 2016.[22] Crude oil prices in excess of $80/bbl would persist for most of the period from 2006 to 2014.[23] Subsequent Alberta and federal governments welcomed this investment, providing reasonable fiscal regimes as well as reasonable environmental assessment and oversight processes.[24] The oil sands flourished in the new millennium, in keeping with Prime Minister Stephen Harper's vision of Canada as an emerging "energy superpower." At the time, a claim with real credibility.[25]

By the mid-2000s, projections for northern Alberta's crude production justified new transportation infrastructure.[26] The producers needed high-volume pipelines to export oil sands-derived crude oil to the mid-continent and to Gulf Coast refining facilities. Even more importantly, they were demonstrating a willingness to commit financially and long-term to ensure this development.

Since the 1990s, TransCanada had been struggling with the long-term economic viability of its Canadian "mainline" gas transmission system, substantially due to the advent of new gas sources in the United States, concerns about the sustainability of western Canadian gas production, and diminished growth in traditional Alberta gas markets. The fundamental purpose of the mainline system was to get western Canadian gas to markets in eastern Canada and the northeastern United States. Costs to carry gas to these markets increased, as volumes shipped declined relative to the installed capacity. To put it simply, the company didn't have enough gas to move, and that was increasing the cost of its gas transmission service for the gas that it did move. TransCanada's executive team asked itself: If the company can't increase the volume of gas it's shipping, can it ship something else? That inspired question laid the foundation for the original base Keystone project.

By 2005, TransCanada's mainline gas transmission system had one virtually unused pipeline between Alberta and Manitoba. The company's engineers were confident that existing technology could be applied to reasonably convert this gas pipe to oil service. Essentially, oil pumps would replace gas compressors, and the company would adapt its control systems and the pipes themselves to complete the conversion. This would not only decrease the cost absorbed by TransCanada's gas customers but it would also provide sufficient competitive advantage to attract crude oil shippers. This pipe conversion would be supplemented with a new pipeline built into the mid-continent United States to crude refineries and terminals around St. Louis and Southern Illinois.

Converting from gas to oil service enabled base Keystone — a genuine commercial and strategic breakthrough for TransCanada.[27] Over 2005 and 2006, the company contracted with credible counterparties from among certain Canadian oil sands producers and American refiners, beating out competitors, including Enbridge, the dominant competitor for oil transport from Alberta, which had expected to gain this new shipping opportunity for itself. TransCanada's contracts with these shippers provided us with an attractive return on a significant investment base.[28] The pipeline project was named base Keystone after the Keystone Centre in Brandon, Manitoba, principally a hockey arena proximate to the pipeline that was to be converted.

Permission to Build

Since the base Keystone pipeline would have sections in both Canada and in the United States, TransCanada required permits in both countries. Canada's National Energy Board would regulate the Canadian section, and applying to them was, of course, a process the company knew well.[29] For the U.S. section, gaining permission was more complicated. The process was governed, fundamentally, by a series of executive orders, dating back to the mid-1960s, which necessitated presidential authority for the approval of cross-border infrastructure, in a manner consistent with the standards established by the National Environmental Protection Act (NEPA).

In the case of base Keystone, the U.S. Department of State (DoS) was designated the lead agency for carrying out the environmental review process and NID. The DoS is, of course, full of diplomats and foreign-policy analysts, not engineers — one might have thought the Environmental Protection Agency (EPA) or Department of Energy (DoE) more obviously suited to assessing the environmental impact of a pipeline. However, since the project involved crossing the border, the DoS asserted its bureaucratic authority. Nevertheless, it followed the prescribed NEPA process, hiring expert consultants to actually assess the application, analyzing whether TransCanada had addressed the requisite issues. Each state the pipeline traversed also had to provide state approval or devolve to the federal process.

In a process that would become so problematic in the years to come, the DoS assessed our application and issued a Draft Environmental Impact Statement (DEIS) in the latter half of 2007. Other relevant agencies reacted to this DEIS, notably the EPA. The DEIS was also available to the public for comment. With inter-agency and public comments taken into account (to whatever extent deemed appropriate), the DoS prepared its Final Environment Impact Statement (FEIS) issued in early 2008.[30] That was followed promptly by a National Interest Determination, a document containing all views on whether the project was in the United States' national interest. Then, the final decision, informed by the FEIS and NID, rested with Secretary of State

Condoleezza Rice, who had been delegated to perform that task by President Bush. On March 14, 2008, the certificate to cross the U.S.-Canada border was in hand for base Keystone.[31]

For base Keystone, TransCanada surmounted some minor controversy in Canada, related to the gas industry's potential need for the pipe we were converting to oil use, and to the merits of exporting crude oil as opposed to upgrading it in Canada.[32] The American process, however, unfolded without any material setbacks — hardly a surprise given the Bush administration's alignment with the hydrocarbon industry. Notably, the DoS reviews incorporated no concerns over climate-change risk attributable to oil sands production. As the Associated Press noted in 2015, "The revamped process Bush created was intended to speed up, not slow down, permits for major infrastructure projects." The article went on to quote Robert McNally, Bush's then–senior energy adviser, who called approving pipeline permits, until KXL, "the most routine, boring thing in the world."[33]

Between late 2006, when TransCanada struck base Keystone's initial commercial agreements, and mid-2010, when the company began commercial operations, the project conformed reasonably to its expectations. Some construction issues related to difficult weather had to be dealt with. But overall, base Keystone was conceptually innovative, strategically significant, and deftly executed. In fact, base Keystone became even bigger than originally conceived when TransCanada, over this period, extended the system from its original southern terminus in Nebraska to the oil-trading hub of Cushing, Oklahoma.[34] The whole project was predicated on long-term transportation contracts with strong counterparties; it was part of an economic value chain that justified the investment of the billions of dollars required. Apart from its size, however, base Keystone was unremarkable. Its construction involved the application of conventional pipelining technology and was subject to reasonable regulatory approval and oversight processes. Base Keystone proved uncontroversial. It was a brilliant investment for TransCanada, but, from a regulatory point of view, just another pipeline.

The Straightest Line: KXL

The economic fundamentals for more crude oil pipeline capacity asserted themselves even more intensely after TransCanada started constructing the base Keystone system. With base Keystone's terminus in mid-continent United States, Canada still had no direct infrastructure to deliver oil sands product to the U.S. Gulf Coast's refineries, many of which were designed to run optimally on heavy crude, of which Canadian diluted bitumen was a competitive alternative — if it could access that market economically. Those refineries had traditionally depended on oil from Venezuela and Mexico, but with the buildup in Alberta oil sands production capacity, as well as potential instability in the traditional supply areas, oil sands supply became an evermore serious supply option. An added bonus for an additional pipeline for Canadian producers was that it would help them avoid potential oversupply and thereby price discounts if it accessed the incremental Gulf Coast markets.[35]

In 2007, TransCanada achieved commercial support to extend the base Keystone system modestly, from the original terminus of Steele City, Nebraska, to the major crude terminalling hub in Cushing, Oklahoma.[36] The Gulf Coast, however, would require a several-hundred-mile extension through Oklahoma and Texas. The company was already using almost all of base Keystone's capacity, from Hardisty, Alberta, to the Nebraska terminus at Steele City, so Canada needed more capacity between those locations. TransCanada considered expanding the existing Keystone system, following its route to Manitoba and then directly south into the mid-continent United States, but also building a new, more direct and cost-efficient pipeline on the diagonal, direct from Keystone's supply terminal in Hardisty, Alberta, to the Steele City, Nebraska, Keystone junction point. The new route was dubbed Keystone XL. It would form the hypotenuse of a right triangle formed with the existing base Keystone system, beginning in Hardisty and moving southeastward out of Canada through Montana and South Dakota.

KXL would enter Nebraska west of the existing Keystone system to cross the state diagonally. The route avoided major crop-growing regions, traversing Nebraska's Sandhills instead; this, TransCanada saw

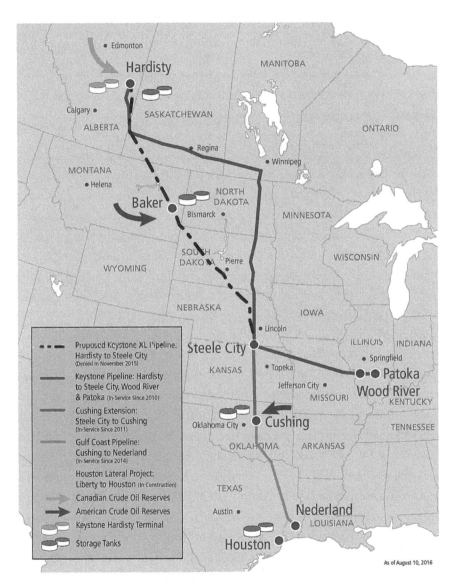

Keystone XL pipeline system.

as a virtue. The Sandhills region's economic activity was devoted to range-land and pastureland applications.[37] KXL's final section would extend from Cushing to the Gulf Coast. KXL's capacity was slightly over 800,000 barrels per day, and when combined with base Keystone's capacity would approach close to 2 million barrels, with most of that expected volume reaching the Gulf Coast.

As the company had for base Keystone, TransCanada signed binding commercial contracts with counterparties that would become KXL's shippers. The commercial foundation for KXL again utilized a similar mix of both producers and refiners as shipper counterparties. For some producers, KXL was the most advantageous route to a premium market; for refiners, the pipeline represented a fundamental new supply option for their required heavy oil. The transportation costs offered for transportation were sufficiently compelling that the company gained contractual commitments despite vigorous competition. Again, the investment opportunity was significant for TransCanada, expected to exceed $8 billion. With some spare capacity built into the KXL design, it expected returns beyond those of conventional pipelines. Not surprisingly, TransCanada's board sanctioned the project in 2008.[38]

TransCanada would follow the same regulatory approach for KXL as had worked for base Keystone. Once again, it needed a presidential permit to cross the U.S. border. The State Department would lead that process. Again, the company would also require construction approvals from those states the pipeline was traversing — at least those that had applicable approval processes in place. We knew the KXL project would not be processed while Bush was still president, and that Barack Obama was very likely to be elected. Base Keystone had been approved by an American government well aligned with the hydrocarbon industry and fundamentally ambivalent toward the entire climate change issue. TransCanada appreciated that an Obama administration was different, but however it dealt with climate change, we at TransCanada expected KXL to essentially receive the same treatment as base Keystone. The company did not see President Obama's presidency as a showstopper.

In September 2008, TransCanada submitted its applications in Canada and the United States.[39] The prospective Obama administration notwithstanding, the regulatory challenge for KXL was seen as well within our competence. This application described the pipeline design and related environmental impacts in sufficient detail and rigour to achieve regulatory approval. Though Obama had meanwhile been elected president, expectations remained that KXL would be treated much the same as base Keystone, with approvals in hands in 2010, sufficiently early to have the pipeline in service by the fall of 2012.

It is worth emphasizing that the Obama administration had, in the same approximate period, approved an Enbridge project known as "Alberta Clipper." That project was essentially an expansion of their existing major crude oil system into the United States, serving the markets in both the upper Great Lakes region and mid-continent. The major product flowing in that project was Alberta oil sands–derived crude.[40] The disposition of that project was essentially consistent with TransCanada's base Keystone experience. No special policy attention was given to the project by the Obama administration.

As TransCanada conceived and developed base Keystone and then KXL, Canada and the world were struggling to come to terms with the risk of climate change, and the outcome of that struggle would clearly impact hydrocarbon development as the millennium unfolded. At this time, I believed that climate change and the policies created for its control posed no serious risk to Canadian hydrocarbon development or the transportation infrastructure it required. Canadian oil sands crude had not, remember, been singled out by the United States as a uniquely problematic supply. The world *was* attempting to deal with the risk of climate change and the environmental movement and its related supporters *were* calling for extreme measures, yet the hydrocarbon industry functioned as though that process, however it unfolded, would not invalidate inherently economic investment opportunities.

That mindset infused TransCanada's approach as the company moved into oil sands–based transportation infrastructure and specifically KXL. The company relied on the reality that modern economies require hydrocarbons, and especially crude oil. It expected to see carbon policy applied fairly across all sectors. It believed North America's regulatory institutions to be rational, technically competent, and fair in respect of due process. It had faith that politicians would respect an obvious economic opportunity that used conventional technology and provided reasonable mitigation to acknowledged risks to public safety and property, acceptably minimizing overall environmental impacts.

In late June of 2009, just as the initial rounds of public consultation began along the American portion of the route, TransCanada chose to acquire full ownership of the Keystone investment by acquiring interests from some of the original shippers on base Keystone, who had held ownership positions.[41] Until then, TransCanada had partners, and therefore less exposure — but less exposure also meant less opportunity, depending on how you looked at it. My colleagues and I were enthusiastic about taking more of a good thing, even the most cautious and risk-averse amongst us.

TransCanada's expectations of when Keystone XL would be in service are best reflected in the language of its 2009 annual report: "TransCanada expects Keystone to begin generating EBITDA in 2010 with earnings increasing through 2011, 2012 and 2013 as expansion phases commence delivery of crude oil. Contracted volumes of 217,500 bbl/d will increase to 910,000 bbl/d from 2010 to 2013 as commercial in service of the Cushing and Gulf Coast phases commence."[42]

TransCanada was solely responsible for obtaining regulatory approval for the project. Capital commitments needed to be made, consistent with those schedule expectations. But oil sands were very much "in the money" in midsummer of 2009. Contracts were in place with strong counterparties. An Alberta pipeline carrying Alberta diluted bitumen (dilbit) to the Gulf Coast was a strategic imperative for the industry, province, and country.

By March of 2010, Canada's National Energy Board had approved the project as expected.[43] But across the border, KXL was becoming a highly politicized emblem for the American environmental movement. What happened?

CHAPTER TWO

2009 TO AUGUST 2011 – NEBRASKA AND THE DEPARTMENT OF STATE

Nebraska

Carbon was the hill KXL ultimately died on, but first the project met significant opposition related to its route through the Sandhills of Nebraska. TransCanada's response to that opposition, essentially dismissing any consideration of a reroute, began the chain of events that led to KXL's ultimate rejection. Could the company have reasonably predicted what would unfold? A nexus between a Sandhills route to the White House that would culminate in a rejection of the project? TransCanada was convinced that any reasonable environmental assessment of the project, regulatory precedence, and due process would prevail and culminate in approval. And while Nebraskan's concerns, per se, were fundamentally unrelated to carbon, those concerns twice provided President Obama with a justification to defer a seemingly affirmative decision both in 2011 and 2014. Delay justified by the route through Nebraska gave the environmental movement time to seize on KXL as its *cause célèbre* and thereby made President Obama confront how he could ever rationalize the KXL project in terms of his own desired legacy on carbon.

In its original KXL permit application, TransCanada provided alternative routes, but stated that its experts preferred the direct, diagonal route through Nebraska.[1]

Nebraska Sandhills.

It traversed mostly open, relatively unpopulated rangeland, causing minimal disturbance to agriculture, population centres, and existing infrastructure. Since the route was the shortest possible, it would minimize construction and operating costs, but also attributable environmental impacts from the pipeline.[2] As a general rule, the shorter the linear distance of a pipeline, the less the environmental impact.[3] TransCanada had few concerns that an inherently Republican state, historically inclined to accept hydrocarbon infrastructure, would have profound issues with this Sandhills route, or that the governing regulatory process might validate such concerns.

In 2009, however, TransCanada received substantial public feedback from Nebraskans about its route through the state's 19,600 square-mile Sandhills region.[4] Their concern emphasized the region's unique characteristics, including its high concentration of wetlands, extensive areas of groundwater, and sensitive ecosystem. Below the Sandhills' surface lie hundreds of feet of coarse sand and gravel, which act like a giant sponge that quickly absorbs precipitation and allows very little run-off. This massive sand dune formation, stabilized by native grasslands covering 95 percent of its surface, is highly susceptible to wind erosion if that grassland is disturbed. In some areas, the water table reaches the land's surface, creating lakes. The Sandhills, along with most of Nebraska, lie above the Ogallala Aquifer, one of the largest freshwater aquifer systems in the world.[5]

As part of KXL's environmental assessment, TransCanada had, of course, estimated the likelihood of spills and their potential impacts. The KXL pipeline was originally designed consistent with prevailing industry standards and then current regulatory oversight requirements from the U.S. Department of Transportation Pipeline and Hazardous Materials Safety Administration (PHMSA). As for any unique risks related to the Ogallala Aquifer from a dilbit spill, TransCanada determined that given the orientation and depth of the aquifer and the quality of the intervening soils, the possibility of permanent contamination was minimal.

Much of the opposition to the project within the state was led by the left-wing activist Jane Kleeb.[6] Although she never persuaded the DoS to reject TransCanada's Sandhills route in its environmental assessments up to October 2011, she did achieve a considerable profile that would ultimately integrate with environmentalists resisting KXL on the ground of attributed carbon impacts. Kleeb seized on KXL and began rallying the state's left, such as it was, against the route as early as 2009. In 2010, she founded the anti-XL non-governmental organization (NGO) Bold Nebraska to resist KXL, representing the pipeline as an unreasonable risk to the Sandhills and the Ogallala Aquifer.[7] Bold Nebraska became a nucleus of resentment and opposition to the pipeline, representing that Nebraskan sentiment unwilling to accept any risk related to KXL, regardless of reasonable mitigation efforts or any reasonable assessment of the absolute dimension of the attributable environmental risks to the state.

For some Nebraskans, the argument against KXL was that the state would accrue no significant resource rents or other benefits from accommodating it while taking on more environmental risk to the state. Montana and North Dakota were going to use the pipe identified with KXL as an important conduit to move the crude from their own Bakken formations, utilizing fracking technology for oil recovery. But Nebraska had no such oil production potential. The elements within Nebraska argued that the state had no reason to look at this pipe as anything other than a risk. TransCanada's response was that Nebraska's economy would benefit from construction spending in the state, and that for as long as the pipe remained in the ground it would also benefit from TransCanada's substantial property tax payments — an incremental revenue source that would enable various public spending, likely far in excess of any ongoing costs that Nebraska would bear relative to KXL.

Nevertheless, growing agitation from Bold Nebraska had more Nebraskans asking themselves whether accommodating KXL represented a net benefit for the state. Some Nebraskans objected to the regulatory process, since Nebraska did not have, at the time, its own statutory authority for approving a crude oil pipeline such as KXL. Nebraska would participate in the federal regulatory process, in this case led by the DoS, and ultimately defer to its determination. Some opposition, however, had little to do with the potential environmental impacts; rather, it involved landowners concerned about the terms of access payments and the relative bargaining power accorded TransCanada by the federal process. Increasing in-state opposition improved their leverage for land-access negotiations. However, some Nebraskans along the original route had consensually agreed to land access by 2010.[8]

Some right-wing elements tolerated the idea of the pipe, but they, too, expressed unease about the route through the Sandhills. The junior U.S. senator from Nebraska, Mike Johanns, insisted that TransCanada must change the route, abandon the diagonal across the Sandhills, and return to a route parallel to the existing north-south Keystone line instead. He insisted that Nebraska sentiment against the Sandhills route must be accommodated.[9] Despite Johann's vigorous admonition, TransCanada remained committed to its existing route. A federal regulatory process culminating in a sufficiently mitigated risk would adjudicate local concerns in Nebraska. TransCanada expected all stakeholders to defer to that determination. From 2009 to August of 2011, Nebraska governor David Heineman had not opposed the project or its route, largely deferring to the federal regulatory process.

TransCanada tried various tactics to influence public opinion within the state, explaining its bona fides and the potential benefits arising from the project, raising its profile with various community investments, including even becoming a major advertising booster at University of Nebraska football games.

Some element of xenophobia existed within the state, however. Despite the fact that the project would provide genuine net benefits to the state, the reality was that a Canadian resource via a pipeline owned and operated by Canadians would impose some risk, however reasonably mitigated. However, most of the polling that TransCanada conducted over this period suggested that it enjoyed public support typically in the range of 50 to 60 percent amongst Nebraskans.[10] Would it have been higher for a American company with an American resource? Probably, but any company would have aroused animus from the likes of Kleeb and Johanns. TransCanada would persist with its existing route until President Obama's intervention in November of 2011.

The company's 2008 application had actually included a route alternative that passed through Nebraska but avoided the Sandhills, but its assessment found that this route would impact Nebraska environmentally more than the selected diagonal "straight line" to Steele City, primarily because it would have to be longer and more disruptive to cropland. And it would also, of course, cost more. Certainly, committing to a reroute would have impacted in-service expectations. And that could have eroded TransCanada's expected return. The company was not ready to make the concession of a reroute. Governor David Heineman remained tolerant of the project. Overall, Nebraskan public opinion was not deemed so hostile to the Sandhills route to impact the de facto neutrality of the Heineman administration. Still, those Nebraskans who opposed the project did so vehemently and implacably. So, the company cast its fate with the federal process, trusting the DoS would validate its technical and environmental assessments. Nebraskan reaction in 2009 and early 2010 caused no fundamental change in the project.

The State Department's Draft Environmental Impact Statement

On April 16, 2010, the DoS released its Draft Environmental Impact Statement (DEIS) for KXL.[11] In short, the assessment substantially validated TransCanada's route and overall environmental assessment, confirming minimal environmental impacts relative to alternatives and a tolerable risk of spills, with reasonable industry standard emergency response undertakings. The DoS identified no "showstopping" risk to the Ogallala Aquifer or the Sandhills. This DEIS largely conformed to TransCanada's expectations.

As part of the DoS process under NEPA, relevant government agencies and the public had a chance to comment on this DEIS. Throughout May, various public consultation sessions in Nebraska gained reaction to this draft report.[12] U.S. environmental non-governmental organizations (ENGOs) had been focusing on the project since midsummer 2009, after Canadian ENGOs had laid out their frustration with the seemingly unchecked pace of oil sands development. With the election of the federal Conservative government in 2006, the Canadian environmental movement had faced enormous obstacles in their efforts to constrain oil sands development, since Conservative governments controlled both Alberta and Ottawa. The provincial Conservative government held the authority to issue permits for oil sands production. The environmental movement had seen the provincial government fail to deny essentially any production facilities, regardless of concerns about cumulative effects on local air, water quality, biodiversity, or ultimate carbon emission effects. Those concerns had no practical impact on the approval process.

In the face of this frustration, the Canadian ENGOs asked their U.S. counterparts for support to frustrate pipeline development. Granted, the U.S. ENGOs had more pressing concerns, such as how the Copenhagen climate conference would unfold. Nevertheless, it became seized with the oil sands issue. National Resources Defense Council (NRDC) president Frances Beinecke told the *Globe and Mail*, "The meeting with the Canadian groups really made a difference.... It was a very important session for elevating our attention in the US to this issue and the interrelationship between the two countries." Beinecke went on to visit the oil sands herself, and recounted in the *Huffington Post* that the development lacked government oversight, and wreaked havoc on the land, water, and air, as well as emitting three times the carbon of developing lighter crude.[13]

A year later, in the spring of 2010, the DoS DEIS incited the U.S. environmental movement's first substantial reaction to KXL. NRDC responded to the DEIS sixty days after its publication, with a 150-page critique that lambasted virtually every aspect of the DEIS. Other ENGOs submitted similar comments, along with landowner groups, principally from Nebraska.[14] On June 23, 2010, fifty of the most left-of-centre Democrats in Congress wrote to Secretary Clinton, stating that "building this pipeline has the potential to undermine

America's clean energy future and international leadership on climate change," referencing the emissions created by refining the bitumen, compared to conventionally derived fossil fuels.[15] More importantly, Henry Waxman, chairman of the House Energy and Commerce Committee, endorsed that critique with a letter to Secretary Clinton. Waxman emphasized the carbon intensity of oil sands crude and the overall carbon emission impacts attributable to the pipeline. He opined that the DoS had provided insufficient time for comment.[16]

The DoS NEPA process requires inter-agency comment on the DEIS, notably from the EPA. On July, 10, 2010, the EPA issued a withering critique, rating the DEIS "inadequate" — from its perspective, it failed the DoS environmental assessment. The EPA expressed particular concern over "potential greenhouse gas (GHG) emissions associated with the project, air pollutant emissions at the receiving refineries, pipeline safety/ spill response, potential impacts to environmental justice communities, wetlands, and migratory birds." Most significant, for the EPA, were the unaddressed potential climate impacts that could be directly or indirectly attributed to the project.[17]

Concerns about pipeline safety and spill response had been heightened at the time by two concurrent and highly publicized oil spills — Macondo and Kalamazoo. BP's Macondo oil spill had occurred only months earlier, in mid-April. Otherwise known as Deepwater Horizon, the spill was the largest of its kind of American history; for roughly eighty-seven days, oil flowed into the Gulf of Mexico. Macondo had nothing to do with the oil sands per se, but it did draw significant public attention to reliance on crude oil and the related issues of operational safety and corporate responsibility.[18] More unfortunate for TransCanada was a second and more relevant incident that occurred in July, when Enbridge's main system in Michigan spilled diluted bitumen into the Kalamazoo River, creating the largest inland oil spill in U.S. history. The problematic emergency response sparked a major controversy over pipeline operations, emergency response, and diluted bitumen. In response to concerns about pipelining dilbit, the U.S. Department of Transportation's PHMSA contracted the National Academy of Sciences to conduct a full and independent study. And despite an eventual assessment that "did not find any pipeline failures unique to the transportation of diluted bitumen or evidence of physical or chemical properties of diluted bitumen that are outside the range of those of other crude oil shipments,"[19] the Enbridge spill in particular contributed to greater public concern about any pipeline transporting Canadian dilbit within the United States.

The First Delay

In the summer of 2010, TransCanada faced the first real deviation from business as usual, creating unease about the regulatory process for KXL under the Obama administration. The DoS communicated its decision to embark on an extended reconsideration of the DEIS. In spite of writing a fundamentally supportive initial DEIS, representing close to two years of analysis and assessment, the cumulative effect of the resistance in Nebraska, the breakdown of carbon pricing in the U.S. Congress, increased ENGO attention, and the recent major oil spills had the DoS backtracking to accede to a supplemental assessment exercise. For TransCanada, a supplemental environmental assessment meant a twelve- to fourteen-month delay in its original schedule. In the middle of June 2010, just before Russ Girling became CEO on July 1, news that a supplemental process was to be imposed on the project was received. The reality was that this would have to be accommodated if approval of the project was to be achieved. At best, TransCanada could hope for a decision before the end of 2011. The DoS conveyed that expectation on timing to TransCanada.[20]

Dismay and incredulity abounded within TransCanada about this delay and the extension to the expected normal course assessment. But the cumulative impact of Congressional Democrats, the EPA, and elements within the Obama White House, all catalyzed by the ENGO community, had asserted enough pressure that the supplemental review had become non-negotiable. Evidently, a kind of consensus had emerged amongst Democratic thought leaders that the oil sands were a problematic energy supply alternative. On June 22, 2010, John Podesta, head of left-wing think tank Center for American Progress and formerly President Bill Clinton's chief of staff, told a Georgetown audience, "Oil extraction from oil sands is polluting, destructive, expensive, and energy intensive…. Suggesting that this process can come close to approximating being 'green' is largely misleading or far too optimistic or both." Easy for the smug, and unctuous, Podesta to say.[21]

The DoS claimed "new information" had come to light, which legitimized further review. The specifics of that new information were never clear. The first DEIS represented a standard, entirely logical outcome, consistent with conventional environmental assessment. It approached KXL as a pipeline traversing relatively benign topography, carrying a hydrocarbon fundamentally similar to what was already moving across North America's existing and extensive pipeline network. But of course, the DEIS did not consider upstream carbon impacts, because the emissions created before the oil entered the pipeline were not considered within the scope of our project's environmental assessment. For those skeptical or outright opposed to the project, that justified further assessment. Now, given the recent Kalamazoo incident, agitation over potential spills and the unique effects of dilbit was to be expected.

TransCanada had to accept the dictates of the DoS for this supplemental review or abandon the project. In doing so, the company also had to accept that climate impacts previously considered outside of the scope of standard environmental impacts were now in play.

Could the U.S. administration be trusted to deliver a rational decision in the end when it had clearly altered the normal course of the decision-making process essentially due to political and ideological pressure? This would be first of several occasions that TransCanada confronted that question. The supplemental review was problematic, but the company would persist and deal professionally with concerns and issues raised by the DoS, relying on its professionalism and intellectual integrity. Although never within TransCanada's control, the supplemental review would likely take about six to nine months to respond to the additional issues now in play, such as the incremental climate impacts reasonably ascribable to KXL, further market analysis on the necessity of KXL, and reconsideration of operating and design conditions to better mitigate the possibility of spills. TransCanada had to work with its commercial counterparties to accept this delay — but even more problematic was the challenge of maintaining sufficient project spending to avoid further erosion in the schedule.

Later in 2010 and into 2011, TransCanada began negotiations with the DoS and the Department of Transportation, mediated by PHMSA, about adding operating and construction conditions, beyond conventional industry standards, to assuage concerns post-Kalamazoo. As the supplement DEIS process unfolded, resentment over the route increased. The company had achieved a disquieting level of notoriety in Nebraska; but nevertheless, it carried on, convinced the DoS process and its inherent professional environmental assessments would not deliver a conclusion that differed fundamentally from the original DEIS. The company expected any accommodations demanded of it to be manageable.

Senator Mike Johanns exhorted TransCanada to fundamentally change KXL's route — to abandon the diagonal straight line and instead follow the route of base Keystone, thereby avoiding not only the Sandhills but the Ogallala Aquifer altogether. Johanns's stance bolstered the efforts of the state's activist groups. Unlike Johanns, however, these elements would not accept the project on any terms, reroute or no reroute. Resisting the project was an opportunity to lever left-wing political influence in a fundamentally conservative state. Despite their political differences in other areas, Johanns and Kleeb found themselves in a de facto coalition on Keystone resistance within Nebraska.

Throughout 2010, Nebraska's Republican administration, led by Governor David Heineman, voiced no active support — but no active opposition either — to the pipeline. His position was not one of tremendous significance, though. Since Nebraska did not have its own regulatory authority for pipeline approvals, the state's determination would devolve to the federal DoS process, and Heineman seemingly recognized this and that KXL provided considerable economic benefits to Nebraska.

Despite the extended review process and the significant opposition within Nebraska, TransCanada persisted in its application focused on obtaining a positive SDEIS, never considering a route change in Nebraska.

In October 2010, the company was delighted to hear Secretary Clinton tell a San Francisco audience that she was "inclined to approve" KXL.[22] The event was not devoted to KXL, but when an audience member asked about Enbridge's Alberta Clipper project, she took the opportunity to mention KXL's approval process as well. "We haven't finished all of the analysis," she said, "but we are inclined ... to do so and we are [so inclined] for several reasons ... we're either going to be dependent on dirty oil from the Gulf or dirty oil from Canada." She did not define what she meant by "dirty," and of course that was an adjective TransCanada was never pleased to hear applied to oil sands crude. However, Clinton's language was consistent with the essential determination implicit in the original DEIS. She cited no environmental showstoppers associated with the project related to routing, operations, or even, ironically, carbon emissions. Her recognition that the United States already used "dirty" oil from Venezuela and Mexico implied that the United States was already culpable for incremental special climate impacts that could be ascribed to oil sands–derived production. Clinton's perhaps unintended candour was significant, as it implied that a professional assessment of the overall merits, considered in appropriate context, would rationalize approval.

Not surprisingly, critics of the project, including some members of Congress and the Senate, objected to Secretary Clinton's remarks. Senator Johanns wrote a letter expressing his concern that her statement made the pipeline's approval appear a foregone conclusion.[23] TransCanada publicly rebutted Johanns's argument in an open letter to Hillary Clinton, restating the basic rationale laid out in its original application, which the DoS DEIS had validated: the shortest diagonal route across Nebraska minimized environmental impacts, certainly relative to the reroute demanded by Johanns along the state's eastern border.[24]

In the spring of 2011, the U.S. government asked TransCanada to implement fifty-seven special conditions never before imposed on a pipeline (by 2014 those special conditions would be supplemented by two others, bringing the ultimate total to fifty-nine). These included using high-quality, puncture-resistant carbon steel; adding a layer of corrosion-resistant coating; building around water, roads, and structures with horizontal directional drilling; automatic shut-off valves; and ultrasonic weld inspections. Again, TransCanada needed to accept that any chance for gaining approval from the Obama administration required taking on these fifty-nine conditions. The options were to accede to the conditions, despite the consequent erosion these would have on in its return and the doubts about the utility of some of these conditions, or walk away from the project, despite what had been invested financially and reputationally up to that point. The company agreed to all fifty-nine, which would make KXL the safest pipeline ever built in North America.[25]

Perseverance was seemingly vindicated when the DoS issued its supplement DEIS in April 2011.[26] The fifty-nine special operating and construction conditions, the supplement DSEIS stated, gave KXL "a degree of safety over any other typically contracted domestic oil pipeline." In respect of attributable climate impacts, the entire supplemental DEIS pointed to three major questions: Is oil sands crude oil responsible for more carbon emissions than other crude oil? Would building KXL allow Canada to produce more oil sands–derived oil than it would otherwise? And if oil sands oil is responsible for incremental emissions, are those emissions substantial enough to matter? The SDEIS acknowledged that oil sands-derived crude was "somewhat more" carbon intensive than the crude it would displace from the market, but found that KXL would have very little impact on the growth of oil sands development since the resource would be developed anyway. More importantly, the SDIES found that the project would not substantively increase global GHG emissions.[27]

The SDEIS concluded, "Although the DoS received thousands of comments on a wide variety of topics addressed in the draft EIS during the comment period, no new issues of substance emerged ... the information provided in the SDEIS does not alter the conclusions reached in the draft EIS regarding the need for and the potential impacts of the proposed project." Once again, the DoS sanctioned TransCanada's route through the Sandhills. A maddening irony was emerging, however: although the project continued to receive professional validation, Nebraska resistance continued unabated, impervious to a rational assessment of attendant risks and benefits.

The SDEIS's release began a forty-five-day comment period, and TransCanada expected to have its permit by the end of the year. Several ENGOs objected vigorously to the SDEIS. Sierra Club, National Wildlife Federation, Friends of the Earth, and the NRDC called the forty-five-day comment period too brief, and chided the DoS for failing to hold further public hearings in Nebraska or to seek route options that avoided the Sandhills and Ogallala Aquifer. The ENGOs claimed the United States did not need more crude options, and argued that access to Gulf Coast markets would increase the price of oil mid-continent. The four major substantive issues remained: pipeline safety, notwithstanding the fifty-nine new conditions; routing through Nebraska; climate impacts; and disproportionate local air and water impacts on minorities. In other words, no surprises. The ENGOs had already opposed the pipeline on those grounds. Their reaction to the SDEIS was as the company expected, but it seemed, perhaps, to be tinged with a tone of grudging resignation. Their request for more time and process doubtless betrayed a belief that they expected the pipeline's approval eventually. No attempt at accommodation came from the ENGO community in this period to TransCanada. More left-wing elements amongst the Democratic Congressional Caucus also registered their opposition to the SDEIS.[28]

On June 6, 2011, the EPA submitted a terse, seven-page letter disputing the DoS's conclusions about KXL's climate-change implications and urging a new route to avoid the Sandhills and the Ogallala Aquifer.[29] They acknowledged many of the new safety conditions as improvements, but still provided a rating of "insufficient." Regardless, would EPA abide a grudging acceptance of the project? The EPA certainly had bigger issues to contend with that year, as it tried to develop a regulatory mechanism to deal with carbon emissions in the electric generation sector using executive authorities available within the Clean Air Act, an essential breakthrough if the United States were to meet its Copenhagen reduction targets. This initiative was much more significant than KXL in terms of actually impacting the future level of U.S. carbon emissions. Perhaps the EPA was prepared to settle for TransCanada's concessions, and in effect hold its nose as the project moved forward. In any case, the EPA had tabled objections consistent with ENGO expectations. Of course, the decision was Obama's in any case.

Although the DoS extended its public comment period, TransCanada expected the final environmental assessment and National Interest Determination later in the fall, with an actual certificate before the end of 2011. Based on the DSEIS, the company was confident the DoS would remain consistent with its previous findings, regardless of continuing opposition from national ENGOs and from within Nebraska.

But from April to November 2011, other events would evolve that would derail our seemingly inexorable march to approval.

CHAPTER THREE

THE ENVIRONMENTAL MOVEMENT DISCOVERS KEYSTONE XL

The Climate Trinity: The Greenhouse Effect, Climate Sensitivity, and 2 °C

Since the late 1980s, in a seemingly separate, parallel world from that occupied by the hydrocarbon industry, the environmental movement had been striving to compel the world to seriously deal with the risk of climate change. No authority on world energy markets or environmental policy could have predicted these two polarities would intersect over the KXL pipeline — that KXL would become the "tipping point" for how the world responded to climate change risk. But it happened. And it started in earnest in the summer of 2011, just as TransCanada savoured the State Department's supplemental DEIS.

Almost a quarter of a century had passed since the world had seemingly accepted the need to genuinely deal with the risk of climate change, but the ENGO movement had little to show for its efforts. The environmental movement was frustrated, even desperate. To understand what awaited KXL, we must first understand the environmental movement's efforts and failures leading up to 2011, the year the pipeline seemed so near its regulatory approval.

In the late 1960s, major U.S. environmental advocacy groups emerged, ENGOs such as the Natural Resources Defense Council and the

Environmental Defense Fund, dedicated to ensuring the government took account of environmental issues based on scientific analysis, legal engagement, and broad public advocacy.[1] American academics played the major role in developing the various climate models (essentially mathematical simulations of the effect of rising concentrations of GHGs on global temperature) that the subsequent U.N. climate process would rely upon heavily.[2] As early as 1975, Yale economist William Nordhaus, in a seminal paper, alluded to the risk of exceeding the range of observed global temperature over the past centuries.[3]

In 1988, James Hansen, then head of NASA's Goddard Institute of Space Studies, testified before the U.S. Senate in hearings convened by then Tennessee senator Al Gore. Hansen told the Senate that global temperatures were increasing observably, beyond natural variation, and that human activity was the cause. Largely by burning fossil fuels, and to a lesser degree by deforestation, humans had contributed to increased atmospheric concentrations of CO_2 and other greenhouse gases (GHGs) since the Industrial Revolution. Since those gases break down only very slowly over time, they had built up in the atmosphere, and continued to do so. Carbon

Dr. James Hansen, testifying before the U.S. House Energy Committee, June 1988.

dioxide and other GHG gases, most notably methane, absorb heat in the atmosphere. Ergo, combust enough hydrocarbons, emit enough GHGs, and global temperature will increase. That growing temperature, Hansen explained, would, over time, impact the Earth's environment, increasing sea level, ocean acidity, drought, and other extreme weather events.[4]

Hansen's testimony pointed to the two big questions that climate scientists grapple with to this day. First, how much GHG increase in the atmosphere causes how much temperature increase? This relationship between growing concentrations of GHGs and temperature is called "climate sensitivity." Second, what consequences can we expect from each degree of average global temperature increase? Scientists have relied on climate models to predict probable global temperature increases from rising GHG concentrations in the atmosphere. These models comprise complicated sets of mathematical equations intended to replicate physical interactions on a global scale; that in itself suggests the models' limitations and challenges. Virtually no one denies that observed increases in CO_2 concentrations are "anthropogenic" — caused by human activity — or that these increased concentrations in turn increase the probability of the greenhouse effect: raising global average temperatures. Debate exists, however, over how much of any observed temperature increase may be attributed to natural variability rather than human activity.[5]

Hansen's testimony in 1988 marked the seminal moment in the world's efforts to seriously deal with this potential climate risk. Within a year, the U.N. set up its Intergovernmental Panel on Climate Change (IPCC) to provide scientific analysis on the risk.[6] The panel has essentially represented scientific consensus on the issue ever since. The IPCC's first assessment report in 1990, based on existing analysis and modelling, validated that GHGs generated by human consumption of fossil fuels would continue to enhance the Earth's natural greenhouse effect, leading to additional warming of the Earth's surface. Stabilizing the concentrations of such gases would require reducing emissions caused by human activity. The IPCC conceded limitations in its predictive capacity and gaps in current scientific understanding of certain key physical phenomena that impact the natural variability on climate. But despite these admitted limitations, and most importantly, the report called for action to deal with the risk of climate change.[7]

The United Nations' 1992 conference in Rio De Janeiro created the U.N. Framework Convention on Climate Change (UNFCCC), essentially its process for addressing the climate change risk. It remains the only such global process. The UNFCCC's objective was the "stabilization of greenhouse gas concentrations in the atmosphere at a level that would prevent dangerous anthropogenic interference with the climate system." The framework did not, however, embrace a specific temperature containment target; it stopped short of defining at what temperature increase climate change would become dangerous. The IPCC's second assessment, issued in 1996, reaffirmed the risk of climate change due to increased concentrations of GHGs caused principally by fossil fuel emissions, but still did not explicitly advocate for a specific containment target.[8]

Also in 1996, however, the European council of environmental ministers, including Angela Merkel, then Germany's minister of the environment and nuclear safety, stated that emission targets must be designed with the goal that "global average temperatures should not exceed 2 degrees above pre-industrial levels."[9] A team of physicists assembled by Merkel had found that in the annals in human history, the average temperature had never deviated much more than 2 °C from the historical mean. They concluded that, therefore, keeping the temperature increase within 2 °C would be a sufficient, practical objective to contain the risk of climate change. Hans Joachim Schellnhuber, a scientist on that advisory panel, explained later, "We said that, at the very least, it would be better not to depart from the conditions under which our species developed. Otherwise we'd be pushing the whole climate system outside the range we've adapted to."[10]

The environmental movement has since come to speak of the 2 °C target as something to be adhered to with absolute scientific and moral certitude. But its genesis came more from practical reasoning than absolute scientific certainty of a fundamental physical threshold. It did provide the U.N. process a practical benchmark for carbon policy, notwithstanding the lack of full scientific understanding or consensus on climate sensitivity itself. The target's value was fundamentally hortatory — a readily graspable rallying point for climate policy. Most credible forecasts show global emissions doubling throughout this century without policy intervention. In turn, the climate models show that doubling that Earth's concentration of GHGs, principally CO_2, would cause an average global temperature change beyond 2 °C and likely between 3 and 4 degrees. That became the scientific justification for a major policy intervention on a global basis to contain GHG emissions. The costs of actually meeting the 2 °C containment limit remains, however, a difficult and open question. Debate persists over whether this is a reasonable goal for climate policy, whether the future benefits of achieving the 2 °C target justify the near-term economic impact. Nevertheless, containing 2 °C remains the environmental movement's minimum objective for global climate policy.

Of course, dealing with this climate-change risk would require virtual global consensus on the urgency of the risk, and, even more challenging, on how to allocate the burden.

Prime Minister Jean Chrétien after signing the Kyoto Protocol, December 2002.

Kyoto, Waxman-Markey, and Copenhagen

Over the UNFCCC's first five years, most of the world's developed countries and various other nations worked toward meaningful collective action. Efforts culminated in 1997 with the Kyoto climate-change treaty. According to Kyoto, the developed world would, by 2012, emit 5 percent fewer GHGs than it had in 1990, and thereby stabilize emissions. Kyoto did not explicitly mention 2 °C, but its targets were designed to stabilize CO_2 concentrations at 450 parts per million (ppm), a level that would prevent dangerous anthropogenic interference with the global climate system. A limit of 450 ppm, according to the IPCC, provided a fifty-fifty chance of containing global warming within the 2 °C limit. Kyoto was a first step for the environmental movement — a beginning, not an end in itself, for the efforts of containing GHG emissions.[11]

The United Nations struggled to achieve necessary ratifications, fulsome participation, and serious implementation of the Kyoto Protocol. A vast disconnect grew between Kyoto's ambition and the actual emission reductions achieved, even by the developed economies that substantially negotiated it. The United States was a major participant at the Kyoto negotiations, in the person of Vice President Gore. Although President Bill Clinton signed the treaty, the United States never ratified Kyoto. In fact, after the 2000 election of George W. Bush, the treaty was never submitted for ratification. Kyoto had no legal effect on the United States. Others such as Canada and Japan simply failed to meet their Kyoto obligations. Russia ignored the process entirely. Meanwhile, growing emitters, such as China, India, and Brazil, were exempt from the treaty's core obligations, primarily due to their contentions that they were still developing economies, deserving the opportunity to fully utilize hydrocarbons as had the developed world for most of the prior two centuries. Global emissions rose steadily over the ten years after Kyoto was signed, well beyond the emission reduction levels mandated in the first reporting period, and well beyond the reductions required to stabilize GHGs at 450 ppm.

The environmental movement and the hydrocarbon industry functioned in parallel realities over this period: from the point of view of those who embraced 2 °C, the world had identified the interventions required to deal with the risk of climate change and then had failed to commit to those interventions. Concurrently, the hydrocarbon industry was committed to meeting global demands for its production, as economically efficiently as possible.

Kyoto's breakdown meant further GHGs had accumulated in the atmosphere between the early 1990s and 2009, making eventual containment of GHG levels and the meeting of the 2 °C limit ever more difficult. The third IPCC assessment report, published in 2001, predicted that without significant policy intervention, the global average temperature would likely increase within a range between 1.5 to nearly 6 °C over the remainder of the century.[12]

Simultaneously, the world crude price was escalating, enabling the development of various unconventional hydrocarbons, including the Canadian oil sands. From the point of view of the hydrocarbon industry and the political entities levered to that industry, Kyoto's failure served as a reassurance. If industry leaders had ever seriously accepted that climate policy would materially affect their business, Kyoto's breakdown confirmed that the world could not bring itself to constrain its reliance on fossil fuels.

In the mid-2000s, the U.K. government charged British economist Lord Nicolas Stern with analyzing the effects of global warming on the global economy. In his resulting report, Stern made the basic argument that the economic cost of dealing with climate change was reasonable relative to the attendant risks — in other words, that dealing with the risk of climate change was economically worthwhile, and that the sooner developed economies started dealing with it, the lower the cost would eventually be.[13] Although the report was contentious both for its methodology, in terms of how it treated, economically, future costs and benefits, and its assumptions about future technological improvements, it still represented a significant challenge to the developed world. Most significantly, Stern recommended carbon pricing as the foundational policy tool for moving forward. He later noted that if the fourth IPCC assessment issued in 2007 had been available before he released his report, he would have couched his recommendations in even greater urgency.[14]

We can see the disparity between environmentalists and industry in stark relief by contrasting the 2006 Stern Report with ExxonMobil's public positions report of the same year. ExxonMobil acknowledged human culpability for rising GHG concentrations, but argued that any current policy must account for various uncertainties about the IPCC assessment. As for urgent intervention to deal with the risk of climate change, ExxonMobil was equivocal, reflecting the mindset shared by most of the hydrocarbon industry: cautious and skeptical, and vaguely optimistic about technological improvement.[15]

In 2000, George W. Bush was elected, and environmentalists, quite rightly, recognized that the U.S. government would not be leading climate-change initiatives. With Bush as president and the Republican Party in control of the Senate, the United States not only failed to ratify Kyoto, but failed to deal with the issue of climate-change risk at the federal level of government, whether through legislative or executive initiatives, federally or internationally. The United States effectively contributed nothing to emission reductions demanded by IPCC climate models to achieve the 2 °C target. In fact, it didn't even relate to the target. Granted, Bush did attempt to reframe dealing with climate-change risk as a gradual process of improving technology, but he showed no interest in pricing carbon, mandates for low-carbon alternatives, or regulation of emission reductions. The Bush administration's indifference, like that of the hydrocarbon industry, had climate-change denial at its core, despite a consistently growing scientific consensus on the nature of risk, as demonstrated in the third IPCC assessment report of 2001.[16]

So much for the U.S. response up to 2008.

With no incumbent running and grim prospects for any Republican candidate for the 2008 presidential elections given the other policy failures of the Bush administration, the U.S. environmental movement — if not the global environmental movement — set their hopes on the election of a Democratic president. Far from denying climate change, the Democrats almost unanimously accepted that the risk called for urgent action both domestically and internationally. In 2006, they gained control of both houses of the U.S. Congress. The Republicans lost whatever slim chance they might have retained of holding the presidency with the financial crisis in September 2008. At that point, the victory of the junior senator from Illinois, Barack Obama, was all but guaranteed. Ironically, President Obama's position on climate policy was virtually identical to that of his Republican opponent, Senator John McCain, who had made significant efforts in 2007 and 2008 to advance comprehensive federal carbon pricing legislation within the U.S. Congress. However, most Congressional Republicans resisted climate legislation, typically seeking to protect hydrocarbon interests and holding to outright denialism of any material climate-change risk.

Optimism for Democrats and climate activists reached ecstatic heights when, during his nomination victory speech in St. Paul, Minnesota, on June 3, 2008, Barack Obama intoned that future generations would look back on his presidency as "the moment when the rise of the oceans began to slow and our planet began to heal." He didn't mention the 2 °C target explicitly, but every environmentalist understood meeting that target as his implicit promise.

Obama was elected in November of 2008 with a formidable personal mandate, bolstered by a Democratic Congress, and equipped with a filibuster-proof sixty Democratic senators. He set out to implement an aggressive progressive agenda of social and economic transformation. However, in 2009, the Obama administration prioritized delivering on its promise of a national health-care program. His administration would use all of its political capital to persuade equivocal Senate and House Democrats required for passage of the legislation that would come to be known as the Affordable Care Act, or Obamacare. All of this unfolded against the backdrop of extreme partisanship and heightened ideological polarization between Republicans and Democrats over the public sector's rightful place in the American economy.

Where did all this leave the initiative for national climate legislation?

Despite the United States' withdrawal from Kyoto and the Bush administration's indifference, Congress had in fact been working on policy alternatives, informed by input from some elements of American industry and the environmental movement. In 2009, liberal Democrat Henry Waxman, chairman of the House Energy and Commerce Committee, and Edward J. Markey, chairman of that committee's Energy and Power Subcommittee, came forward with an economy-wide cap-and-trade system that synthesized the various formulations from previous congressional legislative efforts. "Waxman-Markey" was formally known as the American Clean Energy and Security Act.[17]

Cap and trade limits (caps) overall emissions, and provides certain emitters free allowances to emit, while other emitters must bid amongst themselves for sufficient allowances. Some allowances are simply auctioned by the government directly. For those most in need of more allowances than originally allocated to them by the initial government allocation, a bidding process would emerge to generate sufficient willing sellers of existing allowances. Out of such a process an effective carbon price emerges. At least that is the theory. The Waxman-Markey cap was formulated to replicate the United States' intended Kyoto commitments, which in turn had some link to the fundamental 2 °C containment objective. The cap-and-trade policy put a price on carbon without calling it a tax, which proponents thought increased its chance for bipartisan support. A carbon tax, by contrast, specifies the price of emitting without specifying actual emission reductions. Emission reductions under a carbon tax regime result from the pressure of increased prices on consumption.

A policy specifying the level of permissible emissions would have aligned government action with the environmental movement's concern about the absolute level of U.S. emissions relative to the global containment goal. Trading of allowances resembles the dynamics of any conventional market, allowing participants to determine the value of emitting, with the difference that the government controls the overall emission cap. The cap would also encourage industry to avoid emitting altogether if it could find viable, economic substitutes for hydrocarbons.

Other compliance mechanisms, notably "offsets," were also an element of Waxman-Markey. An "offset" is the term used to describe the situation when an emitter operating under the cap system compensates another party, not subject to the cap, to reduce or eliminate an emission. Typically this takes the form of finding emissions reductions in other countries or special sectors in the national economy not subject to the cap. Using international offsets can become a source of foreign aid for some countries, or a subsidy for some sectors outside the cap, pointing to a peculiar nexus of climate, international development, and income redistribution objectives for many within the broad climate-change community.

The Waxman-Markey cap and trade clearly required initial choices on what sectors would be provided with what allocation of free allowances, what would be deemed to be acceptable "offsets," and how, if at all, the cap would change with time — all contentious political choices. That Waxman-Markey placed an overall cap on national emissions was its most basic accomplishment. For that reason alone it enjoyed support from much of the American environmental movement, despite its significant accommodations to certain industrial sectors, notably coal and renewables. Some private sector entities in the utilities sector supported the program, as did some elements of Wall Street, as they saw a new business opportunity in trading allowances. But most, if not all, of the American hydrocarbon industry opposed the bill.[18]

The bill was complicated, often politically arbitrary, likely to generate many unintended consequences, and fundamentally unclear about what level of pricing would emerge from its mechanics. Nevertheless, Waxman-Markey passed the U.S. House of Representatives in the summer of 2009, well before Waxman's infamous letter about the first DEIS on KXL. Given the different procedural rules in the U.S. Senate and some equivocal Democrats, passage of Waxman-Markey was uncertain in that body, but the bill did at least provide the Obama administration with some tangible credibility as it prepared for the December 2009 U.N. climate conference in Copenhagen. The United States was tangibly enacting legislation to replicate its past, unmet, promises from the Kyoto process, and thereby reclaim some global leadership on the issue.

The United Nations' most significant climate conference since Kyoto unfolded in the shadow of that treaty's breakdown and failure. Copenhagen, optimists hoped, would pick up the pieces. Many countries considered setting global emission goals as the conference's minimum objective, leading to binding agreements that would restore the possibility of 2 °C containment. The participation of the United States and China was vital. The global environmental movement and developing countries awaited the conference with great anticipation of a real breakthrough. But Copenhagen failed. The Copenhagen Accord, signed by most developed countries, represented more a statement of defeat rather than a blueprint of future intervention to deal with the climate-change risk. Although the participating countries did specify some national emission reduction targets, and reaffirmed the global 2 °C containment target — both of these "aspirationally" — Copenhagen generated unenforceable "pledges" rather than real legal obligations. Further, the voluntary carbon reduction pledges, even if honoured, would not contain emissions sufficient to achieve the 2 °C containment. Although, like Kyoto, the Copenhagen Accord contained provisions that would see the world's richer nations providing funding to poorer nations for climate mitigation and adaptation, the reality was more a promise than a legal obligation.[19]

In her book *This Changes Everything: Capitalism vs. the Climate*, author and activist Naomi Klein recalls the night Copenhagen fell apart, and describes fellow environmentalists despairing to the point of sobbing. "I have come to think of that night as the climate movement's coming of age," she writes, "it was the moment when the realization truly sank in that no one was coming to save us."[20]

For the environmental movement, the outcome was a crushing disappointment despite various rationalizations to the contrary. The developed world could not, apparently, commit to the kinds of interventions necessary to stay within GHG concentrations the IPCC had defined as reasonable to avoid the worst impacts of climate change. For that matter, neither could China nor India, though they claimed they should not be asked to do so, considering that Europe and North America had contributed disproportionally to the risk and benefitted disproportionally from carbon-based industrialization and development.

The Copenhagen Accord asked developed countries to submit emission targets by the end of January 2010. But it was really only a commitment to more process. Klein articulates the catalyzing impact of Copenhagen's failure very well: "No matter how many times we [the environmental movement] have been disappointed by the failings of our politicians, this realization still comes as a blow. It really is the case that we are on our own and any credible source of hope in this crisis will have to come from below."

Kyoto and Copenhagen both attempted to allocate the burden of dealing with the risk of climate change primarily to the developed nations — those countries most responsible for the accumulated emissions. The underdeveloped world would likely experience more impacts from climate change than those who had caused the risk, so Kyoto included a global offset trading system to help provide vulnerable nations with funds to mitigate or adapt. That system was, of course, never really implemented in any material manner. Copenhagen failed to improve on what had been architected at Kyoto. Carbon mitigation as the justification for increased north-south wealth transfer would have to wait for some future breakthrough.[21]

Back in August 2009, just after passage of Waxman-Markey in the House of Representatives, Senator Ted Kennedy died, and in early 2010, to the great surprise of most, Massachusetts elected a Republican to replace him. The Senate had devoted 2009, with the Democrats' sixty-senator, filibuster-proof majority, to the passage of Obamacare, not a Senate complement to Waxman-Markey. Could Waxman-Markey find enough bipartisan support in the Senate in 2010? Could Senate Democrats find sufficient compromise with some moderate Republicans to salvage cap-and-trade legislation? The answer was no. The bill was essentially defeated in the Senate by its failure to even vote on Waxman-Markey outright or even develop an alternative. The efforts of forty Republican senators and a handful of hydrocarbon-state Democrats proved too difficult to overcome, reflecting the reality of U.S. politics and its equivocation on dealing with the climate risk.

Kyoto had failed; Copenhagen had generated only uncertainty and concern; and the environmental movement's best chance ever for comprehensive climate pricing legislation was irreparably stalled in the U.S. Congress. And then came the 2010 mid-term elections, which brought significant Democratic losses in the Senate, though leadership remained in Democratic hands. More importantly, the House of Representatives fell to the Republicans. One essential branch of the U.S. federal government was not controlled by President Obama — control was vested in Republicans, who were fundamentally skeptical of climate-change science, and generally aligned with the interests of the hydrocarbon industry. Moreover, cap and trade as a major policy instrument was profoundly problematic to them, with its "top-down" prescriptive emissions cap and the largely political process of allowance allocation. By June 2010, the Senate's efforts to find a comprehensive climate bill were over.[22] It's not difficult to understand the American environmental movement's despair. Despite the IPCC's findings and despite reports such as Lord Stern's, efforts for American legislation consistent with containing global warming at a level of 2 °C had been rendered impotent. Moreover, post-Copenhagen, the path forward within the U.N. process was uncertain.

For industry, including TransCanada, Copenhagen and Waxman-Markey's failures corroborated the long-held intuition that the world simply did not have the capacity to embrace the costs of dealing with climate-change risk to the degree scientific consensus demanded. Why would a company volunteer to acquiesce to, much less advocate for, carbon policy that the world had shown itself incapable of enacting? At the end of 2010's first quarter, crude prices had substantially recovered from the decline suffered in 2008, reflecting rising global supply and demand. All this amounted to validation of oil sands investment, and, in turn, investment in related transportation infrastructure including KXL.

At the end of 2010, the American environmental movement was in a difficult position to advance its carbon agenda. It could have reinvented itself to focus more on adaptation than mitigation of the impacts

President Barack Obama with European leaders at the United Nations Climate Change Conference in Copenhagen.

of climate change. It could try to find a conciliatory approach with the hydrocarbon industry and the body politic generally by developing a political consensus for comprehensive carbon pricing legislation. Or it could adopt more obstructionist tactics, relying in part on their greatest political asset for support, Barack Obama.

In the early spring 2011, the DoS released its supplemental assessment, concluding that attributable incremental emissions from KXL were fundamentally immaterial to the dynamics of global climate change. Soon after, some elements of the U.S. environmental movement explicitly chose the path of obstruction, hoping that resistance to KXL would revalidate their reason for being, reassert their political clout, and reinvigorate their funding and human resources.

CHAPTER FOUR

HOW KEYSTONE XL BECAME AN ICON

James Hansen and His Saint Paul

Until the State Department issued its Draft Supplemental Environmental Impact Statement for Keystone XL, the pipeline's approval process proceeded without undue national media attention, despite opposition from Nebraska activists and extensive objections from the major ENGOs. On June 11, 2011, however, Dr. James Hansen responded publicly to the DoS's DSEIS. This intervention would prove to be a game changer. Hansen had of course been one of the first scientists to evaluate and publicize the risk of anthropogenic climate change. Hansen now composed a pointed polemic against the oil sands. In "Silence Is Deadly," a seven-hundred-word blog post, he stated that "the tar sands monster," if developed, would mean "game over" for the climate. He conceded that the regulatory process was unlikely to stop the project, and called on the scientific community to submit to the DoS written objections to KXL.[1]

Hansen's basic argument and rhetoric aimed to animate the American environmental movement and general public against the pipeline. Simply put, he singled out the oil sands as a vast reserve of hydrocarbons and, in turn, potential carbon emissions— 400 gigatons of in situ carbon or the equivalent of 200 ppm of atmospheric carbon.

Dr. James Hansen
(above) and
Bill McKibben (left),
circa 2011.

This, in a world that, according to his view of allowable further emissions, could tolerate no more than 350 ppm in the atmosphere if it was to meet the 2 °C limit and avoid environmental disaster. Existing conventional oil and gas reserves could already contribute sufficient future emissions to exceed the 400 ppm benchmark, without even taking into account the future contribution from coal. Adding oil sands to the crude oil supply mix, Hansen claimed, would render "implausible" any possibility of containing aggregate emissions within 350 to 400 ppm. If the world ceased using coal and unconventional sources of crude, however, stabilization was "conceivable."

His methodology attributed to these various hydrocarbon resources potential emissions impacts as if produced and combusted all at once, immediately adding to the atmospheric concentration of GHGs. This was hardly a reasonable standard given that their rates of production, absent extreme policy intervention, have always been primarily a function of economic considerations moderating their actual production. Nevertheless, his approach allowed him to contextualize the oil sands resource as served his purpose, regardless of its inherent sophistry. Hansen further added that developing the oil sands irreversibly affected regional biodiversity, reduced water quality, destroyed pristine boreal forest and associated wetlands, disrupted life cycles of birds and caribou, caused fish deformities, and harmed human health in downstream communities. All this without even mentioning the Nebraska Sandhills or the Ogallala Aquifer.

"Silence Is Deadly" was a call to arms, not a nuanced argument. Hansen later, and famously, called the oil sands a "carbon bomb," containing enough carbon to overwhelm any prospect of containing global temperature increase to acceptable levels. This metaphor contributed to the special animus toward the oil sands. At its core, it was based on a logic that ignores the recovery limitations of the processes used to produce the actual bitumen from the oil sands and other economic constraints such as global crude oil demand and alternative sources of crude oil supply.

Hansen's claim that the oil sands could increase atmospheric CO_2 by 200 ppm was rebutted by various commentators, who determined that the annual incremental emissions attributable to oil sands were on the order of 0.02 ppm, based on reasonable assumptions of future crude oil demand, oil sands production economics, and technology improvements. This issue of what was a fair attribution of incremental emissions to oil sands production would eventually become the key question in the technocratic assessment of environmental impacts of the projects.[2] Incrementality has to account for the fact that for each barrel of oil sands–derived oil, some other crude oil barrel could have served that same demand. The emissions attributable to that other supply alternative have to be netted out. Demand for the crude oil is also independent of whether the oil sands are developed or not. The debate, if any, should have been about the materiality of the incremental emissions of oil sands production. But "Silence is Deadly" contained none of that nuance or fairness. Even assuming an aggressive rate of oil sands–derived crude production anticipated for the period post-2015 of up to 3 to 4 million barrels per year, producing the 2.5 trillion barrels of oil sands resource required to reach Hansen's 200 ppm impact would take until the year 3316.

But his sophistry still had impact. Contain the oil sands or lose all hope of dealing with the risk of climate change: the oil sands, like coal, simply have to stay out of the energy supply mix. Of course, oil sands already had a controversial reputation; environmentalists detested the resource not only for its alleged carbon impacts but also for the various impacts of its production processes, both current and cumulative. As early as 2009, *National Geographic* had published its aerial photos of the surface mining operations, showing a seemingly black lunar landscape interspersed with yellow robotic bugs, stretching on as far as the eye could see — a kind of modern-day Mordor, the ENGO's favorite metaphor for the McMurray oil sands mining operations. Strip mining and tailings ponds are problematic visuals for those unwilling to put them into context and acknowledge the considerable reclamation and remediation efforts of oil sands operators.[3]

Environmentalists had been singularly unsuccessful in containing development, however, because of the oil sands' inherent economic value and the fundamental alignment of the governments of Alberta and Canada to developing the resource, including a belief that overall environmental impacts could be reasonably mitigated and managed over time.

Despite that, Hansen pointed out that oil sands–related transportation infrastructure could be just the Achilles heel the environmental movement needed to fundamentally alter its prospects.

A month later, in July, as TransCanada anticipated the DoS's Final EIS on KXL, environmentalist Bill McKibben took up Hansen's challenge, and issued a clarion call for widespread demonstrations, and even civil disobedience, against the pipeline. Legend has it that Hansen told McKibben building KXL would mean "game over for the planet" — a conversation that inspired McKibben to become the Saint Paul to Hansen's Saint Peter. Hansen handed McKibben the basic theology, and McKibben turned it into an actual significant resistance movement. Charismatic, articulate, ascetic, and unctuously moralizing in a classically socialist manner, McKibben proved a perfect leader for such a resistance movement. Already leader of the anti-carbon ENGO 350.org, author of various books on environmental issues, while holding the sinecure of a professorship in English at Vermont's Middlebury College, he had significant profile in the U.S. ENGO community. He had never really been a player with the major ENGO efforts to win a fundamental carbon pricing breakthrough with the cap-and-trade initiatives of the prior three to four years in the United States, but with Waxman-Markey's breakdown in 2010, plus the failures of Copenhagen and the seeming momentum for hydrocarbon development of even the most carbon intensive of crude oil alternatives, the Canadian oil sands, he appreciated perhaps more than most the need for a tangible cause that could reinvigorate the entire environmental movement. A cause that could not only be depicted as significant in the entire context of dealing with climate-change risk but one that had some reasonable prospects of success. He discovered KXL for that purpose.

In summer of 2011, McKibben invoked Hansen, calling concerned Americans to Washington, D.C., where they would protest the KXL pipeline outside the White House. He deployed the techniques of the American civil rights movement: public protests and acts of civil disobedience to provoke ever greater media attention, which would in turn exert pressure on fundamentally empathetic politicos with legal authority for the actual decision. That was the first test for the environmental movement of whether KXL could rally sufficient attention based on its connection to a resource declared entirely antithetical to the cause of containing the risk of climate change.

McKibben was hardly a constructive force, if compromise and gradualism are to be valued. He eschewed any effort to find a pragmatic approach to dealing with the risk of climate change, and never devoted his energies to finding potential common ground with the hydrocarbon industry or with politicians around carbon pricing. Instead, he chose to demonize a particular project as a test of what political leverage the environmental movement could exert on President Obama — who undoubtedly led the most empathetic administration environmentalists might ever find in the White House. Nevertheless, McKibben was a formidable propagandist and agitator. Employing tactics long perfected in other areas of social activism, he used KXL to make an abstract issue concrete, giving people somewhere to focus their inchoate desire to deal tangibly with the risk of climate change.[4]

McKibben offered a simple pitch: stopping KXL amounted to a moral issue for anyone who cared about the environment. "Twenty years of patiently explaining the climate crisis to our leaders hasn't worked," he wrote, truthfully enough. Did that imply that civil disobedience was, therefore, long overdue? He called KXL "a horror," characterizing it as a "fifteen hundred mile fuse to the biggest carbon bomb on the continent, a way to make it easier and faster to trigger the final overheating of our planet, the one place to which we are all indigenous."[5] McKibben emphasized that the KXL decision lay entirely with President Obama, a president who promised in his nomination speech that future generations would look back on his presidency as "the moment when the rise of the oceans began to slow and our planet began to heal." This formulation was powerful to those who saw dealing with the climate risk as a self-validating moral imperative. But it was fundamentally unfair to particularize a single infrastructure project and ignore other constructive policy alternatives that dealt more proportionately with the risk. That more nuanced and constructive approach did not serve McKibben's purpose.

In mid-August 2011, McKibben elaborated in a *Greenbiz* article that the hydrocarbon industry posed a serious threat to the planet, and it had just received a huge boost from the demise of Waxman-Markey. He lamented that the federal government had failed to provide incentives for renewable energy alternatives, and called on the electric utility and renewables industries to join his fight. Resisting KXL, McKibben wrote, could re-energize the American environmental movement: "What we are planning is civil disobedience, the broadest in the history of climate activism." His logic was explicit: the environmental movement could use KXL to regain its power, taking advantage of the unique circumstances around the project.[6]

McKibben did make the valid point that North America and most of the world had no credible price on carbon. He further contended that the world lay at the mercy of the hydrocarbon value chain. An overstatement, yes, but his lament for the lack of carbon pricing was legitimate. As I will discuss at length in the latter part of this book, the failure of the hydrocarbon industry and the ENGO movement to find common ground on carbon pricing — via carbon taxes rather than the tortuous cap-and-trade mechanism or outright regulated market interventions — was a real tragedy. If such a dialogue had begun in 2011, then KXL may not have evolved into the phenomenon it did. But in the summer of 2011, instead of inspiring a more constructive reconsideration of carbon policy based on carbon taxes, McKibben remained focused on thwarting KXL. His choice was profound, ultimately, for TransCanada and Canada. KXL became the *cause célèbre* to restore significant resistance to hydrocarbons in North America.

Supplementing McKibben's calls for public protest on KXL, early in August 2011, Hansen, with other noted scientists, issued a statement calling on President Obama to reject the pipeline. They stated KXL would access a "huge pool of carbon, but one that does not make sense to exploit."[7] Near the end of that month, just before the DoS released its Final EIS, environmental groups, including the Environmental Defense Fund, the NRDC, the Sierra Club, and Greenpeace, came together and urged President Obama to reject KXL. They stated that the "green base" would obstruct KXL even if that required civil disobedience. Notably, the EDF and the NRDC, who had both participated in the effort to realize an American cap-and-trade system only a few years earlier, and were the country's best funded and most analytically rigorous ENGOs, were conscripted into supporting McKibben's activities. Their support indicated the leverage that must have been exerted on them — they succumbed to fatuous symbolism rather than constructive policy.[8]

KXL's Vulnerabilities

Of all the pipelines in the world, why did the environmental movement seize on KXL? First, as I have already discussed at length, the pipeline crossed the Canada-U.S. border and consequently required a presidential permit. McKibben recognized the unique opportunity that circumstance provided: "If it had been Congress in charge of it, I don't know that we would have invested the hope and passion, because what's the odds of getting our Congress of doing anything," he'd tell *Al Jazeera* in 2015. "It was a decision that the president was going to make, which gave the glimmer of a chance of winning."[9]

Second, despite the fact that KXL would not have increased global carbon emissions materially, the oil sands-derived crude oil it was designed to ship was more carbon intensive than conventionally produced crude oils, though it should be pointed out not materially more carbon intensive that most other heavy oils produced by steam-assisted recovery methods. From the perspective of KXL's environmental opponents, however, any incremental emissions were intolerable. TransCanada and the hydrocarbon industry never disputed that the oil sands resource did create more incremental emissions than some other crude oils. It was the materiality of those incremental emissions that was the real issue.[10]

Third, the pipeline was routed through the United States for most of its length but was owned and operated by a Canadian company shipping primarily Canadian oil. The oil shipped on KXL would be delivered to American refineries and so American interests would capture the majority of the value of the refined products derived from that Canadian resource, but opponents still made the inaccurate and unfair assertion that the pipeline shipped "foreign oil" for export, with no apparent economic benefit to the United States. It was never remotely true that KXL's economic benefit would be enjoyed by Canada exclusively. But the ENGOs and our other political opponents never acknowledged even KXL's obvious positive employment impacts. Most of TransCanada's shippers were U.S. controlled, in fact. Nevertheless, the project's "Canadianness" became an issue. Ironically, this xenophobia came mostly from the U.S. left. However, it was most acutely evident in Nebraska — did the state derive enough benefit from accommodating any minimal pipeline risk? Why abide a Canadian project?[11]

And fourth, KXL was vulnerable because Barack Obama was president. McKibben vigorously asserted that President Obama had the right to make the decision on whatever terms he saw fit, virtually regardless of the regulatory record that had been generated in respect of the project. And so it became a question of whether Obama would relate to the Hansen-McKibben sophistry, or defer to the technocratic assessment of his own Department of State? McKibben set out to prove that the environmental movement could actually influence this administration, vulnerable because it had defined itself, from the moment it secured the Democratic nomination, with the loftiest of environmentalist ideals. Ideals President Obama presumably intended to live up to.

One doubts if McKibben ever exercised due diligence on the materiality of incremental emissions attributable to KXL; by the summer of 2011, the DoS in its DEIS had already evaluated KXL's emissions as minimal in a global context. But for McKibben's purposes, that was beside the point. He saw that resisting KXL could motivate the American environmental movement and its donors, plus left-wing politicians, to assert their influence over President Obama both financially and ideologically. The 2012 re-election was a point of leverage for them. At stake were Obama's credibility on climate versus the potential economic benefits to the United States from the advent of KXL, his legacy, and his bona fides on climate.

The reality was inescapable that the final decision would be President Obama's. A man with no experience in the private sector, and no affiliation at all with the hydrocarbon industry. A man reliant on a political base with significant elements largely alienated from the interests of capital. A man of obviously more left-wing instincts than the Clintons or most of the other conventional Democratic politicians that ever held the Oval Office. A man fully conscious that the polarization within the American political system would likely force him to rely solely on his existing executive authorities to deal with the climate-change risk over the remainder of his term as president. What capacity would he have to put KXL into its proper context? Would he actually support his own bureaucracy? Could he arbitrate between the DoS and EPA? Would he be capable of seeking out accommodation with Canada?

Some always asserted that the decision actually rested with Secretary Clinton, a moderate Democrat eminently capable of rationalizing approval. I instinctively knew otherwise. In 2010, President Obama seemingly had little direct engagement on KXL, but as events unfolded in the summer and autumn of 2011, KXL was elevated by McKibben and his movement as the test case of the president's climate legacy. President Obama had of course set the bar sky-high for himself when he claimed in his nomination acceptance speech that the Earth would begin to heal under his watch. He would own this decision regardless of any nominal delegation to the secretary of state.

A final vulnerability for KXL was that Canadian Prime Minister Harper had little ideological common ground or personal chemistry with the American president. Harper's failure to connect with President Obama made it even less likely that the president would factor Canada's economic interests or enduring damage to bilateral relations into his deliberations. Nothing typified the Harper mindset more perfectly than his comment in the early fall of 2011, when he called approving KXL a "no-brainer."[12] It's hardly a surprise that Harper would hold such a view. But implicit in his remark was an assumption that Obama would defer to the expectations of the North American private sector, which almost universally supported TransCanada's pursuit of the project.[13]

Keystone XL Undone: When Carbon and Sandhills Converged

On August 21, 2011, McKibben began a series of KXL protests in front of the White House.[14] By August 24, even the more moderate elements of the U.S. environmental movement, such as the EDF, declared their support for the KXL protestors and their demand for an outright denial of the project.[15]

On August 26, however, TransCanada gained a substantive victory. The DoS finally released the long-awaited KXL FEIS, which TransCanada characterized as having "reaffirmed the environmental integrity of the project."[16] Once again, the DoS cited no material environmental impacts and judged the pipeline's proposed route "the shortest," which "would disturb the least amount of land and water bodies resulting in reduced environmental impacts. Alternative routes that were considered to avoid the Ogallala Aquifer and the Nebraska Sandhills are not preferable environmentally or otherwise." The DoS had accepted the company's analysis of the route, despite the obvious resistance in Nebraska, and had not ascribed to any of Hansen and McKibben's apocalyptic claims about the pipeline's climate impacts.

The governing regulatory process now required a final National Interest Determination, to be carried out over ninety days. Relevant government agencies would provide their views, for the president's consideration, on whether the project was in the national interest. The company had waited three years — a long time — but now it was seemingly poised to have the final presidential permit in hand by year-end. At TransCanada, we felt reassured: as vulnerable as President Obama may have been to left-wing pressure, we still believed we would receive the permit. The company had played by the rules — had accommodated the DoS, responded to substantive issues, remained professional in its public posture, and avoided vitriol and ad hominem accusations, despite provocations. At TransCanada, we existed in a technocratic world, and so from our point of view, this civil disobedience had nothing to do with the regulatory process that dealt professionally with the fundamental merits of the project. All of which was, of course, consistent with our Alberta mindset. Moreover, despite the extremely publicized protests, at least 60 percent of the American public supported KXL in the fall of 2011, though support within the Democratic base was well below 50 percent.[17]

The various ENGOs that had objected to KXL were, of course, dismayed by DoS's assessment. For the ENGOs, KXL's environmental review could never end until the pipeline was rejected. No conditions, our fifty-nine or otherwise, could assuage their opposition. Opposing KXL had become a kind of religion for them. Nevertheless, the major ENGOS must have known that the existing bureaucratic process was headed inexorably toward approval. Only at the highest political level could an intervention reverse that outcome. McKibben's mobilization planned for late August was the best and only game in town on that front.

Elation with the FEIS was followed, within a few weeks, by a shock out of Nebraska. Nebraska governor Dave Heineman — who had passively abided KXL for nearly three years — reversed his position and declared he would no longer tolerate the route through the Sandhills.[18] He wanted to establish for Nebraska a new in-state process for the approval of crude pipelines such as KXL. TransCanada's political consultants had suggested that Heineman would stay the course of de facto neutrality on the project, deferring to the federal process despite growing resentment of the project within the state. What happened? Had tensions within the state finally risen to the point that he thought he had to come out against KXL to serve his own political interests? Perhaps he believed that the FEIS assured the president's approval of the project, so that he could have it both ways, opposing the pipeline but not actually stopping it. Through September and October, no accommodations on the route occurred, despite the governor's newfound objections. In any event, at that point it was not clear that Nebraska objections to the route would ultimately matter to the federal approval of the project.

Of course, the FEIS seemingly only encouraged environmentalist resistance. KXL protests continued through September and October, now across North America. In October, McKibben called on the major American ENGOs to sign a letter to President Obama, calling for his decisive action to block the pipeline. "We expect nothing less," they wrote. They described the pipeline battle as "perhaps the biggest climate test you face between now and the [2012] election," adding that denying the permit would trigger a "surge of enthusiasm from the green base that supported you so strongly in the last election."[19] Most significant was the clear threat that failure to block KXL would cause the ENGO movement and its donors to reconsider their support for President Obama's re-election.

By the end of October 2012, McKibben ratcheted up the American environmental movement's influence on the Obama administration, and that movement expected Obama to identify with the basic argument against the project:

- Containing a 2 °C temperature increase to mitigate the prospect of climate disaster remains the basis of the U.N.'s climate process.

- The Copenhagen Accord acknowledges as much, implying that deep cuts in emissions are required to achieve that target.
- Global annual emissions will likely persist, almost assuredly exceeding, in the next twenty years, atmospheric concentrations necessary to contain 2 °C. Unless, of course, the world embraces more committed and urgent climate policy.
- Potential carbon emissions embedded in the proven global hydrocarbon resources base exceeds this global "carbon budget" many times over.
- The vast majority of proven hydrocarbons must, therefore, stay in the ground to contain 2 °C.
- The Canadian oil sands represent potential carbon emissions almost sufficient to exceed that target, and, worst of all, is one of the world's most carbon intensive potential crude oil sources. Each oil sands–derived barrel accelerates emissions toward the necessary limit.
- President Obama has the KXL decision solely in his hands, independent of Congress and any regulatory authority. He must recognize the imperative of this denial to his own credibility on climate. Failing to deny KXL would have consequences for his re-election, enacted by donors and activists.

Materiality, mitigation, pricing, and accommodation were not part of the pitch.[20] This argument unfolded in fall 2011, as the protests continued and the final NID process moved toward closure.

Despite Heineman, McKibben, and increasingly difficult press attention, TransCanada steadfastly held to the existing process running its course, issuing a press release in late September emphasizing the FEIS determination that "the analyses of potential impacts associated with construction and normal operation of the proposed Project suggest that there would be no significant impact to most resources along the proposed Project corridor." The company reminded Nebraskans that the Heineman administration had fully participated in the DoS process, implicitly supporting the FEIS conclusion that TransCanada's fifty-nine special conditions "would result in a project that would have a degree of safety over any other typically constructed domestic oil pipeline system under current code."[21]

Be that as it may, Heineman held to his new position, and convened a special session of the Nebraska legislature for November 1 to deal with the public's growing concern over the pipeline route and creating for Nebraska a new regulatory authority for the approval of crude oil pipelines traversing the state, albeit in the context of KXL, all after the fact.[22] TransCanada countered with the line that it could not prejudice its project timeline for a route change; the company insisted that it would not reconsider its route.

McKibben's momentum, meanwhile, culminated on November 6, with another major anti-KXL rally in D.C., attracting an estimated ten-thousand-plus protesters, including both environmentalists and Nebraskans.[23] If nothing else, the protest affirmed that KXL, in McKibben's hands, could mobilize public participation and media attention as no other environmental issue had.

Although 2011 public opinion polls showed that American support for KXL remained at or above 60 percent, a poll of registered Democrats would surely have found support below 50 percent. Congressional support for KXL had never penetrated the Democratic caucus in any substantial manner; notwithstanding that a few Democratic senators and members of Congress from hydrocarbon-levered states such as West Virginia and Louisiana had supported the project, virtually no Democrat from a genuine "blue state" had ever supported it. Nevertheless, the inter-agency National Interest Determination was well underway in October.

Expectations were that TransCanada was to receive, by the end of November, a positive National Interest Determination aligned with the August FEIS — and following that a decision by President Obama in which he ultimately deferred to the DoS's three years of rigorous professional analysis, especially in respect of the immateriality of any fairly attributed incremental carbon impacts.

Yet, uncertainty persisted on what would be the final disposition of KXL by Obama. Would he land closer to the view held by the *Washington Post* — that his decision about KXL was immaterial to serious climate policy — and eschew the line taken by the *New York*

Times, which argued he should dismiss the entire technocratic efforts of the DoS and deny KXL as a necessary symbolic resistance, because his credibility on climate policy rested on granting the environmental movement this symbolic victory.[24] The *Post* still espoused cautious optimism of an approval, if the process simply ground inexorably forward. The Obama administration needed to focus, the paper said, on more serious environmental initiatives, such as removing coal from the electric generation supply mix, various low-carbon technology developments, and adaptation investment, not acceding to fatuous symbols of environmental resistance.[25]

Reversal of Fortune

On November 10, 2011, I was in Seattle, negotiating TransCanada's position in a major pipeline development in Alaska, when my phone lit up with a blitz of emails, and then the flurry of internal TransCanada notes arrived. The DoS had announced the whole approval process for KXL was on hold, despite their completed FEIS process. President Obama had intervened, and suspended KXL's regulatory process until TransCanada redesigned the route to avoid Nebraska's Sandhills.

This was clearly another significant delay. How long would it take to complete this reroute and the incremental environmental assessment related to it? Early indications from DoS suggested the possibility of completing such a review as early as the first quarter of 2013, although the company was skeptical about that estimate.

President Obama had found a way to provide the environmental movement with a major tactical victory, while putting off his own substantive decision until well after the 2012 election. Although a week earlier, in an interview on local Nebraska television, President Obama had stated he would "make the KXL decision" personally — in fact, on November 10 the DoS announced the delay. Meanwhile, Secretary Clinton was missing in action, willing to abdicate to President Obama if he insisted. She saw no political upside to resolving the KXL dilemma. KXL was not the political hill she would die on.[26]

Though President Obama never admitted McKibben's protests triggered his intervention, they were doubtlessly the determining factor. Obama could have rationalized KXL as laid out by the DoS FEIS, citing its immateriality to global carbon emissions and Canada's capacity to develop the oil sands resource in any case, national economic benefits for the United States, and the importance of maintaining good relations with Canada. Moreover, he could have rationalized the approval with a commitment to seek more genuine policy breakthroughs via carbon pricing. But that was all eschewed with this decision.

It was frustrating to see that opposition to the Nebraska route had given President Obama a politically viable rationalization to delay the project, placating his base while deferring the actual issue at hand. Procrastination was the real objective, not the dubious merits of a Nebraska reroute. Had the company been more responsive to Nebraska's obsession over the Sandhills route, would the pipeline be approved now, I wondered? It was maddening that President Obama's own DoS had validated the original TransCanada route through Nebraska after close to three years of review. But none of that mattered.

The ENGO movement celebrated KXL's 2011 delay as a major tactical victory but recognized that it was not a decisive rejection of the project. But McKibben had to have felt great personal satisfaction. He had identified a project that people could relate to, and shown he could mobilize the otherwise passive but empathetic sympathizers. He hadn't articulated or defined real climate policy, but that wasn't his goal. Practicality and complexities were not McKibben's problem, and neither were the economic prospects of his country or Canada. But he understood the power of metaphor.

At TransCanada, we faced a major dilemma. We had to make a choice within hours of learning of Obama's intervention. We had contracts with shippers, and didn't know if they would grant us concessions to accommodate more delay. The influence of the ENGO movement on Obama's administration had proven more powerful than we had ever imagined. Was the KXL business case still reasonable, or had the environmental movement taken the whole process past a genuine tipping point? Essentially, we had two options: we could abandon a project in which we had already sunk $2.4 billion and four years of effort, which had so much to offer the Canadian and Albertan economies and that based on any professional technocratic assessment ought to have been approved, or we could go forward with the reroute, spending millions more, against an increasingly hostile media and environmental movement, plus at best a very equivocal Obama administration. If we did reroute, the entire project would be delayed, even if the Obama administration dealt expeditiously with the reroute regulatory process and ultimately approved it.

We trusted in the good faith of Barack Obama. We chose the reroute.

CHAPTER FIVE

2012 AND 2013

"What Were You Thinking?"

Many may wonder why TransCanada persevered after President Obama's demand for a reroute. Why didn't the company see the intervention as a real signal he would eventually say no? Didn't we understand that Obama ignoring the DoS's findings meant he hoped the project would just go away? Certainly McKibben had raised the approval of this pipeline into a test of Obama's credibility on the entire climate issue. Did the company's political consultants in Washington not have the insight to foresee and the willingness to convey to TransCanada where this would end up? And if we were determined to persevere, why did we not try different tactics or work harder to gain support from elements that might influence Obama?

My view is that any executive in Girling's position would have found it extremely difficult, if not impossible, to end the project at that point rather than go forward with the reroute. Obviously, given what transpired over the next four years, TransCanada could have minimized its financial losses by simply ending the project in November of 2011. But that would have required the realization that President Obama was being utterly disingenuous in rationalizing the delay on the basis of a reroute through Nebraska. Up to that point, the company had no real evidence that Obama was ultimately in the same place as McKibben. His administration's public statements on the merits of the project included Clinton's now irrelevant remark that she was "inclined to approve," the DoS's FEIS, and the obvious resistance to the project from the EPA. But from inside the White House, we had nothing tangible other than the November 10 intervention to insist on a reroute. Everything up to that point had been about respecting the process for TransCanada. Its significant financial exposure and contractual commitments, amounting to a figure well over $2 billion, could only be recovered by persevering and ultimately gaining the approval.

Girling made the decision to accept the reroute within hours of President Obama's November 10 announcement, and TransCanada issued a press release confirming that later the same day.[1] Work began almost immediately with Governor Heineman's administration, both on the reroute itself and on the form of the new statute that would give

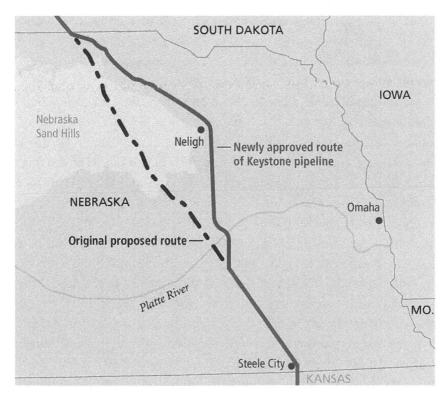

Keystone XL reroute through Nebraska.

Nebraska authority to approve the project and its route within the state. Whatever impact these actions had on our credibility in Nebraska, the company had to live with it. TransCanada was not abandoning the project. It commenced discussions with DoS officials on how much of the existing FEIS could be retained, without having to do a complete "do-over."

At the end of 2011, a reasonable assessment of the balance of probabilities justified persisting. It was estimated that Obama had a 60 to 75 percent chance of being re-elected later that year, and, conversely, there was a 35 to 40 percent chance that Republican Mitt Romney would become president. If Obama was elected, the company believed that there was no worse than a 50 percent chance that he would approve KXL. If Romney was elected, it was believed that he would almost certainly approve the pipeline. So, given all of that, it was believed that the probability of approval was slightly over 60 percent. Ascribing a significantly higher probability of rejection of the project at that time, and acting on that view, would have been difficult to justify.

Continuing with the project meant that returns would have to absorb the incremental costs arising from the delay and additional regulatory review beyond those planned for when the company made its original investment decisions back in 2008 and 2009.

Girling and his Keystone XL team, meanwhile, had the idea to build the southern portion of KXL, from Cushing, Oklahoma, through the rest of that state and through Texas to the Gulf Coast. Without the northern section, the pipe would transport mostly American oil in the short term. TransCanada anticipated less resistance to this abbreviated pipeline since it was expected that President Obama would welcome the economic activity arising from constructing this section in an election year. Moreover, the U.S. federal government had less legal authority to stop the company from constructing this section, since it did not cross an international border. A presidential permit was not required. Most of the necessary approvals required fell within state authority, though the Departments of the Interior and Transportation did still need to provide certain permits and accommodations. Although TransCanada did not expect the project to realize the same returns from this shortened pipeline as it originally anticipated for the entire KXL, it nevertheless believed that it was economically justifiable on an incremental

President Obama at Keystone Pipe Yard, Cushing, OK, March 2012.

basis. Moreover, the project allowed TransCanada to utilize a signifi cant portion of what had already been spent on the project in terms of engineering and environmental assessment.[2] That southern build, which was named the "Gulf Coast Pipeline," represented a constructive way to mitigate a worst-case outcome of rejection of the northern section of KXL. The company's board endorsed the project. This southern portion would be a test of the reasonableness of the Obama administration, even as the northern section was enmeshed in the reroute and potentially another complete EIS.

Steps Forward and Back

Just as work commenced to initiate the reroute and the adjustments to the federal environmental review with both the Heineman administration and the DoS, an unexpected development occurred in Washington.

The House Republicans, who controlled that part of Congress in 2011 and 2012, decided to exploit the Obama intervention by trying to force him to legislatively approve the pipeline. A budgetary resolution was required to keep the U.S. federal government running, and its consideration by both Houses would occur in January of 2012. The House Republicans added a rider that would force President Obama to make a decision on the fundamental merits of KXL, based on the existing FEIS from August 2011 and ignoring his demand for a reroute. Even the U.S. Senate, controlled by the Democrats, acquiesced to this rider. By mid-January, President Obama would have to make a decision: yes or no on KXL.[3]

As comforting as it was to have Obama's opposition so firmly in the company's camp, this legislative gambit would at best call Obama's bluff on a denial of KXL. It hardly imposed on him a decision to approve. Predictably, when President Obama had to make a decision at the end of January 2012, he formally rejected KXL.[4] Mercifully, however, for TransCanada, the Obama administration invited it to submit a new application reflecting the reroute, which made the administration appear open-minded about the pipeline's fundamental merits, and concerned only about the Nebraska route. Obama's rejection was rationalized on the grounds that the Republicans disrupted the due process of the existing regulatory approach. That was ironic if not utterly disingenuous, given Obama's disruption of three years of due process back in November of 2011. TransCanada displayed all requisite pragmatism, letting the Republican gambit run its course, without alienating the Obama administration by being collusive with the Republicans. Preserving the chances of the project's approval was paramount. TransCanada tried to be even-handed in its Washington dealings, holding no overt political empathies or biases, per se, and working only to advance TransCanada's interests in respect of KXL. The Republicans had overplayed their hand, actually giving President Obama an opportunity to end the project full stop, which he chose not to do.[5]

TransCanada publicly announced the Gulf Coast Pipeline in the first quarter of 2012, receiving thereafter requisite approvals in reasonable fashion from both the state and federal level. To achieve those approvals, the company had to overcome a number of hurdles. A notable example that presented itself was the result of an environmental assessment, which found that the American burying beetle, a species at risk, would be disturbed by the construction of the pipeline. TransCanada created sanctuaries for the insect in other locations to help protect it and to conform to the regulations laid down by the federal authorities. The Obama administration's willingness to accept this offset essentially confirmed the alignment we had found with it, at least with respect to the Gulf Coast Pipeline. Giving a short speech in a Keystone pipe yard in Oklahoma in the spring of 2012, Obama extolled the economic impact of the Gulf Coast Pipeline as another example of his avowed "all-of-the-above" approach to U.S. energy strategy.[6] Notably, at this photo op, he made no mention of KXL in the context of the climate change debate. This event represented the high-water point of relations between the Obama administration and TransCanada on KXL. The Gulf Coast Pipeline would be in service by the middle of 2013.

As all of this unfolded, Alex Pourbaix, TransCanada's senior officer responsible for the project, in line after Russ Girling, negotiated first with the Heineman administration and then later with officials from the newly formed Nebraska regulatory entity resolving what specific reroute the company would apply for early in 2012.[7] The route replicated an alternative put forward in the original 2008 application, avoiding a direct route through the Sandhills but preserving the northwest to southeast route through Nebraska, albeit with a considerable "dogleg" in northern Nebraska.

Opposition continued from hardline resistors, however, typified by the Bold Nebraska movement led by Jane Kleeb. No reroute would assuage them. Defeating KXL was a political imperative — economic benefit and mitigated risk notwithstanding. At the same time, conventional landowners focused on gaining greater monetary settlements from TransCanada, justified to some degree since the reroute required traversing more valuable agricultural land in eastern Nebraska than the original route through the Sandhills.[8]

At the same time as it was negotiating with Nebraska officials, TransCanada held negotiations with the DoS on the extent to which the completed FEIS of 2011 could be modestly reworked to reflect the reroute. Logic and reasonableness did not prevail, sadly. The DoS insisted on a "do-over" of the entire environmental assessment from the Montana-Alberta border to Steel City, Nebraska, though they cited no reasonable justification to invalidate the entire August 2011 FEIS. The EIS do-over meant no permit to cross the border could be obtained until at least 2013, well after the 2012 presidential election.

President Obama would avoid directly alienating his environmental base of support in 2012. For Republicans, KXL was a perfect metaphor for the misguided climate and energy policy orientation of Obama's administration, but President Obama held to the line that the project was still "in process." Retrospectively, this decision on an entirely new EIS on the whole project from the Canada-Montana border crossing to Steele City was an early indicator that the Obama administration was committed to stretching out the process until the project imploded financially or other events emerged to make a decision more politically obvious and palatable. The EIS do-over was unsettling, but TransCanada could only deal with what was available to it for preserving hopes of realizing the project.[9]

Construction of southern section of Keystone XL.

Adapting to Mounting Hostility

Every Monday morning from 2011 onwards, TransCanada's senior executive team, along with key members of the Keystone project team, met to consider tactical issues related to KXL that had emerged over the past week, such as right-of-way acquisition, construction progress on the southern section, and the legal and regulatory status of the pipeline within both the Nebraska and federal processes. Our discussions reflected the corporate mindset that we would get the work done, stay professional and civil, and respect the process — with the hope that the company would ultimately prevail.

While maintaining its commitment to professionalism and civility, TransCanada was forced from midsummer of 2011 to confront conventional and social media campaigns, waged against the project across North America, of a tone and on a scale no one in the industry had reckoned with before. For example, immediately after President Obama suspended KXL's assessment process in November 2011, TransCanada was barraged with a blitz of organized phone calls from the mobilized supporters aligned with McKibben's advocacy against KXL, essentially exhorting TransCanada to stand down on the project as a consequence

Keystone XL protests near the Washington Monument, February 2013.

of President Obama's intervention. The callers used a consistent word-for-word script, repeating that the inherent "immorality" of KXL should cause TransCanada to simply capitulate. The callers' intent was to intimidate by sheer force of numbers and persistence. Mercifully, this was not sustained long-term.

In the following days and months, McKibben's network maintained the drumbeat, using both conventional media platforms and social media to make the case that a fundamental turning point had occurred in the KXL story, and that TransCanada should accede to it.[10] McKibben and his associates succeeded in making KXL and TransCanada the *bêtes noires* for those who cared about seriously dealing with the issue of climate change.

Predictable elements of the media fully aligned with the meme McKibben created, with the *New York Times* the most notable example. More centrist media outlets were more even-handed, both in reporting and in the editorial positions they took with respect to the project, but in general press coverage still framed the oil sands as a problematic source of crude oil, and depicted a TransCanada under duress from a very equivocal Obama administration.

All of TransCanada's people personally felt the impact of the profile the project had gained. Even in the normal course of our lives, we were compelled to defend both TransCanada's corporate interest and their personal commitment to it. How does one rationalize in a short conversation the overall merits of a project, when the media is teeming with extreme but simplistic characterizations of building KXL as the moral equivalent of destroying the planet? It is difficult to compare the polemical impact of anti-XL statements from celebrities like Robert Redford with that of corporate support from the American Petroleum Institute and the American Chamber of Commerce.[11]

Many have critiqued TransCanada's entire public relations effort on KXL as deficient, lamenting that if TransCanada had explained itself better, had been more creative and sensitive in its media and advertising efforts, public tolerance of the project could have increased. The fact is that by 2012 TransCanada had significantly increased its communication resources, with many employees focused solely on KXL. When reporters and others made negative claims, our communications team restated the facts about TransCanada's practices and materials, and reiterated our safety measures. They rebuffed the constant stream of attacks in the mainstream media and on social media. When people cast aspersions on our dealings with landowners, the toxicity of dilbit, and so on, our team gave as good as they got.

However, TransCanada's communications and community relations teams had much more to deal with than merely negative editorial opinion. Along the pipeline's southern route, activists attracted media attention almost every day, chaining themselves to adjacent construction equipment, and lying down in the actual pipeline trenches. The state authorities had their hands full, and dealt with the situation professionally. In terms of public relations, the company could only respond by restating that the activists' actions were fundamentally unsafe, not to mention illegal.

TransCanada improved its capability to compete in the social media world, as well as in the more conventional media outlets, by developing relationships with journalists to whom the company could share its side of the story as well as by, on occasion, purchasing advertising. Full-page ads showing a pristine prairie with a bright shiny cylinder about to go into the ground were created. The text highlighted the additional jobs and energy security KXL offered. This advertising was focused, in particular, in the Washington, D.C. suburban area, to ensure that both Congress and the administration were confronted with some basic facts and advocacy for KXL.[12]

Russ Girling, meanwhile, achieved a significant public profile, certainly relative to most hydrocarbon sector CEOs. As the CEO of TransCanada, he was the primary public advocate for the project. He appeared on virtually all U.S. media outlets, including Fox News, Bloomberg Television, CNBC, and so on. He met with all of the editorial boards of the major national newspapers, notably the *New York Times* and the *Washington Post*. Not surprisingly, he was criticized heavily in the ENGO blogosphere. Ultimately, he was the subject of unfair attack ads sponsored by Thomas Steyer, ex-investment banker and environmental advocate. Throughout, I deeply admired Girling's civility and commitment to truth and forthrightness, and his ability to avoid indulging in any undue vitriol or recriminations.

TransCanada found itself in a war of attrition in terms of accusation versus rebuttal. Our communications team ensured the facts were available, along with a legitimate interpretation of those facts in terms of technical issues, attributed economic benefits, or legitimately ascribed climate impacts. They dealt with moralizing rhetoric, often bombastic and sanctimonious.[13]

The effect of this extensive media battle on public opinion was minimal. According to extensive internal polling, TransCanada always had at least 60 percent national support for KXL. Those 60 to 65 percent of Americans held no special animus against the project into 2012 and beyond.[14]

A similar circumstance held on the government side. Even with near unanimous Republican support, however, TransCanada could not win over any Democratic congressional support beyond a few isolated hydrocarbon-levered senators, such as Mary Landrieu of Louisiana. Even fundamentally intelligent and fair-minded Democratic legislators were not prepared to support, or even abide, efforts to enact a legislative approval of KXL. McKibben and most of the U.S. ENGO movement had ensured any wavering Democrats vis-à-vis KXL would pay a real political price. Moreover, the issue was in the hands of "their" president. No majority of Democratic senators saw any political advantage to take that decision out of his hands, as various Republicans gambits tried to do. Many of the most liberal completely identified fully with the McKibben's position. As far as the Democratic senators were concerned, the KXL decision lay squarely in President Obama's hands. No greater quantity or quality of public relations and advertising would have changed their commitment to that position.

Nevertheless, I always found it extremely frustrating that fundamentally reasonable and fair-minded Democratic senators such as Dianne Feinstein would not even engage in an open-minded discussion of KXL's merits. The entire infrastructure of political handlers and related Democratic operatives ensured that such open-mindedness held no political value, only liability. Regardless of the actual merits of the project, to be at odds with the large component of their political base that had declared this rejection an absolute expectation of congressional Democrats was simply not conscionable in their eyes.

The *New York Times* and the *Washington Post* maintained their distinct editorial positions vis-à-vis KXL, as first set out in the fall of 2011. However, noted apolitical climate commentators, such as Michael Levy of the Council of Foreign Relations, provided analysis consistent with that espoused by the *Washington Post*: "The fate of the pipeline will be of limited consequence to long-term U.S. energy security or climate change (though the decision to reject it will probably be ugly for U.S.-Canada relations). But the Keystone decision [has] ultimately [become] far more about symbolism than substance. It's a shame that so much attention [has been] diverted from things that matter more."[15] As the regulatory process dragged on, Democratic advisors continued to assert that the Obama administration would ultimately accede to that view as well.

But for the *New York Times*, KXL was a genuine threat to the Obama administration's credibility. Any practical progress on containing carbon emissions meant carbon intensive hydrocarbon alternatives must "stay in the ground." Denying KXL was too good an opportunity to lose, regardless of its impact to Canada, the materiality of the pipeline's fairly attributable climate impacts, or how this obsession with KXL diverted attention from genuine and substantive policies to genuinely deal with the climate risk, such as carbon pricing. The *Times* bought the entire McKibben line. Certain Democratic climate-policy thought leaders, such as John Podesta, did the same, smugly advising Canadians to turn away from its oil sands, as if Canada should align with left-wing American opinion regardless of the cost.[16]

The schism was reflected across the political spectrum. The left and the environmentalists essentially melded together in opposition. Private sector interests, their advocates, and some moderate opinion leaders and analysts supported approval.

It should be noted that TransCanada did enjoy selective support from American labour groups. Unions most directly positioned to benefit from the project were logically staunch supporters.[17] Major consolidated labour groups such as the AFL-CIO had by 2013 cautiously joined in the endorsement.[18] However, major public sector and service industry unions remained largely indifferent to the Keystone XL issue. KXL's labour support was never strong enough to impact

Congressional Democrats to any meaningful degree. In any case, by avoiding a decision in 2012, Obama avoided the possibility of potentially alienating a significant portion of his labour support, and delaying a decision meant that whatever was decided would not affect him since he would obviously not confront re-election again. Alienating one major element of the Democratic coalition with a Keystone XL decision, be it labour or environmentalists, would no longer directly impact him.

TransCanada remained cautiously, perhaps neurotically, optimistic throughout 2012 and into 2013. Despite the ongoing media campaign of accusation and rebuttal, TransCanada was engaged in the particulars of the Nebraska reroute, the DoS EIS "do-over," and the construction process of the southern section. At the same time, President Obama was fully consumed with his own re-election. Despite the critiques from Republicans for failing to approve KXL, Obama consistently relied on the rebuttal that the project was "in process." TransCanada's political advisors told us to endure this additional "process" to enable a better foundation for approval. TransCanada never managed to directly engage with the White House on KXL during this time period. Letting us meet with Obama was deemed unfair while the project was still in its regulatory process. Were TransCanada's ENGO opponents accorded the same treatment? Probably not, I speculate.

November 2012 came and went. Obama was re-elected, with an even bigger mandate than his 2008 victory. The Republicans retained control of the House of Representatives and modestly improved their minority position in the Senate. President Obama would have to govern by his executive authority, not by achieving any legislative breakthroughs that would advance his fundamental agenda. But regardless, these four years would be his last. For him, legacy became an ever more weighty consideration.

2013: It Rained, It Poured

In early January of 2013, TransCanada received its evaluation report from the newly formed Nebraska regulator. That report essentially validated the reroute in its recommendation to the governor. Before the end of January, Governor Heineman approved the reroute, despite continued agitation within the state for a total rejection of the project or greater financial compensation for land access.[19]

In March 2013, the DoS released its third draft environmental assessment. Despite essentially redoing the entire exercise, they had changed virtually nothing. The assessment, once again, found no substantial environmental problems with KXL, climate related or otherwise — it would effect "no substantive change in global GHG emissions" and it was "unlikely to have a substantial impact on the rate of development in the oil sands, or on the amount of heavy crude oil refined in the Gulf Coast area."[20]

TransCanada continued to acquire right-of-way in Nebraska in a methodical fashion over the second quarter of 2013. The company also took heart in early May when one of the issues that had been touted by certain ENGOs — the higher risks attributable to dilbit relative to other crude oils in pipeline transport — was debunked by a report by the National Academy of Sciences in the United States.[21] The DEIS public comment process unfolded over the second quarter, and TransCanada hoped for an expeditious release of an FEIS later in 2013.

At this point, I still believed President Obama capable of approving KXL. Logically, the administration had more at stake in advancing the Clean Air Act to regulate the American electricity sector and reduce GHG emissions. Removing coal from the U.S. fuel mix would more significantly improve Obama's climate legacy than rejecting one pipeline with substantially immaterial direct climate effects. Approving KXL might actually facilitate support from other elements more typically hostile to his climate initiatives.

On balance, even given the pressure that McKibben et al. had generated amongst Democratic politicians and their climate-policy advisors, the possibility of a positive outcome still seemed to be possible by the midsummer of 2013. Persevering with the KXL project remained reasonable. The same was true of the other major pipeline projects the company was developing in Canada, and the smaller-scale projects underway in both the United States and Mexico in same time period. Even then, I believed the Obama administration and the entire North American polity could still deal with these projects reasonably, despite McKibben's having elevated the rejection of KXL as the "litmus test" for "bona fides" on climate change for Democratic politicians.

In June of 2013, a historic flood occurred in the Calgary region. [22] Within days, much of downtown Calgary was underwater, and 100,000 people were displaced. TransCanada's head office was inaccessible, along with most of the city's businesses. The flood proved to be one of the costliest natural disasters to impact urban Canada, with a cleanup bill of $1.7 billion. Calgarians were all trying to help each other in those days, the lucky amongst us welcoming evacuated family and friends into our homes. Spontaneously formed gangs of volunteers visited affected neighbourhoods in the coming weeks, helping strangers rip out destroyed carpets and drywall, emptying flooded underground parking garages with buckets, and emerging at the end of the day as dirty as a mud-soaked army. Girling and others on the TransCanada management were altruistic volunteers. His home unaffected, he went to help another colleague flush water from his house in Elbow Park, another riverside neighbourhood. As this unfolded in Calgary, a significant development in respect of KXL occurred in Washington, D.C.

On June 25, 2013, with none of the TransCanada executives in the office, President Obama gave a speech on climate-change risk at Washington, D.C.'s Georgetown University.[23] As it happened, I learned of the contents of his speech almost in real time from my lawyer in Washington. It's worth quoting him in full:

> I know there's been … a lot of controversy surrounding
> the proposal to build a pipeline, the Keystone pipeline,
> that would carry oil from Canadian tar sands down

to refineries in the Gulf. And the State Department is going through the final stages of evaluating the proposal. That's how it's always been done. But I do want to be clear: allowing the Keystone pipeline to be built requires a finding that doing so would be in our nation's interest. And our national interest will be served only if this project does not significantly exacerbate the problem of carbon pollution. The net effects of the pipeline's impact on our climate will be absolutely critical to determining whether this project is allowed to go forward.

For KXL, this statement from Obama setting out his KXL decision criteria was perhaps the most important development in the project since his intervention back in November of 2011. But what did it mean precisely? Many were elated with his language, in particular, the word "significant." KXL climate impacts came nowhere close to "significant," as the DoS's determinations in their formal environmental assessments kept confirming. Perhaps Obama had laid a path to approving KXL. McKibben and other environmental entities predictably took an opposite view, seeing in the Obama language a straightforward basis for rejection.[24]

Obama had apparently insisted on referring to KXL in this speech after an original draft of the speech ignored it entirely. His language was perhaps intentionally ambiguous. He provided no elaboration on how "significant" would be determined, or recognition of where the DoS process stood on the issue of the materiality of fairly attributable incremental emissions, or even that TransCanada had responded to the nominal reason for his intervention back in November 2011. The Heineman administration and TransCanada had affected the reroute via a state regulatory process as required. Further, TransCanada diligently complied with the DoS insistence on an entire do-over of the EIS process. There was no recognition of TransCanada's respectful and apolitical approach since November 2011 in Obama's speech, however. Despite all the procrastination and reinvention of due process, Obama had at least now clarified that his decision would come down to one issue: carbon.

The March 2013 DEIS had found no significant climate effects. If Obama really wanted to reject the pipeline, wouldn't he have ensured that the EIS provided the justification to do so? When I coupled Obama's words with the DoS's latest draft, approval still seemed plausible, perhaps even probable.

Was such a belief just wishful thinking on our part? Had President Obama already decided in June 2013 that KXL would never be approved? I am not sure that was the case. He doubtless wished the project would simply disappear, allowing him to avoid the decision. Was his language intended to be interpreted by Canadian interests, and especially the Harper government, as indicating that he needed more in terms of Canadian carbon-policy initiatives, regardless of what had been generated by the DEIS process to date to justify an approval? Obama's language was ambivalent. But was that very ambivalence intended to challenge Canada? What could Canada, let alone TransCanada, provide beyond what had already been agreed to within the DoS process? What other undertakings with respect to Canadian carbon policy could be made that would alter the Keystone XL dynamic? And regardless of what could be done, would Canada collectively respond to this implicit challenge — would TransCanada, Alberta, the hydrocarbon industry, and most importantly the Harper government itself? These questions would dominate the remainder of 2013 on the Canadian side.[25]

On the American side, further opposition to KXL was gathering steam. At the same time as Obama gave his Georgetown speech, Thomas Steyer, a wealthy San Francisco hedge-fund manager, began to attract attention by spending large sums of money on anti-XL advocacy with special emphasis on that fact that KXL would primarily transport Canadian oil through the United States for export.[26] The United States would incur all the risk of this "dirty oil," flowing through its soil, Steyer told the American public, and see little economic benefit from the pipeline. His efforts only added to keeping the public profile of KXL high through the remainder of 2013 and into 2014.[27]

But the key next steps, regardless of Steyer or McKibben, were the issuing of the FEIS, which Obama himself ultimately controlled, and determining whether Canada would offer up any carbon-policy concessions that might improve the prospects of approval. However, as 2013 closed out, no FEIS had been released. Unease within the environmental community grew due to the fact that the Georgetown decision criteria had not expeditiously led to a KXL rejection. Frustration with Obama was growing. Many in the environmental movement questioned how committed he could be to his carbon ideals if the possibility of KXL still persisted.[28]

CHAPTER SIX

THE END OF KEYSTONE XL

Carbon Taxes, An Opportunity Missed

President Obama's Georgetown speech lacked any recognition of the existing record of assessment by the DoS. The keywords "significantly exacerbate" could be interpreted in whatever manner Obama would ultimately wish. I believed the speech offered a subtle request of Canada that incremental emissions from crude oil produced from the oil sands had to be acknowledged and in some way rationalized, technically or economically — either reduce them physically, acquire foreign offsets, or, perhaps, apply a sufficient carbon price to them. But Obama did not articulate what standard of materiality he would apply, or give any explicit guidance on what he expected of Canada. Everything was left to inference. If only he had said outright that Canada must impose a price on its carbon emissions as the quid pro quo for KXL approval, at least some genuine negotiation might have been possible. President Obama could have gained the credit for compelling Canada to "do the right thing," and in turn redeem its carbon-intensive oil sands resource.

Harper was prime minister of Canada when TransCanada first submitted its KXL proposal, and he remained prime minister until just days before Obama's denial of the project. His relationship with Obama would impact the fate of KXL. From the inception of KXL, TransCanada enjoyed the wholehearted support of Harper's Conservative government. He famously characterized President Obama's choice about KXL as a "no-brainer," a characterization that was entirely consistent with his government's belief in the importance of the hydrocarbon industry and its goal that Canada become a global "energy superpower."[1]

That view was essentially shared by the American hydrocarbon industry, as embodied in various industry associations, most notably the American Petroleum Institute (API), which held the broadest representation across the entire spectrum of the U.S. hydrocarbon value chain, from production to retail distribution. They appropriated the KXL fight as much as McKibben did; denial would be an affront to the reasonable expectations of a functional and substantially apolitical regulatory process. Other U.S. business organizations including the American Chamber of Commerce and the Business Roundtable were supportive, though they engaged less in the day-to-day rebuttal process with ENGO assertions and the media. The Canadian Association of Petroleum Producers (CAPP), Canada's equivalent of API, and virtually all of TransCanada's customers, fully supported the project as well. Prime Minister Harper certainly had private sector validation for his belief that KXL was a "no-brainer."

The Harper government and "big oil" held to the view that the case for KXL was a compelling one, based on the DoS assessments up to November 2011 — assessments that were reaffirmed by the DEIS of 2013. What more should or could be offered up to actually ensure that Obama provide the permit? Prime Minister Harper and the industry leaders believed nothing was actually necessary beyond simply deferring to the record, which repeatedly reaffirmed that fairly attributed incremental carbon impacts were immaterial. This attitude dismissed the impact of McKibben et al. on Democratic politicians generally and Barack Obama in particular. Given the technological limitations of the oil sands production processes and the reality of how recently most of the oil sands production capacity had been installed, all that Canada had left to offer was carbon pricing of its emissions, most credibly via a national carbon tax, which would obviously be applicable to the incremental emissions derived from oil sands production. Climate economists had long advocated such a tax as the cornerstone of any rational carbon policy balancing climate and economic considerations.

Ironically, within Alberta, large industrial emitters had paid a "carbon levy" on their carbon emissions since 2009.[2] However, the actual applicable carbon price was minimal, less than $5/tonne of emitted carbon on an overall basis. This levy was not sufficient to convince the U.S. ENGO movement, or, seemingly, the Obama administration, that Alberta had adequately "internalized the externality." That most of the funds would be redeployed in low-carbon technology development, notably carbon capture and sequestration (CCS) inside the province, gained Alberta little consideration. But perhaps the potential existed to engage in a negotiation where Canada would impose a national carbon tax within the range of $15 to $30/tonne of emitted carbon dioxide, which might be seen as a material carbon-policy concession — in effect, "redeeming" the higher carbon intensity of its oil sands resource. Moreover, it would be a fundamentally legitimate carbon policy for Canada, independent of KXL. It might even serve as a major advance, providing a precedent for how other countries would approach carbon policy, relying on pricing instead of mandated emission reductions.

Sadly, Prime Minister Harper had won the 2008 election, albeit with a minority government, on his vigorous denunciation of the Liberal opposition leader Stéphane Dion's major election policy initiative known as the "Green Shift."[3] Dion proposed imposing a national carbon tax that would be set off against existing taxes payable; that is, the government would tax carbon rather than income, personal or corporate. Harper campaigned against Dion's proposal as an incremental tax — obviously an unfair characterization.[4] For Harper, any new tax was seemingly to be resisted, especially one grounded in the perhaps still dubious contentions of a U.N. process that seemed more about north-south redistribution of wealth than finding a proportionate response to the climate-change risk. During his term as prime minister, Harper remained implacably resistant to any suggestion of a federal carbon tax or carbon price standard.[5]

Even at the Copenhagen climate conference, Canada chose to impose implausible reduction targets rather than espouse carbon taxes as a legitimate compliance equivalent to physical emission reductions. It was a cynical approach — committing to a national target that Canada would likely never achieve, safe in the knowledge that the U.N. process included no enforcement mechanism, no actual binding obligations. Canada's growing oil sands and natural gas potential meant the country would emit more, not less, during the period it had ostensibly committed to reductions. The Copenhagen target required an almost 25 percent reduction of Canadian emissions current in 2009. If growth in oil sands and natural gas production occurred as forecast by industry, Canadian carbon emissions would grow by 10 to 15 percent by 2030. Were these targets going to imply the contraction of the Canadian hydrocarbon industry? Or require other massive economic interventions to achieve compliance? The Harper government suggested neither. This inherent contradiction between Canadian targets and energy production potential was not lost on the Obama administration, let alone the entire ENGO community.[6] The leadership of the various key companies in both CAPP and API were fundamentally complicit with Prime Minister Harper. Although many conceptually endorsed carbon taxes as the preferred policy instrument to deal with the carbon risk, none were prepared to advocate publicly for specific terms.

The American hydrocarbon majors apparently relied on the U.S. government's inherent political gridlock to avoid any such tax. Canadian energy leaders knew advocating publicly for a carbon tax contradicted the deeply held convictions of Harper, and remained unconvinced that advocacy would necessarily realize KXL or more strategically reduce the long-run resistance of the ENGO movement. Prime Minister Harper was viewed as hardly generous to those who chose to confront him on this most visceral of issues. It also had to be conceded that even if Canada were to impose such a tax in the range of $30/tonne on itself economy-wide, the United States had no capacity to reciprocate, given the inherent legislative gridlock in place in the U.S. Congress at the time. Even with the obvious necessity of revenue neutrality and export/import adjustments to address Canadian competitiveness as part of any carbon tax design, many within CAPP and the Harper inner circle resisted, resenting Canada having to "go first and unilaterally" on a carbon tax, for a "quid pro quo" that should be already in hand based on the fundamental merits of the project.

Despite some vigorous debate across the Canadian oil sands industry, it collectively did not choose to advocate publicly for credible Canadian carbon taxes, despite how much was at stake. Some within CAPP recognized that a carbon tax was the only viable carbon-policy instrument, given the real differences between Canada's energy mix and the United States with respect to ever meeting Copenhagen carbon targets. Canada had relatively little coal to remove from the fuel mix, and world demand for crude oil was growing. Canada's oil sands sector could compete for that opportunity while internalizing a carbon tax. Advocating for a carbon tax as an explicit quid pro quo may well have been the only option left to salvage the project as we closed out 2013.

TransCanada found itself at the very vanguard of the fight for the oil sands' future, carrying the financial burden of the KXL fight, but still expected to keep its advocacy constrained to keep alignment with its stakeholders (customers, Canadian governments, and other hydrocarbon interests). Admittedly, many of these stakeholders would ultimately bear much of the impact of carbon taxes on their value chain. Yet TransCanada had invested literally billions in keeping the KXL option intact. Who would have blamed it if it had been more aggressive in carbon tax advocacy in this last, endgame manoeuvre for KXL?

Alberta's then premier Alison Redford did try to affect some change in the Alberta carbon levy to better approximate what might have been considered a more credible carbon price applicable to oil sands emissions. That effort had tepid support from CAPP, and less still from Prime Minister Harper. This move had little impact, however, since Redford was not in a position to directly bargain with the Obama administration, nor did she have any national mandate.[7]

I believe that most corporate leaders in the oil sands knew only carbon taxes could rationalize growing oil sands exploitation to a world committed to seriously dealing with climate-change risk. But such carbon taxes would mean increases in their companies' cost structures and along the entire hydrocarbon value chain. Of course, that was the whole point of carbon taxes. Carbon taxes should have been seen as strategically compelling, but extra costs were difficult to rationalize, especially since a carbon tax didn't necessarily guarantee KXL's approval or any reduction in ENGO resistance.[8] But it was difficult to understand the unwillingness to negotiate seriously on this basic premise. Or at least try to catalyze such a negotiation.

Sadly, by the end of 2013, the status quo prevailed. President Obama was provided no incremental incentive to approve KXL. Collectively,

Canada, TransCanada, Alberta, and the Canadian hydrocarbon industry would stand pat, implicitly relying on the expected second FEIS to provide a sufficient foundation for approval.

2014 and 2015

At the end of January 2014, the DoS released the FEIS for KXL, including the Nebraska reroute. "This is not too bad," my colleagues and I agreed. After the torturously stretched out ordeal the company had endured, the DoS had still found no substantive reason to reject KXL. If Obama planned to deny the pipeline, then, we wondered, wouldn't he and Secretary of State John Kerry have used the FEIS to cite "significant" climate impact? But the actual FEIS could not provide such a rationalization for denial. It identified minimal environmental impact attributable to the project and said the pipeline was unlikely to impact either the continental demand for heavy oil or the rate of production from the oil sands.[9]

TransCanada CEO Russ Girling at Keystone XL
Houston Pipe Yard, March 2014.

The FEIS said pipeline transportation via KXL represented a superior transportation alternative in terms of cost and safety. The fifty-nine special operating conditions would provide a level of mitigation of spill-related risk above traditional industry practice (representing a final concession of two additional special conditions on the part of TransCanada). The assessment acknowledged substantial economic benefits for the United States, and found "no material" attributable carbon impacts. Even the *New York Times* confirmed our vindication, with the headline "Report Opens Way to Approval." The article conceded that if the pipe were not built, the same oil would still move via rail, if not some alternative pipeline infrastructure.

Of course, the ENGO community expressed pervasive dismay.[10] They had their chance to air their grievances during the ninety-day comment period followed the FEIS. Then the final phase of the governing regulatory process, the National Interest Determination, would commence, leading to an ultimate decision by mid-year. The DoS asked for final input from eight federal departments and agencies by mid-May, consistent with that timeline for a final decision. TransCanada could perhaps genuinely feel some optimism in those early days of 2014.

But only a few weeks later after the FEIS was issued, on February 19, 2014, TransCanada received news from our legal staff that a judge in a Nebraska county court had ruled in favour of an action brought by disgruntled Nebraskan landowners and activists with respect to Governor Heineman sanctioning the reroute. The judge found the statute granting Nebraska's governor the final decision on KXL's route unconstitutional. She held that the decision should have been with a state regulatory commission, not the governor. This was another frustrating distraction, like so many that had beset KXL; however, the federal NEPA process was still going forward. We took solace in that.[11]

Yet, incredibly, on Good Friday, April 14, 2014, the Obama administration announced that it would suspend the NEPA process for KXL a second time, this time to await clarification of the Nebraska's reroute sanction. Now any final decision on KXL would not occur until after the November mid-term elections. Of course, political opponents of the Obama administration and other supporters of KXL viewed the suspension as another transparent gambit to both delay a decision as long as possible and to disable the project with more delay.

At this point, I admitted to myself that this administration would never approve KXL. It had resorted to every possible excuse to prolong the regulatory process on this project. It could not even acknowledge the logical implications of its own bureaucracy's environmental assessment. President Obama might prefer to never decide, but if forced, he would reject it. Of course, this realization was difficult to accept, and never became TransCanada's official position. The company only expressed disappointment and frustration, but restated it was committed to persevering.[12] I would retire from TransCanada in August of 2014. It was a sombre and difficult time in the face of what had occurred and was seemingly evolving with respect to KXL. I was not to savour its approval while still part of TransCanada.

The year closed with the Republicans gaining control of the U.S. Senate, with sufficient numbers to all but ensure a legislative approval of KXL. That would force Obama to veto or acquiesce to the will of Congress. The Republicans did not have the numbers to sustain a veto. Senate Democrats would certainly not defect in sufficient numbers. The Republicans would persist regardless. In late November, President Obama delivered an unfair and inaccurate characterization of KXL, responding to a resolution passed in the House to force him to approve it: "Understand what this project is: It is providing the ability of Canada to pump their oil, send it through our land, down to the Gulf, where it will be sold everywhere else. It doesn't have an impact on U.S. gas prices."[13] Later that same month, Obama, simplistically and inaccurately, described Keystone XL as "a pipeline shipping Canadian oil to world markets, not to the U.S."[14] This comment betrayed his own indifference to the benefits the project, which would bring the U.S. economy. It was as though he'd quoted an NRDC talking point.

Further dampening prospects, the year closed with continued decline in crude oil prices, caused in part by the unwillingness of traditional OPEC swing producers to sustain prices by cutting back production. Increased global supply, notably from increased domestic production from American shale oil sources, impacted the global market substantially. Reduced oil prices would challenge all crude oil producers, but especially relatively high-cost producers such as the Canadian oil sands. Whatever this decline in commodity prices would portend for future investment in the oil sands, it did not cause the shippers supporting KXL to abandon the project. KXL still represented value to them in the short-term, in terms of superior transportation economics, and in the longer-term as capacity for future incremental production.

2015: Endgame

Obama's two most substantive climate policy initiatives were applying the Clean Air Act to gradually remove coal from the electricity-generating fuel mix, and ensuring that the 2015 Paris U.N. climate conference was deemed a success, based on bringing sufficient countries together with nationally determined voluntary emissions targets ultimately intended to contain a global temperature increase within 1.5 to 2 °C. The second directly affected Obama's final decision on KXL.

President Obama announces decision to reject Keystone XL pipeline proposal.

Harper and Obama never engaged on KXL. The Harper government offered no movement on carbon pricing. Canada did remain part of the U.N. climate process. Its contribution to the Paris conference was essentially to maintain the scale of emission reduction ambition implicit in its existing Copenhagen emission reduction targets, reframing the goals terms as "30 percent below 2005 levels by 2030."[15] This created doubt about how committed any Harper-led government would ever be to actually realizing such a target, especially given his long-standing resistance to carbon pricing. All of which would be relevant as the mandated 2015 election approached, with his already doubtful prospects for retaining a majority government.

Predictably, in the first quarter of 2015, the Republican-controlled U.S. Congress passed legislation requiring Obama to approve KXL. He vetoed this legislation, citing that it represented an unreasonable intrusion into the project's regulatory process. That rationale in the total context of the Obama administration's regulatory disposition of Keystone XL was both ironic and insulting to Canadian interests, but was nonetheless provided with no contrition, notwithstanding his record of procrastination and indecision. The required number of Democratic senators sustained his veto, and the Obama administration stated that KXL's possible approval remained intact, despite this veto. Ultimately, thirty-eight Democratic senators held firm with Obama on Keystone XL.[16]

On January 9, the Nebraska Supreme Court ruled that the project's route as sanctioned by Governor Heineman could go forward. Nebraska presented no further legal obstruction.[17] Long-standing opponents and landowner advocates registered typical resentment toward the decision,[18] but the Obama administration allowed the suspended National Interest Determination phase of the regulatory process to resume.

As part of that process, the EPA finally provided its public comments on the DoS's 2014 FEIS. TransCanada vigorously rebutted the EPA assertions that the DoS had not "fully and completely assessed the environmental impacts of KXL," especially the EPA's contention that at lower crude oil prices Keystone would cause incremental oil sands production and increased emissions. Various independent energy economists and analysts also refuted that claim. The EPA's logic was that without KXL, oil sands production levels would decline with lower crude oil prices, but that with the pipeline, production would increase, due in part to the fixed obligations of producers to TransCanada.[19]

Typically, the U.S. government would require two or three months to obtain input from the relevant agencies to complete the NID. But the process stretched through the spring and summer. Obviously, the decision was squarely President Obama's. No new facts had been brought forward.

Notably, in March 2015, Obama announced a more stringent national target for emission reductions by 2025, roughly 10 percent greater than the existing 2030 target, and in June, his administration claimed credit for persuading the Chinese to accept a goal of stabilizing carbon emissions by 2030. Obama fully identified with the Paris climate conference as a decisive opportunity to advance global efforts to materially deal with the risk of climate change.[20] Throughout 2015, the world's nations prepared for the December U.N. climate conference in Paris, most submitting their voluntary emissions reductions as hoped for. Obama would go into that conference wanting to appear a climate champion, having done all that he could with the tools that were available to him. That could hardly portend well for KXL. The public discourse on the oil sands and climate policy had become ever more strident, with the usual suspects calling for extreme reduction targets achievable at a short- and medium-term economic cost that was rarely, if ever, acknowledged.

That spring, efforts at accommodation from some third parties were unsuccessful. Neither the Obama nor Harper administrations showed any inclination to reach out for direct discussions.[21] By midsummer, still no decision had been reached. President Obama's administration would evidently wait until the Canadian election had run its course, presumably not wanting its KXL decision to have any impact on how that election would unfold.

That summer, the left pressed the nexus between climate change and the economy as a new rationalization for socialism. Framing climate change as the means to deconstruct a capitalism epitomized by "evil energy corporations" became alarmingly *de rigueur*. Activist Naomi Klein released her book *This Changes Everything*, which called for a socialist world order, celebrating climate-change risk as the unlikely pathway to a better (as she saw it) world. The book discusses at length the evil oil sands, which Klein argues should be shut down. She writes about KXL specifically, and about the heroic Bill McKibben working to prevent the project. The book was followed by a film of the same name, directed by Klein's husband, Avi Lewis, which received significant attention. At the same time, Pope Francis disseminated a similar and similarly dangerous message in his June 2015 encyclical, "On Care For Our Common Home,"[22] which he took around the world, including the United States. He managed, amazingly, to unite the Catholic Church, the U.S. Democratic Party, and far-left environmental movement all in the name of dealing with climate-change risk, regardless of the cost.

In early November of 2015, about three weeks after Harper lost to Justin Trudeau, whose Liberals won a surprising majority government, Obama announced at long last his decision on the fate of KXL.[23] He rejected the permit, stating that "America is now a global leader when it comes to taking serious action to fight climate change … frankly, approving this project would have undercut that leadership." Instead of identifying the project as a conventional infrastructure project, he transformed it into a symbol of the era that he presided over. Secretary John Kerry restated the same rationalization, that "moving forward with this project would significantly undermine our ability to continue leading the world in combating climate change."

But the most outrageous justification was contained in Kerry's press statement, wherein he stated that "this decision could not be made solely on the numbers." This was doubtless a truthful reflection of President Obama and Secretary Kerry's mindset.[24] Due process and technocratic assessment counted for nothing.

Kerry at least chose to acknowledge the impact the decision would have on Canada, but relied on the newly installed Trudeau government simply to "move on." Sadly, that is exactly what the Canadian government proceeded to do. "We are disappointed by the decision but respect the right of the U.S. to make the decision," Trudeau stated. "The Canada-U.S. relationship is much bigger than any one project and I look forward to a fresh start with President Obama to strengthen our remarkable ties in a spirit of friendship and co-operation."[25]

Girling issued a statement shortly after Obama's announcement: "Today, misplaced symbolism was chosen over merit and science — rhetoric won out over reason." What else could he say? "Today's decision," Girling continued, "cannot be reconciled with the conclusions of the State Department's comprehensive seven-year review of the project."[26] The epitaph for the demise of KXL. All those years of assessments, of rerouting, of playing ball, had amounted to nothing but rejection. All justified to preserve Obama's climate credibility. Sadly and ironically, over the same period, as KXL played out, U.S. crude oil production was restored to near historic peak levels. All with no apparent impact on the president's credibility.[27]

CHAPTER SEVEN

KEYSTONE XL'S HAUNTING QUESTIONS

The nightmare of endless process did end, but only with defeat for TransCanada. My former colleagues and I persisted for seven years, only to lose KXL. Was the prize worth the commitment? Yes, unequivocally. Was TransCanada treated cynically? Absolutely. Throughout, TransCanada assumed it was dealing with a more rational and balanced world than the one it actually faced. The company's senior management was certainly more sinned against than sinning. Would an appropriate set of fundamentally different tactical and strategic choices have altered the ultimate outcome? Or was President Obama's perverse and obviously political choice inevitable? This chapter will consider these difficult, haunting questions related to the demise of KXL.

The Route Through Nebraska

Many Nebraskans called for us to reroute in 2009, and that issue ultimately gave President Obama a rationalization to disrupt the established regulatory process — he used it twice, in 2011 and 2014. Between Obama's 2011 demand for a reroute and his 2015 denial, time worked against

TransCanada. ENGOs continued to frame KXL's denial as the proxy for any bona fides for President Obama on the climate-change issue, regardless of other, more substantial, carbon-policy initiatives and alternatives. His re-election in 2012 allowed him to decide the KXL issue without any consideration of his participation in future presidential election campaigns; he was liberated to follow his own biases. As the final decision extended into 2015, a denial became, from his perspective, more essential for the climate legacy he so desired.

Could TransCanada have reduced the opposition in Nebraska early in the process, thereby defusing the controversy and resistance in the state? Did the company adequately understand the risk of relying on Nebraska's political leadership to support due process for a "foreign" infrastructure company? Could it have reasonably anticipated that the DoS's validation for the original route through Nebraska would mean nothing? That Obama would not defer to the actual regulatory process? And the most haunting question of all: If TransCanada had changed the route as early as 2009, would it have received a permit in 2011?

In my view, TransCanada could have been more sensitive to the original concerns expressed over the Sandhills route back in 2009, despite the results of our own environmental assessments and our resulting confidence that the DoS would find no show-stopping risks related to the Sandhills or Ogallala Aquifer attributable to the project. We could have switched routes to avoid the Sandhills substantially, if not entirely. But I also know that a reroute would not have eliminated all the resistance or opposition within the state, much of which was fundamentally and implacably opposed, independent of the route. Some of that opposition took the form of classic landowner demands for greater financial compensation for land access, but more perversely, a minority of landowners were intent on denying us access on any terms — despite the inevitable legal rights of pipeline developers to gain access for a project judged to be in the public interest. TransCanada also faced some xenophobic resentment, not only as a nominally foreign company, but also as a foreign industry in a state with no indigenous hydrocarbon potential and therefore no share in the significant economic rents associated with the hydrocarbons traversing their state. For other Nebraskans essentially indifferent to the project, it was at best a mitigated, long-term risk, with only modest enduring economic benefits to claim in its favour. This same point could be made of much of the hydrocarbon pipeline infrastructure already traversing the state.

A small minority of Nebraskans, meanwhile, used KXL to advance a progressive political agenda fundamentally out of sync with the state's majority conservative political mindset. Resisting KXL provided a rallying point for them. That political opportunism transcended the specifics of the route, as their continued resistance after 2011 proved. Avoiding the Sandhills would not have changed the positions of some Nebraskans' regarding their excessive financial demands for access, or resistance to accepting any pipeline-related risk.

Also, frustratingly for TransCanada, Nebraskans had no consensus on what a reroute should look like. For some, such as Senator Johanns, "reroute" meant not only avoiding the Sandhills but also essentially abandoning the entire notion of a diagonal across Nebraska. What would have placated them, presumably, was for TransCanada to abandon the entire KXL concept and build instead a parallel expansion of base Keystone, traversing Nebraska north to south at the state's eastern border. That would have meant greater distance and cost. For others, a reroute meant merely avoiding the Sandhills, and for others still, a reroute meant avoiding Nebraska altogether.

As for Nebraska's Governor Heineman, TransCanada's capacity to understand his true intentions proved deficient. We did not anticipate that resistance to the pipeline would eventually persuade him to come out against the route. But this is exactly what he did in late August 2011. The timing of his reversal was enormously unfair to TransCanada, as it occurred just a few weeks before KXL could have potentially achieved a final and positive NID from the Obama administration. Heineman should have either clarified his terms much earlier, or continued deferring to the federal process. I remain unsure whether he ever genuinely wanted to obstruct KXL or even the Sandhills route. His opposition was an opportunistic political gesture, allowing him to finally register opposition while still relying on the governing federal process to grant approval. He could have reasonably expected that his opposition would come too late to materially impact the actual outcome. That way he could blame the Obama administration when the pipeline went ahead, and still gain significant economic benefits for the state from the construction process and ongoing land access and property tax payments.

As a Canadian company, TransCanada relied on the U.S. regulatory process to function reasonably. It assumed that that process would operate consistent with historic standards of professional competence and intellectual integrity, and it especially relied on the political leadership to defer to the technocratic assessment of their own regulatory system. At least with respect to the DoS itself, that expectation was met. Notably, the state of Nebraska participated in that process from late 2008 into 2011. The DoS substantially validated our original route, despite contentions from various interveners, primarily from within Nebraska, about the risks of traversing the Sandhills near the Ogallala Aquifer. The 2011 FEIS represented close to three years of regulatory process, public consultation, and special accommodations acceded to by TransCanada. Of course, Obama did not ultimately support that determination, for reasons that had nothing to do the merits of the route through Nebraska. Nevertheless, in the following years, TransCanada went on to accommodate a route change to placate the avowed concerns of Nebraskans with the original.

If TransCanada had shown more sensitivity to Nebraskan concerns, trusted the state's leadership less, and relied less heavily on the presumption that the DoS process would be validated by the Obama administration — if the company had rerouted in 2009 — would dilbit flow through the KXL pipeline today? Some argue that rerouting in 2009 might have forestalled the DoS's first supplemental DEIS, the first major delay in the anticipated regulatory time frame. The U.S. ENGOs demanded this SDEIS, with support from the likes of Henry Waxman, all of whom insisted on a more fundamental examination of the project's attributable carbon emissions and a revisiting of the existing pipeline operating standards, not simply the route through Nebraska. The resistance in Nebraska certainly contributed to the demand for more review, but the ENGO's fundamental objection was always oil sands production and its incremental carbon emissions enabled by the KXL project, not primarily, if at all, the Sandhills route. The ENGOs would have persisted with resistance even if TransCanada made all the accommodations Nebraskans wanted.

Sadly, that original route simply became a convenient rationalization for President Obama to avoid a decision in late 2011. But the real question is whether, without the Sandhills route in play, Obama would have been able to avoid a decision on KXL in 2011. If TransCanada had rerouted voluntarily as early as 2009, it would not have changed the opposition led by McKibben, which related fundamentally to carbon, not routing or pipeline safety. KXL would have remained a conduit of the world's most carbon-intensive source of crude oil regardless of how it moved through Nebraska. Yet the route issue did give Obama a convenient and plausible excuse to defer a decision in 2011, a delay that allowed him to placate the resistance. The deferral also allowed him to avoid alienating the few elements within the Democratic political coalition, primarily certain labour unions, who supported the project. His deferral was an example of political finesse, enabled by the controversy in Nebraska on routing, and especially legitimized by the state's own governor's ultimate opposition to the route.

My view remains that a reroute would not have ensured a positive decision in either 2010 or 2011. It was not a sufficient conditional for approval back then, nor, as we know now, was it one even in 2015. Would the odds of approval have been higher in 2010 and 2011 than what they were ultimately in 2015 if a reroute had been acceded earlier? Yes, but not sufficiently higher to ensure approval.

The Business Deal

TransCanada faced competition from other pipeline entities offering alternative projects, which used more circuitous routes to provide comparable Gulf Coast access for Alberta oil sands–derived crude oil. When it negotiated the underpinning commercial agreements with its prospective shippers, TransCanada had to find acceptable compromises amongst various key considerations relating to the project. Those agreements were rationalized based on the overall potential value of the project to TransCanada (initial scale, available return, and future expansion capacity) and internalizing anticipated risks, including those related to obtaining regulatory approvals.

No private sector pipeline developer can realistically expect to earn a reasonable financial return if it assumes no risk. It can reasonably expose its prospective returns as a function of its performance as pipeline developer and operator. That is fundamental to the value proposition it offers its shippers. It ultimately seeks to provide a service "on time" and within an agreed range of expected costs, relying on its experience and competencies.

Even as the Obama administration stretched out KXL's regulatory process over the entire period from 2008 to 2015, TransCanada maintained its shipper support. By November of 2011, TransCanada had spent in excess of $2 billion,[1] and in the first quarter of 2016, TransCanada announced a write-down of $2.9 billion,[2] a direct consequence of the denial of the project by the Obama administration.

In my view, the business deal that TransCanada committed to was reasonable, given the context of TransCanada's past regulatory experience, the compelling economics of the project as originally anticipated, and the application of conventional technology over relatively benign topography. Commitments to shippers as well as the obvious imperative to realize the anticipated financial value for TransCanada were material factors in the persistence of the company in wanting to realize the project throughout the entire course of the KXL experience right up to November of 2015, when the final denial occurred. How reasonable would it have been in 2007 to 2009 — when the underlying contractual commitments were entered into and the TransCanada position in Keystone increased to 100 percent — to have anticipated the perverse unfolding of events that actually occurred? What informed industry observer in those years would have placed any significant probability on such an outcome? Who would have advised to not seize the KXL opportunity? Very few, if any, I submit.

TransCanada's Communications Strategy

TransCanada adapted over the course of the entire KXL process to unprecedented scrutiny from both mainstream and social media. Our communications team responded to what evolved into almost daily high-profile rebuttal and advocacy, and did so civilly, adhering to the facts, as TransCanada understood them.

Overall, American public support for KXL held steady at 60 to 65 percent. Virtually all Republicans were onside with the project, but we never won over the vast majority of Democrats. This never changed, despite our communications team's efforts across all kinds of media. Nor did it change as a result of the various DoS determinations in favour of the project. Did TransCanada fail to find the right message on KXL or on the Canadian oil sands? Did it fail to find the right communications experts to get that message out? Could it have argued more persuasively that denying KXL would have no material impact on curtailing climate-change risk in the United States and beyond? Could the company have persuaded fair-minded people in the ENGO movement and the Democratic Party to support it?

I believe that public advocacy for a Canadian carbon-policy framework centred on carbon pricing, as opposed to mandated emission reductions or mandated production constraints as a quid pro quo for rationalizing a KXL approval, despite the reservations of elements within industry and the Harper government, could have improved the dynamic, both in terms of the public debate and how that might have impacted the Obama administration. TransCanada never chose that path, and consequently its own communications message was constrained. Advocating for carbon pricing may well have improved how TransCanada was perceived within the environmental movement and Democratic policy circles, if not by the Obama administration itself.

If TransCanada had publicly advocated for carbon pricing in Canada to "redeem" Keystone's incremental emissions, its communications story would have improved. As I will discuss later, carbon pricing in Canada might have influenced the Obama administration's decision on KXL; however, the American ENGO movement had already invested too much in achieving an outright KXL denial to change their minds, and the Democratic Party Congressional leadership would not have abided KXL if the ENGOs didn't. Certainly not until Obama himself accepted such a quid pro quo as reason to approve KXL.

Even more fundamentally, corporate interests, however indispensable to sustaining living standards and functional world economies, struggle to win broad public support beyond grudging acceptance. Advocates from the left enjoy an advantage, if only because their basic ethos is to redistribute wealth, not create it. It is always easier to promise free things with other people's money. As well, there is a special animus that exists for the hydrocarbon industry as a result of the climate-change risk. Popular culture reinforces a basic empathy for the left, and a narrative in which the environmental movement offers a future both more sustainable and moral than one that serves the interests of capital and encompasses hydrocarbon development. Never mind the long-term consequences of constrained development. Never mind that economic progress has historically correlated demonstrably with freer markets and increased hydrocarbon use.

My view remains that regardless of how much more intensive or inventive it might have been, our communication strategy could not have materially altered the positions of sufficient Democratic politicians, directly or indirectly, especially without embracing carbon-pricing advocacy. After 2011, any breakthrough on Keystone sufficient to sway the Obama administration would have had to occur in the policy arena. It would not merely come from reiterating the basic net benefits of the project. Those could be restated as much as possible, and validated by various DoS processes and other fair-minded analysts, but sadly they were never sufficient to change opinions within the Democratic base or the ENGO movement.

Did TransCanada Persist Too Long?

It bears repeating that TransCanada came to its most significant crossroads in the hours and days after Obama announced his decision to demand a reroute in November of 2011. When the company chose to persist at that time, it implicitly took Obama at his word — that the route through Nebraska was the issue at hand, an issue it could respond to. Its decision was consistent with the mindset it had applied to Keystone from the beginning — traditional regulatory processes would apply and be deferred to politically, notwithstanding President Obama's re-election. As noted earlier, that same conviction applied in midsummer of 2009, when TransCanada became sole owner of the entire project. Even as the 2010 supplemental environmental assessment was imposed, TransCanada accommodated the mandated additional operating conditions, despite their impact on project return. Even to that point, it had not yet encountered demands fundamentally beyond our capacity to accommodate.

At the end of 2011 and beginning of 2012, who would have unequivocally and compellingly argued that persevering with KXL was futile? On the other hand, despite Obama's 2011 intervention and TransCanada's accommodation of a reroute through Nebraska, who could confirm that this was the actual necessary and sufficient "must-have" for the Obama administration to commit to approval? Who really knew the ultimate mindset guiding Obama on KXL? It was reasonable to expect that Obama appreciated the immateriality of incremental emissions attributable to KXL, would simply defer to his DoS assessments, and that his initiative to deal with coal in the electric generation sector by using existing executive authorities under the Clean Air Act was a bigger element of his legacy on dealing with the climate-change risk. A prevailing view persisted that Obama was, after all, ultimately a moderate Democrat, and most assumed that he was aligned more to the mindset of Secretary Clinton circa 2010: "inclined to approve."

As mentioned earlier, a reasonable balance of probabilities at the end of 2011 would have suggested that with Obama there was at worst a 50/50 chance of approval and a re-election prospect on the order of 60/40. If a Republican was elected, the probability of a KXL approval was virtually 100 percent. The balance of those probabilities was in the range of 70 percent, validating the belief that persisting with the project was a reasonable risk to accept.

TransCanada's most basic assumption, that Obama was ultimately capable of rationalizing a KXL approval, proved to be wrong. But I do not believe he had already made an absolute decision to deny the project in November 2011. The continued vigorous advocacy by American environmentalists, including the later interventions of the billionaire Thomas Steyer over the 2012 to 2014 period, suggests they were not yet sure of the outcome either, and so their actions to some extent validate TransCanada's wary confidence to persist. Moreover, by "playing ball" with the Obama administration, TransCanada won a consolation prize — the southern Gulf Coast Pipeline. That represented value, and the Obama administration did actually facilitate that project throughout 2012 and 2013.

My view unequivocally remains that it was an entirely reasonable business judgment to persist with the project at that critical moment in November of 2011, based on the actual demand made of TransCanada, a reroute through Nebraska. It was, after all, a demand that could be accommodated. Admittedly, when the Obama administration insisted on a do-over of the environmental assessment in early 2012, concerns arose that Obama was not acting in good faith. Why was an entire environmental do-over required if the route through Nebraska was the only issue? Of course, it was apparent that Obama wanted to defer a decision beyond the 2012 election. More process served his political interests.

Once the decision to persist had been made by TransCanada, there was really no turning back until the entire do-over had run its course. Sadly, the length of that do-over would work to TransCanada's ultimate disadvantage.

Changes in Canadian Carbon Policy: A Rationalization Obama Needed

Beginning in 2012, I came to the view that Obama required more than the 2011 DoS FEIS to overcome McKibben's argument against KXL. What more could be offered up that might provide some further rationalization for approving the project? The only card left was for Canada to impose a credible carbon tax on its national carbon emissions, including those incremental emissions attributable to the volumes carried by KXL. By the end of 2013, economically internalizing the potential impact of those incremental emissions was Canada's only hope to gain the economic benefits of that production while showing itself genuinely responsive to the climate risk. By setting a carbon price on those emissions via a national carbon tax, Canada could have taken the lead in North America on carbon policy, using carbon pricing to deal with the risk of climate change rather than setting disingenuous carbon targets. This was all the more necessary since Canada would emit increasing carbon if it developed its hydrocarbon resources to the extent anticipated by the Canadian industry, facilitated by infrastructure like KXL.

But Prime Minister Harper's government remained adamantly opposed not only to carbon taxes but to carbon pricing in any form. TransCanada's shippers and other industry supporters also resisted such a concept. Carbon pricing would mean a real incremental cost, both short- and long-term, and doubt persisted that offering it up might not achieve an approval. TransCanada chose not to challenge its shippers, the Canadian hydrocarbon industry collectively, and the Harper government with a public demand to embrace a carbon tax as a quid pro quo for KXL approval.

Prime Minister Stephen Harper and President Obama.

Many disagreed with me at the time, and disagree with me still, that offering carbon tax as a quid pro quo for a Keystone XL approval would have made a real difference. Few disputed, however, that by 2013 it was the only card left to play for TransCanada, the industry, Alberta, and Canada. The belief persisted that Obama would approve KXL based on the existing regulatory analysis of the project inclusive of its carbon effects, as of mid-year 2013. The 2013 DEIS was still viewed as a template for approval. Even Obama's Georgetown speech suggested an approval was still possible, as long as he concurred that the DoS determination of the materiality of incremental emissions attributable to KXL conformed to his "not significantly exacerbate" standard. Of course, TransCanada was never able to penetrate the inner sanctum of Obama's administration to corroborate what the Georgetown speech really signalled. But if Canada kept defining its carbon policy in terms of disingenuous targets, indifferently pursued, why wouldn't the Obama administration remain skeptical, even contemptuous, of the Harper government with respect to its climate bona fides? And if that was the case, why wouldn't KXL end up as collateral damage?

Yet the rebuttal was always the same: Could Obama be sufficiently trusted for us to presume that a national carbon tax would a sufficient quid pro quo for approval? A legitimate concern, but not sufficient to prevent, in my judgment, approaching the Obama administration. Admittedly, a carbon tax would imply higher costs for Canadian crude oil production, but the improved economics offered by KXL alone, relative to rail transport, would have offset those costs substantially. Over time, new pipeline capacity would eliminate constraints on market access for potentially significant incremental production. The carbon tax could have paid for itself if it had actually achieved a KXL approval. But this argument was not persuasive enough to compel the industry to vigorously insist that the Harper government put the quid pro quo in play with conviction.

As for the U.S. hydrocarbon industry, its most active vehicle for engagement on the KXL issue was the American Petroleum Institute (API). The API was dominated by major integrated oil companies such as ExxonMobil, Chevron, and ConocoPhilips — entities with major interests in the Canadian oil sands and LNG (liquid natural gas) developments. Those entities supported the idea of carbon pricing conceptually, and even preferred carbon taxes as the specific policy instrument for responding to pressure to deal with GHGs, but always placed the onus on governments to lead with specific terms. Meanwhile, since losing Waxman-Markey and the House of Representatives in 2010, the Obama administration had effectively written off carbon pricing as a federal initiative. This tension resulted in a bizarre default. Neither side advocated specific carbon pricing terms, but the Obama administration relied on its regulatory authorities to advance mandated carbon emission reductions, while the API et al generally resisted these initiatives.

I concede that the Obama administration never explicitly asked for credible carbon pricing on the Canadian oil sands as a quid pro quo on KXL. But the onus surely lay with Canada to make a first move. Prime Minister Harper ostensibly won the 2008 Canadian federal election on the basis of opposing the Liberal opposition's policy initiative to use carbon taxes as a major policy instrument for tax reform and climate policy. He claimed that such a tax would represent an additional cost, as counterproductive as any incremental tax, and would not likely curtail Canadian emissions meaningfully, let alone significantly contribute to lessening the global climate-change risk. He chose to have Canada withdraw from its Kyoto emission commitments, but at Copenhagen chose to commit to other disingenuous carbon reduction targets for Canada. Targets the country could not meet without significant economic contraction of hydrocarbon production capacity or massive intervention in energy systems within Canada, neither of which his government had any intention of imposing. At the heart of Harper's approach was seemingly cynicism, if not real indifference. He showed dubious judgment on Canada's dilemma between dealing credibly with the climate-change risk and its own economic interests.

Perhaps it is possible to attribute to Harper the same mindset held by the most atavistic of American right-wing think tanks — that a carbon tax is ultimately just another tax, never likely to become revenue neutral in practice. No North American carbon tax would ever be sufficiently "global" to preclude free riders, or high enough to meaningfully deal with the risk of climate change, at least not in the short and medium term.

But unlike a U.S. president, with the constraints of division of powers that exist in the United States, Prime Minister Harper had de facto the capacity to enact a revenue-neutral carbon tax, especially after 2011 when he achieved his majority government mandate. Had he done so, he would not have faced much significant political opposition within Canada. Harper's political opposition had been persistent advocates of more aggressive Canadian carbon policy, including carbon pricing. But Harper would have had to publicly recant his previous position, instead of potentially salvaging KXL and all that would have meant economically for Canada, and providing a credible carbon position for the country.

Prime Minister Harper always supported the Canadian hydrocarbon industry, and particularly its infrastructure ambitions. As a leader of the national government, he was seen as sympathetic to hydrocarbon interests, while his political opposition expressed reservations and outright antipathies toward reliance on hydrocarbon production as a major cornerstone of the national economy. He was the best political champion available to that industry, but that does not absolve Harper of his failures on carbon policy for Canada and in turn contributing to the outcome on KXL. Harper did support KXL, but within narrow parameters no longer sufficient by mid-2013 to sway Obama, even assuming they ever had been satisfactory.

I acknowledge again that throughout most of the Keystone approval process, Alberta had in place a "carbon levy" — a de facto low-grade carbon tax that applied only to large industrial emitters, including the oil sands. However, it applied only to emissions incurred after 2005, at $15/tonne of emitted carbon equivalent in lieu of physical reductions. On a total emissions basis, the resulting carbon tax was less than $5/tonne. The levy was not revenue neutral, and the proceeds funded low-carbon technology development in the province. Having a "levy" rather than a "tax" finessed some conservative sensibilities both in Alberta and in the Prime Minister's Office, but it was comparable to what carbon-trading schemes had achieved across the United States and Europe in terms of actual price.[3] Evidently, the levy was not sufficiently stringent to impress the Obama administration.

In 2013, the Alberta government and corporate interests from the oil sands sector discussed expanding the levy in terms of price and applicability so that it would more closely resemble a cutting-edge carbon tax, at least on the order of $30–40/tonne of emitted carbon. Then premier Redford vigorously tried to achieve a breakthrough on the market-access issue, using carbon pricing as a basis of some compromise. Her efforts might have formed the foundation of a proposal to Obama, but it never achieved sufficient industry support, let alone serious consideration from the Prime Minister's Office. It was frustrating that the province did not receive more credit for what it had accomplished with its carbon levy, its transparency on emissions performance, and its commitment to improving technology. The environmental movement and the Obama administration should have recognized more fairly these constructive initiatives occurring with Alberta.

I recognize that a credible Canadian carbon tax may not have persuaded President Obama to approve KXL. I doubt that McKibben would have supported swapping a tax for KXL, and neither would have the likes of the NRDC either; the environmental movement sees such taxes only as complimentary policy instrument to mandated emission reductions. Carbon pricing via carbon taxes, according to the environmental movement, is not a sufficient, stand-alone carbon policy. Still, Obama had already publicly called carbon pricing his preferred policy response, and his 2009 support for Waxman-Markey validated that. However, political gridlock had doubtless hardened him, and in the absence of new legislation, he defaulted to regulation. Approving KXL in exchange for a carbon tax — rationalizing a highly carbon-intense source of crude oil — might have even changed the dynamic unfolding for the 2015 Paris climate conference: instead of voluntary national physical emission reductions commitments, a focus on carbon pricing.

Nevertheless, the fall of 2013 was not November 2015, and engaging with the Obama administration with a credible carbon-pricing proposal as quid pro quo for KXL was both plausible and essential. Canada should have tried. The Canadian industry in its totality should have advocated publicly for that quid pro quo. It was a missed opportunity.

Summary

With respect to KXL, TransCanada was more sinned against than sinning. Ultimately, the company was undone by President Obama's particular vulnerability to the demands of the American ENGO movement as they evolved over the course of the Keystone regulatory process. He viewed the project as a meaningful symbol of his carbon legacy when he should have instead tried to achieve more genuine breakthroughs on carbon policy — breakthroughs that might have been facilitated by an accommodation on KXL via carbon pricing.

If TransCanada had shown greater sensitivity in Nebraska, and enabled a route adjustment, that might have, in turn, reduced in-state hostility and removed Obama's convenient excuse to avoid a decision in 2011. Greater public advocacy of credible carbon pricing in Canada might have improved the prospects of receiving an accommodation from Obama on KXL. However, the fundamental business opportunity for TransCanada was worth all seven years of effort, even in terms of reputational impact and financial exposure. TransCanada management could not have reasonably anticipated that KXL would evolve into a kind of proxy war for the environmental movement, or that even a Democratic administration would accede to those demands. Certainly not in 2008 and 2009, and not even necessarily in 2011. Even in 2013, TransCanada reasonably expected Obama to defer to the professional, intellectually rigorous assessment of his administration's lead agency, the Department of State. That due process and some respect for the basic interests and value of capital within the economy and society at large should have meant something, and should not have been discarded to bolster the ephemeral standard of "credibility" for the uncertain and perhaps dubious Paris climate process of late 2015.

KXL could have represented real economic value to Canada. Many plausible scenarios can be theorized for future crude oil prices, cost structures for Canadian oil sands production, and carbon policy to quantitatively measure that value, primarily as cash flow back to Canada from export revenues.

But how much cash annually, then, would have come back to Canada? Two benchmarks bound plausible estimates. First, assume that KXL, with its 800,000-barrel capacity, moved existing barrels now sent out by rail to U.S. Gulf Coast markets. According to Premier Rachel Notley's spring 2016 pleading before the Trudeau Cabinet, the gain to Canada from improved transportation economics would be on the scale of $8/bbl, an incremental value slightly in excess of $2 billion annually. Second, consider a case where all of the barrels moved on KXL are incremental to what is being currently produced with existing transportation infrastructure. Incremental cash flow will be a function of crude prices net of incremental costs to produce and transport the barrels to market. Assuming a margin of $40/bbl on each barrel moved on KXL on the scale of 800,000-bbl/day capacity, an incremental cash flow of roughly $15 billion annually would be generated.[4]

Directly and indirectly, this cash flow would have paid Canadians employed in oil sands production and transportation, would service Canadian bond and equity holders, and would fund Canadian governments. If crude prices exceeded $60/bbl (a reasonable estimate of average full cost economics for installed oil sands production capacity), the resulting economic rents would provide a greater opportunity for Canadian governments to appropriate them. Consider the impact of incremental cash flow on the range of $2 to 20 billion a year into Canada; Alberta expects an operating deficit of roughly $10 billion for 2017, and the federal government expects its operating deficit to reach close to $30 billion that same year. Even a carbon tax on the order of $30/tonne would cost most operators no more than $2/bbl equivalent to their cost structures — less than the overall transportation cost savings that KXL could have generated.[5]

But Canada's broader body politic, beyond those from hydrocarbon-producing provinces and the right-of-centre political parties and interest groups, did not seemingly appreciate what was at stake. Too many were simply indifferent to Canada losing a significant contribution to its GDP based on private sector investment, and consistent with its actual competitive advantages. Many Canadians still insist the country can resort to economic alternatives to hydrocarbon resource development, despite Canada's inherent scale and geographic disadvantages. This delusion persists.

KXL was always an essential infrastructure option for Canada. It offered the highest value with the least impact within Canada. That should have been recognized and embraced by all Canadians. Canadian resistors to Keystone XL did the country no service.

PART TWO

TO BE OR NOT TO BE
— *Hamlet,* Act 3, Scene 1

CHAPTER EIGHT

CANADA POST-XL

Canada's Other Pipelines:
Northern Gateway, TransMountain, and Energy East

The DoS's five EIS assessments of KXL contended that Canada would move its oil to market with or without the project, and that the pipeline would therefore make no difference to how much the oil sands were exploited. Many American commentators likewise believed that Canada would, and could, look after its own economic interests regardless of whether Obama approved the pipeline; some even worried that without KXL, Canada might sell the oil to China instead of the United States. Canada also had the option to ship its crude back into the United States using tankers if it could access tidewater.[1]

This U.S. expectation that Canada would realize its economic interests strikes me now as a great irony. Does Canada really share the fundamental conviction that developing its hydrocarbon resources is in their public interest? Since KXL's demise, Canada has shown itself profoundly equivocal to that proposition. The demands of some elements within current federal and provincial political leadership, ascendant environmentalists, extreme NIMBY concerns from proximate communities, and resistance from some segments of the

Aboriginal community likely transcend what any pipeline project could ever accommodate.

If Canada is to develop its oil sands potential post-KXL, the country requires pipelines from northern Alberta to tidewater. Of all the pipeline projects conceived and developed to move incremental barrels from the oil sands, KXL was always the best alternative, in terms of maximizing cash flow back to Canada, long-term capacity to accommodate expansions, and direct alignment with the most valuable market available to Alberta crude, namely the U.S. Gulf Coast. However, with KXL's demise, three major Canadian pipeline projects emerged: Enbridge's Northern Gateway, Kinder Morgan's TransMountain expansion, and TransCanada's Energy East. All were logical responses to the same business opportunity that spawned KXL: growing oil sand crude production requiring incremental pipeline access. All offered direct access to Canadian tidewater. And all required approvals only within Canada. As of mid-year 2016, the regulatory, legal, and political dispositions of these projects remain unresolved; none have progressed to the point of actually being under construction. All of which demonstrates that for Canada today, rationalizing economic opportunity based on its hydrocarbon development and a commitment to a lower carbon future is seemingly no easier than it was for Barack Obama.

The Northern Gateway Pipeline, sponsored by TransCanada's major corporate rival and direct competitor, Enbridge, would be the first pipeline committed exclusively to moving oil sands–derived crude from Edmonton terminalling facilities to the northern British Columbia deepwater port of Kitimat, originally developed in the 1950s to transport processed aluminum ore. From the Kitimat terminus, the oil would move out on tankers, navigating the Douglas Channel, then move on to the Pacific. With a current estimated cost approaching nearly $8 billion,[2] the project's capacity is roughly two-thirds of what KXL was expected to provide — slightly more than 500,000 barrels per day.[3] The product could reach Asian and West Coast U.S. markets, distinctly different markets than KXL could directly access, but could

Northern Gateway route map.

also potentially access the U.S. Gulf Coast via the Panama Canal.

Enbridge filed its application with the NEB on May 27, 2010, and the project was conditionally approved roughly four years later by the Harper government.[4] The regulatory process governing Northern Gateway had the NEB and the Canadian Environmental Assessment Agency proceed together under a combined panel, known as the "Joint Review Panel."[5]

Northern Gateway always faced several fundamental challenges; in Canada, its regulatory, legal, and political struggles have become a formidable *cause célèbre*, rivalling, in Canadian terms, the KXL experience in some respects. First, although the basic topography along Northern Gateway's route resembles that of north-central Alberta, once it reaches the coastal mountains, it meets the formidable engineering challenge of moving diluted bitumen at high elevation across difficult mountain passes. Second, most of the Northern Gateway route crosses land subject to unsettled lands claims from various Aboriginal entities. Third, British Columbia would accrue no economic rents from the Alberta oil sands resource moving through it. And fourth: any potential crude oil spills in the channels from Kitimat to the Pacific would impact the coastline of northern British Columbia, an area now referred to as part of the "Great Bear Rainforest." The possibility, however small, of such a spill has been deemed unacceptable to virtually all Canadian environmental entities. As early as April 2010, even before Enbridge had submitted its Northern Gateway application, let alone any regulatory disposition of its risks or proposed mitigations,

Aboriginal Canadian groups proximate to Kitimat called for a crude oil tanker ban for the British Columbia north coast.[6]

Kinder Morgan filed its application for TransMountain in late 2013.[7] The project entailed expanding a pipeline that already supplied Alberta crude oil to the Lower Mainland of British Columbia, following the existing right-of-way west from Edmonton, through Jasper National Park, moving south through Kamloops and along the Fraser River into terminals at Burnaby, B.C. Using that existing right-of-way should have reduced overall costs and stakeholder opposition. The project, involving both new build and debottlenecking existing pipeline sections, offered a capacity of slightly more than 600,000 barrels per day, and would also expand terminalling at Burnaby, B.C.[8] However, TransMountain's unique challenge lay in the increased tanker traffic it would bring to Burrard Inlet and to shipping channels from the Pacific Ocean to Vancouver. Local resistance beset

Kinder Morgan TransMountain expansion route map.

TransMountain, especially in the Burnaby area and ultimately across the entire Lower Mainland — resistance so virulent that Kinder Morgan required intervention by the NEB, courts, and local policing authorities just to complete the environment assessments for its NEB application process.[9] However, using existing right-of-way meant the project faced somewhat less resistance than Northern Gateway from Aboriginal elements, but by no means overwhelming support.

Energy East was spawned as a direct consequence of Obama's November 2011 announcement that KXL required rerouting through Nebraska: in addition to persevering with KXL, TransCanada decided to develop an all-Canadian route alternative. The 4,500-kilometre pipeline would transport approximately 1.1 million barrels of crude oil per day from Alberta and Saskatchewan to the refineries of eastern Canada and then on to a marine terminal in New Brunswick. TransCanada would convert parts of the existing TransCanada natural gas mainline system between Alberta and the Ontario-Quebec border to an oil transportation pipeline, construct new crude oil pipeline capacity primarily in Quebec and New Brunswick to link up with the converted pipe, and construct terminalling facilities in New Brunswick. Energy East would carry Alberta diluted bitumen to Canadian tidewater, and on to markets that KXL would have accessed along the U.S. Gulf Coast, but also markets beyond North America, if market conditions evolved favourably. The scale of Energy East would rival that of KXL at over 800,000 barrels per day, with an expected initial investment of over $10 billion. The project was conceived in late 2011, with underpinning commercial agreements put in place the following year.[10]

Energy East's economic impact would reach across the entire country.[11] It would provide Canadian access to oil sands crude to Quebec and the Maritimes, improve the economic utilization of TransCanada's natural gas system via conversion to crude oil transport, contribute substantially to local property taxes, and, like all of these projects, enable greater direct export revenues back to Canada.

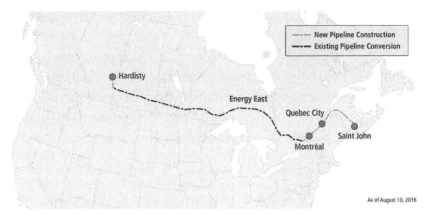

Energy East route map.

TransCanada originally planned for an oil terminal in Quebec, in the upstream sections of the St. Lawrence River, which would increase economic impact in that province. However, that element of the project was cancelled due to concerns over the impact of construction on beluga whale populations.

In early 2016, TransCanada was still working to have its NEB application for Energy East deemed "complete," at which point at which the mandated cycle to render a regulatory decision on the project would begin.[12] This determination was finally achieved in mid-June 2016.[13]

Two basic driving forces gave all three pipelines economic impetus. First, as the pipelines were conceived, the commodity price of crude oil exceeded $80/bbl — enough to reasonably expect as much as 3 million barrels per day of oil sands–derived crude production by the end of the decade, and, therefore, a need for greater pipeline capacity — even perhaps a need for all of these projects. Second, any of the pipelines would provide improved transportation costs relative to the status quo of rail transportation as the alternative of last resort. If all three projects were approved and contracted, Canada might have some surplus pipeline capacity in the short-run; nevertheless, all enjoyed commercial support from strong producing and refining interests, validating the basic economic opportunity provided by the oil sands resource. Although the oil price declined beginning in the fall of 2014, the projects kept their commercial support into 2016.

Northern Gateway: How Canada Resists its Own Hydrocarbon Potential

Northern Gateway was conceived and developed concurrent with KXL, while TransMountain and Energy East were developed mostly after KXL's November 2011 setback. All relied on the expectation that Canada's regulatory and political systems would deliver the required approvals, notwithstanding environmentalist and Aboriginal resistance, based on their inherent economic value and imminently mitigable environmental and stakeholder impacts. Like KXL, these three projects required hundreds of millions of dollars to achieve regulatory approval, all funded at the risk of the proponents and their shippers. None, of course, would have made such expenditures if they thought the projects would not gain approval. In the pre-XL world, pipeline developments had always gained necessary regulatory approvals. Even when losing KXL became a real possibility, the other three pipelines retained private sector contractual support with strong credit-rated counterparties, which had substantially validated their enduring inherent economic credibility. Their approval became a national imperative. At least, that was the view inside the Canadian hydrocarbon industry.

Up to October 2015, Canadian carbon policy offered no material constraints on oil sands development, whether Liberal or Conservative governments held power. Since the Kyoto commitment, the Canadian federal government imposed no physical reduction requirements on the oil sands industry, despite the commitment to meet goals made at Kyoto and Copenhagen. Even Alberta's carbon levy, a de facto low-cost carbon tax, had no material impact on oil sands investment or production. However, Canada's ENGO movement learned from the KXL experience that the regulatory process could be obstructed, all to attract public attention, buy time, and wait for politically empathetic governments to render the ultimate "go/no-go" decision. Like KXL, Northern Gateway,

TransMountain, and Energy East have faced the unrelenting resistance of the entire ENGO community, based substantially on the incremental climate impacts attributed to oil sands development.

Any and all of these projects would obviously enable the prospects for increased crude oil production from the oil sands, both short- and long-term, and in turn for increased carbon emissions, whether measured on an appropriate incremental basis or simply in terms of absolute total emissions generated within Canada. Little, if any, prospects for technology improvements can fundamentally change that reality in the short and medium term.[14] Admittedly, world commodity prices and the inherent cost structure of oil sands production will determine ultimate production levels, but sufficient pipeline infrastructure is essential to realizing this economic potential. Carbon policy will admittedly impact that potential, either via a sufficiently high carbon tax or some absolute regulated limit on allowable emissions from oil sands production. In Canada, however, with no direct carbon policy directed at the oil sands resource, the ENGO community resorted to frustrating the progress of infrastructure.

The Canadian ENGO community shared the same basic attitude of McKibben and Hansen about the oil sands — of all the world's accessible hydrocarbons, why use one of the most carbon intensive? Moreover, given Canada's emission reduction targets and the relative challenge of achieving material emission reductions in other sectors, due to geography, climate, existing capital stock, and political realities, how could any oil sands growth be countenanced? Politicians are less likely to constrain hydrocarbon end use than to simply constrain hydrocarbon output, especially if substantially intended for export. Of course, this regrettably ignores the economic cost to Canada of such a national carbon policy or how that cost compares to what other oil production competitors impose on themselves in terms of carbon policy.

Attributed carbon effects remain the most fundamental source of antipathy to all three pipeline projects, as they were for KXL. In terms of environmental assessment, proponents of the pipeline projects both expected and relied on the Canadian regulatory authorities to disregard emissions beyond those directly attributable to the actual pipeline construction and operation. And for Northern Gateway and TransMountain, the National Energy Board concurred: upstream carbon impacts were not subject to environmental review.[15] This scoping was deeply resented by the Canadian ENGOs, who legally challenged it as a fundamental error of due process, claiming that such attributable effects should at least be considered in the overall environmental assessment. There can be a link between pipeline capacity and the ultimate scale of oil sands production and therefore emissions. Insufficient pipeline infrastructure will ultimately constrain production, even ignoring a scenario of infinite railcar and track capacity. Constrained production means less emissions than would otherwise occur — "all things being equal," as the economists would say.

Frustrating infrastructure should not be a substitute for forthright carbon policy. I certainly acknowledge that the Canadian ENGO movement found itself, before 2015, in a vicious Catch-22. Alberta's regulation of oil sands production facilities has been fundamentally permissive, no federal policy constrained oil sands production or emissions, and upstream effects were out of scope in the regulatory processes on related pipeline infrastructure. All this culminated in Canada emitting more carbon, regardless of its nominal reduction targets. Of course, up to 2015 that reality did have democratic sanction in Alberta as well as federally, in the form of elected Conservative governments. Not surprisingly, Canadian ENGOs resorted to obstruction and delay, and fought for the country to elect a political leadership empathetic to their goals.

But these three pipelines projects also faced, and continue to face, resistance on three fronts apart from carbon: demands from Canada's Aboriginal people, direct stakeholder impacts, and allocation of resource rents from hydrocarbon production.

I use the term "Aboriginal people" as the *Report on the Royal Commission of Aboriginal People* defines it, to include Canada's Inuit, First Nations (Indians), and Métis.[16] The federal government of Canada has a constitutionally enshrined fundamental fiduciary obligation to Canada's Aboriginal people, the implications of which transcend Canadian hydrocarbon resource development. Moreover, Aboriginal people enjoy a unique legal and constitutional position relative to other Canadians. The federal government must "consult" with Aboriginal people on any development's potential impacts on them, and where possible find mutually agreeable accommodations. This obligation applies regardless of whether they have settled land claims or not, and regardless of existing treaties. What constitutes sufficient "consultation" and adequate and equitable "accommodation" is evolving and ambiguous, for both Canadian government and project developers.[17] Project proponents have de facto assumed the Crown's obligation to "consult" with Aboriginal people, and have done so essentially in the same manner as occurs with other landowners and directly impacted stakeholders along pipelines. The fundamental facts of the project, identified impacts and risks, planned mitigations, potential procurement and employment benefits, and finally, where applicable, financial compensation for consensual access are communicated. The regulatory process exists to test the adequacy of proposed mitigations. In many cases, pipeline developers provide funding to impacted stakeholders, particularly Aboriginal people, to ensure they have adequate legal and expert representation. As noted earlier, if proponents and landowners cannot agree consensually, developers can ultimately resort to expropriation remedies.

However, it's not clear whether such remedies are available to proponents with respect to land where Aboriginal people have achieved land settlement agreements with the federal government or even have claims for such settlements. The 2014 Supreme Court of Canada Tsilhqot'in decision has only added to this ambiguity, referring to an undefined standard of "compelling national interest" to compromise the land rights of Aboriginal people. Unfortunately, it offered no practical guidance.[18] If the NEB determines a project in the national interests, is Aboriginal title still subject to the same expropriation processes that apply to any other Canadian landowner? Without that clarity, a developer could still face a circumstance where the failure to achieve consensual land access with certain Aboriginal groups could stymie a project deemed in the national interest.

This legal ambiguity is most difficult in British Columbia, where most of the province has either no treaties or no settled land claim agreements. In particular, Enbridge's Northern Gateway faced the greatest resistance from Aboriginal people proximate to the pipeline route and marine interfaces to the project. Some resisted so ardently that no financial compensation could suffice. Did that resistance represent a de facto veto on the project, regardless of any determinations by the national regulator? If that were actually true, then Canada would be genuinely dysfunctional.

Resisting projects, in part to improve leverage in their negotiations with the federal government on land claim settlements and bilateral disputes, becomes part of the dynamic, just as the ENGOs use delay and obstruction to achieve climate policy objectives not otherwise available. Even if a project proponent actually proceeds with construction sanctioned by the national regulator, risk remains that Canadian courts could grant injunctive relief to certain Aboriginal interests until those same courts have in effect "second-guessed" the prior regulatory determination of national interest. All of which casts doubt whether project proponents will have the right to traditional remedies to ensure land access.

Related to this but distinct in its legal context is the NIMBY phenomenon. NIMBY, of course, stands for "not in my back yard," and I use the term NIMBYism to cover resistance from non-Aboriginal Canadians over matters such as safety impacts to proximate communities from operations and construction, adequacy of specific emergency response commitments, enduring environmental and quality-of-life impacts, potential economic impacts on collateral industries, and adequacy of potential accommodation. The proximate impacts of construction and operations have always been a fundamental concern of the regulatory process, which exists, in part, to ensure reasonable engineering standards and procedures, and adequate compensation and insurance to mitigate anticipated impacts. A well-established, evolving set of industry standards and practices ensure that the operating risks of pipelines, and their marine interfaces, are reasonably mitigated for high-volume hydrocarbon transport. KXL's fifty-nine special conditions beyond traditional operating and construction practice is one recent example. Yet, with respect to Canada's oil sands pipelines, some landowners and related municipalities claim that virtually any risk is unacceptable, regardless of the national economic value at stake. It's a position so extreme that no set of undertakings, mitigations, or insurance funds could rationalize any possibility of oil spills, however minimal that possibility may be.

Traditionally, local resistance ultimately deferred to regulators, who determined an adequate risk-reward balance in the context of net economic benefits. However, local resistance influences both local and provincial politicians, who ask how much risk their particular communities must bear, and who gains the major share of the economic benefits. NIMBYism naturally segues into questions of how the economic rents from these pipelines — and the crude they carry — will be distributed throughout Canada. Some provinces balk at accepting the risk that comes with pipelines traversing their land when most of the economic rents accrue to Alberta and investors in crude oil. Economic impact from the construction process does not endure, and ongoing operational jobs and significant enduring property tax contributions are often seen as insufficient to rationalize acceptance of any risk from operations and construction, regardless of how mitigated. For some provinces and some of their local communities, existing national transfer mechanisms, such as equalization payments between, apparently does not adequately redress the economic imbalance between those who gain and those who bear risk, regardless of Alberta's past and future contributions to those transfer mechanisms.

British Columbia, via Premier Christy Clark government's "five demands," has explicitly called for reinventing some of the basic tenets of Canadian federalism with respect to any potential acquiescence to the Northern Gateway project or the Kinder Morgan TransMountain expansion. Ontario and Quebec may also impose similar demands related to Energy East. Alberta would have to revisit how to share its resource rents, principally oil sands production royalties, with these other provinces. British Columbia, Ontario, and Quebec might then presumably accept risks specific to their jurisdictions, regardless of prior adjudication of net benefits by the national regulator. British Columbia in effect contends that it owns its coastlines and access to them, that they are not a national resource whose access should be adjudicated by federal regulators in the context of national net benefits determinations. The perversity of this logic might compel Alberta to impose transit taxes on goods that enter Canada through B.C. ports and traverse Alberta to eastern markets, breaking down one of the foundations of Canadian federalism — free trade between provinces.

It is worth noting British Columbia's hypocrisy on this matter: its position on LNG development in the province's northeast was always strikingly different from its position on moving oil sands crude, even though the pipeline to access northern B.C. ports would have some comparable environmental impacts. Particularly, LNG facilities represent a significant source of incremental emissions and much of the basic pipelining process is common to carrying either crude oil or natural gas. Of course, Northern Gateway and the TransMountain expansion would carry an out-of-province resource, Alberta's oil sands–derived crude oil, while LNG facilities will process a substantially B.C. resource, natural gas, with the potential for economic rents, if any, accruing substantially to that province.[19]

In September 2012, well after Enbridge filed the Northern Gateway project, British Columbia codified its demands by setting public conditions for its support: acceptably low construction and operational risks for both marine and pipeline elements, sufficient Aboriginal alignment, and a share in economic rents. British Columbia would determine whether these conditions were met, without deferring to the federal process — the province essentially claiming a right to determine the use of its coastline regardless of national public-interest determinations.[20]

Allison Redford's government in Alberta did not so much directly oppose British Columbia's demands as engage in more process and dialogue.[21] If Harper maintained his majority, then Alberta might have a federal ally to confront British Columbia. During his short-lived tenure as premier in 2014 and 2015, Jim Prentice did not differ substantially from Redford in his approach to the Clark government; he never directly called out British Columbia's position as violating the basic tenets of Canadian federalism. Prentice may have believed he could ultimately broker accommodations with the B.C. government, but with the collapse of crude oil prices in the fall of 2014, Alberta lost any financial capacity to buy support for Northern Gateway.[22]

The Harper government proved just as unwilling to call out Christie Clark's B.C. government. Clark, who represented British Columbia's right-of-centre political alternative, won a surprising majority in 2013, in no small part thanks to her strong advocacy for the province's liquid natural gas opportunity and her five conditions to grant any oil sands pipeline access to B.C. tidewater. Her position did not overtly oppose Northern Gateway, but her five conditions were so open-ended, subjective, and self-determined that they amounted to opposition.

In April 2013, the NEB announced 199 conditions for Northern Gateway, and Enbridge set out to analyze and accommodate them.[23] One of the most problematic related to increased Aboriginal alignment. In spite of the Clark government's opposition, by December 2013 the Joint Review Panel recommended Northern Gateway for approval, with the final number of required conditions increased to 209. On June 17, 2014, Harper's government accepted the Joint Review Panel recommendation that Northern Gateway could proceed, conditional on meeting those 209 conditions.[24]

Commercial and regulatory processes continued over this period for both TransMountain and Energy East, despite opposition in British Columbia similar to that directed against Northern Gateway and indifferent support from central Canadian politicians for Energy East.

Without confronting British Columbia's demands, the Harper government accepted the NEB's recommendation to approve Northern Gateway, but left the onus on Enbridge to satisfy the required conditions, and ultimately to request a leave to construct (permission to commence construction) — an inadequate position intended to avoid unduly alienating B.C. voters for the next federal election in 2015. I find it regrettable that Canada's government failed to assert federal jurisdiction and the overall national interest by not actually encouraging Enbridge to vigorously pursue leave to construct and then ultimately granting it.

The Harper government essentially treaded water through the remainder of 2014 and into 2015, remaining ambivalent about whether Enbridge had sufficiently met the NEB conditions, and never signalled that, if Enbridge were to ask for permission to actually commence construction, it would support the project against inevitable legal challenges and on-the-ground civil disobedience. So, Enbridge strove to satisfy the NEB's conditions for certification as best it could, but demurred from forcing the issue with the Harper government by asking the NEB for leave to construct. It did not choose to bring the project's fate to a head, especially without significant Aboriginal support or any accommodation of British Columbia's revenue-sharing demands.

The Harper government missed its opportunity to support Enbridge in commencing construction on Northern Gateway prior to the 2015 election. That failure left open some fundamental questions. Were Premier

Clark's five conditions, regardless of their legal status, actual constraints on any federal government making a decision to allow construction of a federally regulated pipeline project that had already gained a public interest determination? Would the absence of consensual agreements with First Nations proximate to pipeline right-of-way, with or without settled land claims, be sufficient to stall such projects? Or would they be subject to existing remedies applicable to other Canadian landowners? Pressing forward with construction of Northern Gateway would have brought those issues to a head, but, sadly, that did not occur during Prime Minister Harper's watch.

Ineffectual Reform – Northern Gateway Frustrated

The Northern Gateway hearing process took almost three years, from Enbridge's filing in May 2010 to its final argument in the spring of 2013.[25] That included public consultation sessions and formal hearings with extensive cross-examination of both applicant and intervener evidence. The NEB tried to accommodate the project's opponents "right to be heard" and thereby legitimize its own process in the court of public opinion as well as avoid further legal challenges on process, regardless of the probative value of many representations. The public hearings stretched out over two years from late 2010 into 2012, and the Joint Review Panel did not make its recommendation to approve the project until December 2013.[26] Despite this three-year process, the project still faced legal challenges from both Aboriginal people and environmental groups.[27] As has become typical, Aboriginal entities argued the federal government had not adequately met its duty to consult. What would have constituted sufficient consultation, other than abandoning the project, was never articulated. Without such specified limits, consultation would become an endless "do-loop" that an applicant might never escape. As for the ENGO community, it predictably claimed that failure to consider upstream carbon effects delegitimized the entire regulatory process. These suits persist to the present day.

Even as recently as January 2016, a suit brought to the B.C. Supreme Court by an alliance of B.C. Aboriginal people questioned the jurisdiction of the federal regulatory process. In January of 2016, a decision from this court stated that it was necessary for British Columbia to replicate the entire regulatory process in order to adequately meet its obligations as a provincial government to Aboriginal people.[28] This ruling fundamentally questioned "equivalency," the deference of one level of government to another for environmental assessment, including discharging statutory obligations to Aboriginal people. Although the ruling is under appeal, it represents another legal ambiguity burdening the entire regulatory process related to Northern Gateway.

Back in 2011, the Harper government had made regulatory reform of major energy infrastructure a legislative priority, in response to examples of regulatory dysfunction such as the Mackenzie Valley gas pipeline's approval, which took seven years to achieve even with no substantial opposition, and the emerging difficulties with Northern Gateway. Harper's government seemingly understood that the regulatory processes must lead to successful permits in the vast majority of cases, or else no private sector investors would risk the substantial cost of applying. In 2012, the Harper government implemented various reforms in the federal regulatory process. Harper did not reinvent the process, but introduced modest, albeit constructive, adjustments in the existing fundamental process. Nevertheless, these reforms were still bitterly resented by the Canadian ENGO movement and other interest groups that sought to obstruct, or at least materially constrain, hydrocarbon development.[29]

Specifically, Prime Minister Harper's legislation imposed timelines for regulatory decisions. Major projects would follow a twenty-four-month timeline, beginning after their sponsors submitted an application deemed "complete." As well, to deal with conflicting federal and provincial jurisdictions, greater latitude was provided to deem "equivalency" between the processes by the federal government, thereby decreasing the risk of redundancy. Public participation in major environmental assessments would be restricted to "interested parties," those directly impacted or those that brought relevant information or experience. In cases where the regulatory process determined a project contained significant adverse environmental effects, the federal Cabinet could still determine if the project's overall benefits were sufficient to justify proceeding. An ultimate finding of national interest would rest with Cabinet. The regulators would provide recommendations for approval, not decisions, per se. Implicit in this formulation was the potential for Cabinet to approve a project that the regulator had rejected, and vice versa.

These changes, welcomed by the Canadian hydrocarbon industry, were enacted in June 2012 as part of that year's federal budget. Even with these reforms, the fundamental process was not altered. Any major pipeline project still had to prepare a detailed application for the regulator before any timelines came into effect. Proponents would still need to expend hundreds of millions of dollars to satisfy the required rigorous application to launch the prescribed timeline, all with no assurance of the federal government's alignment, regardless of the project's most basic and apparent merits. An initial project description only begins the process of resolving how a project will be processed by the various regulatory entities that may or may not have jurisdiction; it also reveals what identifying major issues relevant to the application must address. When the application is deemed "complete" by the regulator, then the process to determine intervener status begins, leading to formal written information requests and tabling of intervener evidence. Ultimately, filed evidence would be tested via cross-examination at public hearings, or via written interrogatories culminating in final oral argument. The regulators make a recommendation to Cabinet on the project's environmental acceptability, its alignment with overall national interest, and appropriate conditions to impose on the project. Finally, Cabinet accepts or rejects that recommendation.

As a practical matter, Cabinet's disposition of any major project is substantially constrained by the regulatory panel's recommendation, notwithstanding the reforms introduced by the Harper government. To stand entirely at odds with a federal regulator's recommendation, especially one for rejection, would prove politically difficult for any government. Harper's reform package had not really changed the risk or cost of the regulatory process to proponents. Substantive political sanctions for a project would still come late in the process, not early.

Back in summer 2011, then federal Minister of Natural Resources Joe Oliver made the public comment expressing that "Canada has a vision to be a global superpower, so it's critically important that we stay at the forefront of research and development." He continued, "The oilsands are an enormous resource for both Alberta and for Canada.... Clearly, the oil produced there has to be shipped and pipelines is the way to do it. This government is supportive of the Keystone-XL Pipeline and Northern Gateway. Gateway would open up the Asia market to Canadian exports." This comment, along with Harper's regulatory reforms, led the ENGO community to conclude that Northern Gateway's regulatory process had been preordained before it even began.

Regrettably, Prime Minister Harper's reforms neither reinvented the process fundamentally nor built broader public consensus for hydrocarbon development. Public pronouncements such as Oliver's open letter against "radicals" trying to undermine the Canadian economy by resisting oil sands development only antagonized the Canadian left.[30] Such remarks, for all their candour and validity, added further to the sense of resentment and implacable opposition between the Harper government and the ENGO community. The battle between those in favour of economic opportunity and those supportive of obstruction of industrial projects played out in the regulatory and legal forums. Proponents still found themselves committed to an increasingly dysfunctional regulatory process, even when advancing projects that had compelling economic value for the country.

Northern Gateway's process demonstrates what is still broken with the existing Canadian regulatory process for major hydrocarbon infrastructure. In 2014, as Obama strung KXL along, the Harper government accepted the conditional NEB recommendation for Northern Gateway;[31] however, the project had achieved a kind of pariah status in British Columbia, even as Enbridge committed itself to meeting the various conditions imposed on it. Enbridge depended entirely on the integrity of the federal approval process. Yet, it was expected to pursue further Aboriginal alignment, even after government acceptance of the affirmative NEB recommendation, despite the minimal possibility of achieving any substantial breakthrough amongst such groups. The federal NDP and Liberal leaders both opposed the project, but didn't cite any specific deficiencies in the NEB determination; rather, they identified with B.C. resistance and gave no acknowledgement to the integrity or competence of the federal regulator. Certainly, neither opposition leader invoked substantive technical arguments or specific recommendations to improve reasonable mitigation. Sadly, Harper never publically signalled his support or encouragement for the project if it had tried to commence construction.

The project treaded water until the 2015 election concluded. Construction never began in 2015.[32] And then, once Trudeau was elected in October 2015, he implemented a tanker moratorium for the northern B.C. ports, effectively nullifying the project. This, despite the possession of a certificate containing a finding of being in the national interest, and regardless of how Enbridge's compliance with the NEB conditions would evolve.[33]

TransMountain and Energy East: More Heavy Going

After extensive public consultation over two years, Kinder Morgan filed its NEB application for the TransMountain pipeline expansion on December 16, 2013.[34] Hearings related to the project began in early 2014, and then continued for 686 days before the record closed.[35] TransMountain's capacity had expanded to close to 800,000 barrels per day, based on its proposed use of debottlenecking and expansion of selected pipe, a process known as "looping," within existing right-of-way.

This was the Kinder project's presumed competitive advantage — utilization of an existing pipeline right-of-way in British Columbia. The project represented an investment of close to $6 billion. The project faced the fundamental challenge of creating incremental crude oil tanker traffic into Burrard Inlet, down to its Burnaby terminal. Kinder Morgan met persistent resistance, not just in suburban Burnaby, where it needed to conduct studies for its NEB environmental assessment, but across the entire Lower Mainland of British Columbia. Still, by the end of 2015, the project had worked its way through the regulatory process to the point of final argument. Somewhat amazingly, in the final argument phase of that proceeding, British Columbia's Premier Clark came out overtly against the project, based on environmental concerns of increased tanker traffic and the deficiencies of Kinder Morgan's proposed mitigations and operating procedures — concerns that could have been tabled and tested much earlier in the entire process, not in final argument.

In January 2016, the Trudeau government chose to extend existing timelines for regulatory review, ostensibly to allow more Aboriginal consultation, consideration of upstream carbon effects, and additional direct stakeholder consultation.[36] This would be carried out by the government itself, essentially as an adjunct to the NEB process. The B.C. Supreme Court decision on the provincial government's requirement to conduct its own environment assessment also clouded the regulatory process. Nevertheless, on May 19, 2016, the NEB provided its positive recommendation for the project, subject to 157 conditions.[37]

The Trudeau Cabinet would have to sanction or deny this project in the face of a positive regulatory recommendation, notwithstanding local public sentiment, and the implacable opposition of the Canadian environmental movement and selected Aboriginal groups. A final decision from the federal Cabinet is not expected until late December 2016.

TransCanada's Energy East project,[38] as of spring 2016, had yet to achieve substantive progress in its efforts to work through its regulatory process. From its inception, it faced similar opposition as Northern Gateway and Kinder Morgan's TransMountain expansion: carbon, NIMBYism, Aboriginal land claims, and competing claims regarding the distribution of economic rents. Quebec and Ontario were particularly conflicted and equivocal about the project, partly due to hostility from existing gas distribution interests.

The section of pipe that would be converted to oil service, roughly from North Bay, Ontario, to Ottawa, had not generally been in use in recent years, apart from some peak demand days in the winter season, when it was an important conduit of gas to Ontario and Quebec. Loss of that capacity to oil service created a unique issue for gas consumer interests in those provinces. TransCanada owned the pipe, but those eastern Canadian gas consumers, who no longer had any financial responsibility for this infrastructure, still enjoyed benefits from its availability for gas service. The proposed oil conversion could potentially force eastern gas consumers to fund new facilities or accept long-term financial commitment to the existing infrastructure to ensure enduring access.

Both options represented additional cost to their status quo, and consequently those interests resisted the conversion. They claimed a residual right to the pipe, without obligations of ownership. But, as with KXL, TransCanada's own financial interest compelled it to take advantage of oil conversion where new parties would pay for the pipe long-term — in this case, the oil shippers of Energy East. Maintaining the status quo would have necessitated greater new oil pipeline build from North Bay, Ontario to the Quebec-Ontario border, thereby increasing the project's cost and straining its overall economic viability.[39] TransCanada chose to accommodate these Ontario and Quebec gas consumer interests, as represented by gas distribution companies, in midsummer of 2014. Even with this accommodation, however, the project failed to win unequivocal support from the Ontario and Quebec governments. Although there would be significant benefits from the capital spending within their jurisdictions, both provinces remained lukewarm in their support of the project and, in turn, in facilitating further oil sands–related hydrocarbon production. At best, both provinces maintained that continued assessment of the overall merits of the project was necessary before finalizing their ultimate their official position, notwithstanding that it had been close to two years since the project had filed its project application in October 2014.[40]

Federal and provincial environmental ministries expressed concerns that constructing Energy East's oil terminal facility at Gros Cacouna, Quebec, could significantly impact beluga whale populations in the Gulf of St. Lawrence. These concerns led TransCanada to abandon an oil terminal in the upper St. Lawrence at Gros Cacouna, Quebec, a terminal that had been part of the original conception of the project and commercially significant to several of its prospective shippers.

The decision, confirmed in November 2015, meant substantial adjustment in some commercial aspects of the project, as well as an amended regulatory filing. It obviously meant less investment in Quebec, and therefore less enduring economic value and less reason for the province to rationalize various safety and environmental risks. Shortly afterward, TransCanada refiled its amended project configuration with the NEB in late November 2015.[41] Montreal-area mayors came out against the project, citing classic NIMBY considerations and insufficient economic value relative to attendant risks from the project. All of this occurred well before the NEB process had tested TransCanada's mitigations or the interveners' filings in the regulatory process's hearing phases.[42]

In early February 2016, the NEB asked TransCanada to resubmit its refiling, rendering it "easier to read and understand."[43] This was an unprecedented request from the NEB to a sophisticated applicant such as TransCanada. The original application had run about thirty thousand pages; to this TransCanada now added supplemental reports and an amended project description to reflect the deletion of the oil terminal facility at Gros Cacouna, Quebec. Then, in late April 2016, TransCanada further capitulated to Quebec's demands for its own provincial environmental assessment of the project, redundant to the federal process already underway for more than three years.[44] Not until June 16, 2016, would TransCanada achieve a "complete" application determination for Energy East.[45] Statutory timelines for the Energy East regulatory process could theoretically now begin.

The in-service date has shifted; now, at best, it will fall in late 2020. As of spring 2016, TransCanada had yet to receive any outright support for Energy East from the premiers of Quebec or Ontario. The capital cost had escalated to almost $16 billion.[46]

Ineffectual Political Champions

Enbridge and TransCanada are substantial players in the North American oil and gas industry, but are very much run and controlled by Canadians. That partially explains why both have persevered so hard in the face of resistance and equivocation, putting their faith in the Canadian and American regulatory and political processes. At least initially, both companies believed that those processes would not only affirm their projects but also enforce their rights to construct and operate. The American-controlled Kinder Morgan — a company renowned for its often ruthless pursuit of shareholder value — has shown a similar perseverance for its TransMountain expansion despite enduring similar resistance. All of these companies share the conviction that, if approved and constructed, their projects represent real value to industry, and, just as importantly, to Canada. Admittedly, after investing hundreds of millions of dollars in pursuing regulatory sanction, any corporation would persevere, even if in retrospect it would seriously reconsider starting the process at all.

As the market-access crisis started to unfold after 2011, with the delay imposed on KXL and the mounting resistance to Northern Gateway in British Columbia, Alberta's then liberal-leaning Conservative premier, Redford, tried to effect a breakthrough by advocating a "national energy strategy." She proposed that hydrocarbon-producing provinces gain support for their market access requirements with a quid pro quo for a more credible Canadian climate policy. To Redford's credit, she appreciated the threat to the province and its key industry, but she was constrained by a federal government incapable of credibly connecting carbon policy to market access. She began a process to convince Canada's provinces to advance this quid pro quo. It was a process that would grind on for over three years, long after she had been ousted as premier of Alberta. Redford's ultimate vision was provided some notional support from all Canadian premiers in related documents released in July 2015. But like so many such processes, the broad concept still had to connect to actual decisions, most of which lay within federal jurisdiction. What might work as high concept would still break down in the specific.[47]

Redford was challenged by Clark's five conditions, despite advocacy that pipelines carrying Alberta hydrocarbons contributed significant capital investment and enduring employment impacts in British Columbia, and therefore satisfied the fifth condition.[48] She clarified that Alberta would not share its royalties or other hydrocarbon revenues to meet that condition. She might have better served Alberta's, and Canada's, interests, if she had rejected that fifth condition outright. Both premiers knew, regardless of their bilateral discussions, that the fates of Northern Gateway and TransMountain lay in the hands of the federal government, provided it had sufficient political will.

Though Redford's tenure leading the Alberta government did not endure long into 2014, she nonetheless deserves credit for identifying the link between market access and credible Canadian carbon policy. She saw that progress on the latter could only improve the overall social acceptance of increased hydrocarbon production, and potentially ease the political positions of the likes of Clark, who were asked to accept some incremental risk without any fundamental change in their share of resource rents.

Redford's successor, Jim Prentice, had a long resumé within the Conservative Party and Harper government. He had held major portfolios, including the federal environment ministry in the run-up to and during the Copenhagen climate conference. He had also held responsibility for advancing certain northern gas pipeline projects. Like Redford, Prentice was broadly perceived as a liberal-leaning conservative. He left the Harper government in November 2010, after serving close to five years in the federal Cabinet, to join the Canadian banking industry, with a special interest in the Canadian hydrocarbon sector. He was vigorously recruited to return to provincial politics after Redford was ousted in early 2014, and he assumed the premiership with resounding support from the provincial Conservative party.

During his relatively brief nine-month tenure as premier, however, Prentice achieved no major concessions or breakthroughs on market access, despite declaring it a major priority of his government. He made no real public demands of Harper, nor did he provide public elaboration of how he could resolve Alberta's dilemma regarding market access and the creation of a credible climate policy. Granted, Prentice had to reckon with falling crude prices for his entire tenure, and so had no financial capacity to assuage resistors. Still, his brief tenure altered little for any of these projects, despite how obviously he recognized market access as a vital strategic breakthrough for his province.[49]

After almost fifty years of dominating electoral politics in Alberta, the Conservative party was defeated in spring 2015. It suffered a significant loss, falling to the Alberta New Democratic Party — the Alberta left, home of unionized labour and Alberta ENGOs, long alienated from the levers of political power. Edmonton labour lawyer Rachel Notley led the NDP.

The provincial election campaign was not a referendum on the existing tactics pursued in respect of market access or provincial carbon policy, but rather a reaction to a litany of longstanding irritants related to Conservative governance, and to Prentice's intention to implement significant austerity measures in response to falling hydrocarbon revenues.

Sufficient Albertans opted for Notley's promises of reform and redistribution but without undue austerity, falling crude prices notwithstanding. On May 5, 2015, a new government was elected that seemed antithetical to the province's hydrocarbon interests. Championing those clashed with longstanding NDP orthodoxy on environmental issues, from profound skepticism about the morality of oil sands exploitation to whether Alberta had derived its "fair share" from resource development relative to the private capital.[50]

With KXL then still in play, Premier Notley largely held to the federal NDP line that the pipeline would export hydrocarbon, upgrading opportunities from Alberta and Canada.[51] To call her equivocal about the project would have been generous. As for Northern Gateway, her indifference betrayed a belief that she saw the project as a lost cause; fighting for it was not, in her view, worth the risk to Alberta's political credibility with other provinces and the federal NDP. She identified Energy East as a more viable long-term option, but never articulated in any detailed fashion how restoring credibility on carbon policy would directly relate to advancing that project. Doubtless, the Notley government did see carbon taxes as an opportunity for incremental revenue as well.[52]

In November 2015, the Notley government announced a new climate policy initiative for Alberta, founded on an economy-wide carbon tax. Its initial "stringency" was at $30/tonne, rising 2 percent per year in real terms after 2018 — certainly more than competitive with most existing carbon pricing regimes in developed economies. Future price increases were astutely contingent on climate policy and carbon pricing implemented by Alberta's relevant competitors and trading partners. The policy also committed Alberta to phasing out coal-based electric generation facilities. Revenue derived from the new carbon tax would, Premier Notley stated, fund various "green" infrastructure and technology initiatives within the province.

The policy initiative did not specify physical emission reduction targets. Unfortunately, however, Premier Notley built in no link between carbon policy and market access. No conditionality. No quid pro quo. As crude prices fell even lower by early 2016, Notley could not ignore that lack of market access for Alberta's hydrocarbons had become a strategic liability for Alberta's long-term economic interests.[53]

Even as this policy was enacted in June of 2016, controversy continued. Many asked, What had Alberta gained, if anything, from this initiative? Albertans saw no clear market access breakthroughs or concessions from the Canadian left or ENGO community on the legitimacy of Alberta hydrocarbon potential. In fact, in March of 2016, the national NDP convention actually endorsed Naomi Klein's "Leap Manifesto," despite Notley's ardent appeals to the contrary. Even within her own party, her climate policy had seemingly bought her nothing in terms of accommodation.[54]

In October 2015, Prime Minister Harper lost to the Trudeau Liberals, who, surprisingly, won a majority government, restoring traditional control of the federal government to central Canadian interests from inner-city Toronto and Montreal. Alberta, true to its political traditions, had the least representation in this new government. For all of Harper's failures on climate policy and the issue of resolving market access, his Conservative governments had been fundamentally sympathetic to the ambitions of the western Canadian hydrocarbon industry. Justin Trudeau was the son of the most reviled federal leader among western Canadians, Pierre Elliot Trudeau. Although Justin Trudeau did not suggest reopening revenue sharing from hydrocarbon production, he did explicitly envision a Canada no longer reliant significantly on hydrocarbon development. He campaigned on rehabilitating Canada as a player in the fight against climate-change risk. His dream for Canada was that it would be the antithesis of "an energy superpower."[55]

Although the Liberal party trailed in third place for much of the 2015 campaign, it gained momentum in the last weeks, based on promises to renew the nation's economy with deficit spending and higher taxes on wealthier Canadians. Trudeau avoided delving into carbon policy, except to differentiate himself from Harper. He was open to carbon pricing, but vowed to improve on Harper's disingenuous emission reduction targets, to establish a more genuine commitment. He did not call specifically for a national carbon tax, but rather vaguely referred to supporting provincial carbon pricing regimes conforming to some national pricing standard. As for market access, Prime Minister Trudeau and his closest advisors always adamantly opposed Northern Gateway. They offered few specific objections, and no critique of the NEB recommendation, but cited the project's failure to win the "hearts and minds" of British Columbians — whatever that meant, other than the Tories failing to win the greatest number of seats in British Columbia in the federal election. Prime Minister Trudeau offered no conditions Enbridge could meet in order to gain Liberal support for Northern Gateway. He set aside the integrity of the entire NEB process with respect to Northern Gateway. While he was more equivocal about TransMountain, Trudeau never outright endorsed that project either.[56]

As for KXL, Prime Minister Trudeau expressed nominal support throughout his campaign, and cited its looming demise as the epitome of Harper's deficiencies as a national leader — he had failed to manage the U.S. relationship for the best interest of Canada. There was no recognition of the unfairness of Obama toward Canada at all. Despite his criticism of the Harper government, however, Prime Minister Trudeau never offered any specific plan to salvage the project. Allowing the U.S. process to play out served him better than staking some of his political capital on the project, especially if it meant confronting Obama on climate policy just before the Paris climate conference, and right after his own election.

Trudeau claimed to be open-minded on Energy East, which at most meant simply he did not yet overtly oppose it. The project's transnational quality was fashionable. Quebec might abide the project if sufficient investment impacts could still be generated. Prime Minister Trudeau had to welcome any private sector investment in the Maritime provinces, even if predicated on hydrocarbons; however, he never identified Energy East as a vital national priority. The glacial regulatory process for Energy East would grind on, providing cover for Trudeau, much as the American regulatory process had done for Obama.

Within six weeks of his election, Prime Minister Trudeau moved quickly in four areas. First, he predictably eschewed any attempt to engage with Obama and salvage KXL — no urgent meetings or public demands for bilateral negotiations to salvage the project. His indifference betrayed the fact that he didn't really mind seeing the project slip away; the new government didn't really want KXL in play as a major bilateral irritant or as an early failure.[57] Second, Trudeau imposed a moratorium on crude tankers for British Columbia's north coast, effectively scuttling the Northern Gateway project, especially if Enbridge had tried to force the issue with its existing certificate.[58] Third, Trudeau required the new minister of energy to alter the federal regulatory process for major hydrocarbon projects, restoring "trust and confidence."[59] This doubtless portends deconstructing Harper's modest regulatory reforms of 2012. Fourth, at the Paris climate conference Trudeau stated he intended to make Canada's targets more ambitious, and to work with the provinces to achieve them. He offered no comments on how those targets could be met, or what impacts the country and especially Alberta might expect. Trudeau's four initiatives, taken together, are antithetical to the interests of Alberta and its hydrocarbon industry. Whatever the Trudeau government imagined as the basis of economic recovery for Canada, the role of hydrocarbons in that plan appeared ever more dubious.[60]

Even worse, newly appointed Environment Minister Catherine McKenna declared Prime Minister Trudeau's Paris commitments "a floor not a ceiling." An astonishing remark, considering that the current level of GHG emissions attributed to Canada annually is on the order of 700 megatons, and Canada tabled a target to reduce its emissions by roughly 30 percent of 2005 levels by 2030. Depending on how we account for certain forestry and land-use related effects, the actual Canadian target is in the range of 525 to 600 megatons of allowable national emissions by 2030. Emissions attributed to Canadian oil and gas production are currently approaching 200 megatons of carbon dioxide equivalent, not counting, of course, any incremental pipeline infrastructure or LNG production facilities. Alberta's existing coal-based electric generation facilities contribute roughly 65 megatons of carbon dioxide equivalent annually. Any growth in the oil sands or LNG sectors would lead to incremental national emissions, given the constraints of reasonably expectable technology improvement.[61]

The Leach report, generated by the Notley government to provide recommendations on its carbon initiative, did not anticipate stabilization of Alberta's emissions, even with enactment of carbon taxes and coal phase-out until 2030. Reducing carbon emissions in hydrocarbon production sectors to achieve a national target on the order of 500 megatons on annual GHG emissions would require either significant mandated constraints on hydrocarbon use within the country, or carbon taxes likely greater than $150/tonne. But the Trudeau government did not change the basic target from what Harper's government tabled in April 2015. This was a target that originally conformed to the U.S. Copenhagen target of "17 percent reduction from 2005 levels by 2020," which was, in turn, viewed as restoring the U.S. Kyoto commitment. Recall the sum of Kyoto commitments were to provide a fifty-fifty chance of containing global temperature increase to 2 °C.

In total, Alberta generates almost 40 percent of attributed national emissions, despite comprising roughly 11 percent of the national population. Any reasonable analysis can conclude that for Canada to achieve its targets in absolute physical terms, it must contract Alberta's hydrocarbon industry, or intervene in central Canadian and British Columbian energy consumption and fuel mixes. Are any of these interventions politically plausible, despite the "ambitions" of the Trudeau Cabinet?

Finally, Canada's Minister of Natural Resources, Jim Carr, the presumed advocate for the Canadian energy sector within the federal Cabinet, led the process to deconstruct the Harper regulatory reforms of 2012.[62] Though the minister claimed he was responding to public demand to "restore trust and credibility," little evidence existed to substantiate that claim, other than from Canadian ENGOS, whose basic complaint was embodied in the approval of Northern Gateway by the NEB in 2013. For them, the problem was more a wrong answer than a biased process. Does Minister Carr recognize the economic contribution to Canada at stake from increased hydrocarbon production?[63] Later in the spring of 2016, however, the basic dilemma between seizing Canada's hydrocarbon potential with credible climate policy and meeting expectations of stakeholders had perhaps gripped the federal government, as Trudeau publicly mused on finding a palatable path forward on Canada's market-access dilemma.[64]

As a last example of the "dysfunction" impacting hydrocarbon infrastructure in Canada, in late June 2016, the Federal Court of Appeal ruled that the Harper government had inadequately "consulted" on Northern Gateway, that they had done so in a "brief, hurried, and inadequate" manner. "The inadequacies — more than just a handful and more than mere imperfections — left entire subjects of central interest to the affected First

Nations, sometimes subjects affecting their subsistence and well-being, entirely ignored."[65] But the court offered no guidance on what constitutes adequate consultation, did not recognize that access is either resolvable as a matter of financial compensation or it is not, nor did it acknowledge that "right to be consulted" is not the equivalent of a veto.

A breakthrough on market access had never seemed more remote and prospects for Canada's hydrocarbon industry had never been bleaker. And it wasn't just because of low commodity prices. The only way forward requires integrated policy changes related to both Canadian carbon pricing and regulatory reform, changes that will credibly achieve required market access and thereby revalidate hydrocarbon production growth in Canada. The next two chapters outline such a path forward.

CHAPTER NINE

A CREDIBLE AND PROPORTIONATE CANADIAN CARBON TAX

Without credible Canadian climate policy, the Canadian hydrocarbon industry will find no peace, even with the most rational elements of the environmental movement, or with liberal sentiment worldwide. A credible Canadian climate policy must be one of the constructive legacies of the KXL experience. Too much was lost for that not to be the case. And for Canada, a credible and appropriate climate policy must be founded on carbon taxes. I don't hold illusions that such taxes would eliminate all resistance to the oil sands, but they are still essential.

Yet both the Harper Conservatives and the much of the Canadian ENGO movement resisted the notion of a national, revenue-neutral carbon tax, albeit for profoundly differently reasons. For some on the right, any form of carbon policy is misguided — a position based on their outright denial of any material climate-change risk. The Harper conservatives never publicly embraced climate denialism, but they consistently disparaged a carbon tax approach as an untenable cost to the economy. They expressed deep skepticism that any revenue neutrality could be sustained, or that any politically viable level of carbon pricing could deal with the basic climate risk as framed by the U.N. process. So, instead, disingenuous targets and wishful thinking for technology breakthrough became the default of federal climate policy under Prime Minister Harper.

Canadian politicians at Paris climate conference, December 2015.

For many environmentalists, carbon taxes are seen as a subtle ruse to enable and rationalize rather than materially contract hydrocarbon production, particularly in the context of the Canadian oil sands.[1] Thus, they view such taxes with trepidation, almost as a Trojan Horse of climate policy. Why rely on transparent, economy-wide pricing via carbon taxes when regulation, mandates, and subsidies are available? Moreover, carbon taxes do not specify specific carbon emission allowables. The entire policy is dependent on the tax rising over time to levels sufficient to generate the level of ultimately desired emission reductions. All of which has be sustained over time by the political process. For the ENGOs, carbon taxes are at best a supplementary policy instrument to alter various behaviours and investment decisions in the economy, but not a pre-eminent policy tool. Why rely on microeconomics when command and control can be imposed?

There is no better recent example than the Ontario climate plan, "trial balloon," leaked in May of 2016, that shows government climate policy founded on dictate, not pricing.[2] In effect, it imposes infinite carbon prices in certain industrial and end-use demand sectors with little apparent connection to cost or reliability of the resulting energy system. Instead, it is entirely fixated on emission reduction as the pre-eminent goal. It intends to achieve emission reductions on a scale of 15 percent below 1990 levels by 2020, 37 percent by 2030, and 80 percent by 2050 — an almost Kyoto-like ambition.

The goals came with a wide array of planned regulated changes in Ontario energy consumption and systems, such as phasing out natural gas for heating, incentives to retrofit buildings, rebates for owners of electric vehicles, requirements for low-carbon gasoline, mandated building-code rules requiring all new homes to be heated with electricity or geothermal systems by 2030, and a target that 12 percent of all new vehicles be electric by 2025. Implementing all this would cost roughly $7 billion. Ontario's Premier Kathleen Wynne did not specify what carbon-pricing regime would create an equivalent energy transformation, or any other measure of the plan's ongoing costs for Ontario energy consumers relative to other jurisdictions.

Ontario's plan is an instructive example of the kind of intrusive and extensive regulation required to even approach such levels of emission reduction. What environmentalist would not rally to such policy in preference to carbon pricing via carbon taxes? But simply criticizing and resisting such a policy agenda is not reasonable either. Canada must adopt a credible carbon policy. Climate change risk is real. Canada cannot ignore that.

Yet during the Harper and prior Liberal administrations, Canada resorted to disingenuous emission reduction targets, while never seriously articulating how they would be complied with. At best, they could have been clarified as being only aspirational and not fixed obligations. Further, these targets should have been subject to amendment to ensure Canada's competitiveness and proportionality of effort relative to its major trading partners' commitments to dealing with the climate-change risk. But disingenuous targets were no substitute for credible carbon policy, and the country's hydrocarbon potential was compromised because of them. As conceded earlier, an appropriate national carbon tax, imposed with genuine conviction and commitment, may or may not have led to a KXL approval. But it would be an entirely reasonable inference that a credible carbon tax policy for Canada was likely Obama's necessary condition for any KXL approval. Moreover, within Canada, environmental resistance to hydrocarbon production and its related infrastructure cannot be reasonably rebutted without such policy.

On the other hand, Canada should not appease the environmental movement by supplementing such a carbon tax regime with other intrusive "command and control" policy instruments to deal with climate-change risk. For that matter, neither should any Canadian province.

The carbon tax must be the pre-eminent, if not sole, policy instrument of Canadian climate policy. Moreover, Canada must not act out of some sense of misguided altruism, or, worse, out of ignorance of its basic economic interests. Only an appropriate carbon tax regime will allow Canada to demonstrate serious intent to deal with the global climate-change risk while remaining reasonably proportionate with the policy initiatives of relevant nations. Seven basic principles would constitute this "credible and proportionate" carbon tax regime for Canada.

1. The Right to Emit

Any carbon tax must represent a right to emit carbon. Without that consequence, what is the point of such a tax? If some other regulated emission limit applies on specific sectors, then at some point they face an infinite carbon tax. Either the tax is equivalent to physical carbon emission for compliance purposes or it isn't.

This simple principle might strike some as obvious. But as we have seen in practice, for some politicians, carbon taxes are never enough. The problem begins when politicians frame some kinds of carbon emissions as more tolerable than others. Consider the elements of the Notley carbon-policy initiative of November 2015. Despite implementing a credible carbon tax (initial $30/tonne of emitted CO_2), some sectors were subject to absolute limits on allowable emissions, notably in the future oil sands expansion and the coal-based generation sector, implying for those sectors ultimately an infinite carbon tax price level. That element of her policy initiative was inconsistent with the central element of the initiative, namely the credible carbon tax.

The Alberta carbon tax is likely not high enough to generate economically significant short- or medium-term emission reductions in the Alberta oil and gas sector. But other jurisdictions applying taxes of the same stringency may realize greater emission reductions earlier — likely those jurisdictions with greater capacity to replace coal in the fuel mix in the near-term, for example.

The current Alberta tax level is as stringent as any carbon pricing regime operating in the United States or western Europe at the end of 2015.[3]

But until an Alberta carbon tax reaches levels to generate material reductions in crude oil and natural gas production and consumption, those sectors can continue to operate, which implies continued emissions. Still, those sectors will internalize the carbon tax, and therefore reduce their emissions at the margin to the extent economically justified.

2. Applicability

The federal government must be prepared to impose and enforce a national carbon tax. All Canadians should face the same incremental cost for carbon emissions, economy-wide. Carbon taxes must apply to all emissions, with the tax imposed as close as possible to the point at which the emissions occur, essentially where combustion or other GHG emission occurs. Each entity (person or corporation) that generates an emission must pay the tax. The only "set-off" consists in not emitting — by abstaining from combustion or sequestering the resulting carbon emissions. Whether the federal government allows provinces to administer this tax is not as important as ensuring the same carbon price applies across the country.

This principle creates practical accountability for each emitter, whether an individual or corporate entity. Driving, flying, setting one's thermostat, investing in "energy efficient" appliances or facilities, minimizing carbon intensity in engineering design for various industrial processes — all these activities would be impacted by the carbon tax. That is the whole point — to create a microeconomic response to the additional cost of generating an emission.

However, any carbon tax design must account for import-export effects. When Canada exports energy intensive products to jurisdictions without a comparable carbon tax, some border adjustment is justified to ensure the competitiveness of Canadian industry. Imports that don't domestically bear a comparable carbon tax must be subject to an analogous import levy.

3. **Stringency**

Ideally, Canada's carbon tax would be equivalent to a comparable economy-wide carbon tax in the United States, Canada's predominant trading partner. American political gridlock between executive and legislative branches of government has meant that currently no such tax is in effect, and that there is little prospect of implementing one in the short- or medium-term. However, the U.S. government has generated various estimates of the "social cost of carbon," the discounted cost of carbon emissions minus ascribed benefits over time from hydrocarbon utilization. Such estimates are contentious in terms of their methodology, especially with respect to appropriate discount rates and valuing various health and demographic benefits presumed to occur due to a reduced climate risk. Consequently, estimates of an appropriate social cost of carbon can vary widely, from less that $30/tonne of emitted carbon to above $100/tonne. Other models and economic analyses have been developed to determine the carbon price required to achieve specific emission reductions. These efforts have always been challenged due to the evolving economics of various technologies, existing capital stock within the economy, consumer responses to rising energy costs, and fundamental commodity price projections over time. Nevertheless, most such analysis suggests that only carbon prices significantly exceeding $100/tonne of emitted carbon can force global transformational change with respect to demand of crude oil and natural gas.[4]

Alberta has set its carbon tax initially at $30/tonne, rising at 2 percent in real terms after 2018. Regardless of noted challenges in establishing a reasonable initial carbon price, most observers would accept the Alberta tax stringency as "credible," certainly as high as, if not higher than, most existing carbon pricing and trading regimes in North America or Europe.

The effectiveness of any carbon tax regime will depend on prevailing hydrocarbon prices, especially with respect to the ratio of the carbon tax to the commodity price. Lower commodity prices may increase the carbon tax proportionately, but overall combined prices may not significantly impact demand, capital stock, or implementation of low-carbon technologies. Similarly, if the low-carbon technological options become less costly on a normalized basis, the impact of any carbon tax increases. Many observers concede that carbon prices between $30 to $100/tonne would meaningfully reduce coal's share in the fuel mix, especially given prevailing natural gas prices in North America and global LNG pricing since the advent of natural gas fracking, recent declines in crude oil prices from levels prevailing last decade, and improvements in the economics of renewable technology. However, transforming the transportation sectors will require carbon taxes well beyond $100/tonne, also depending on prevailing crude oil prices and all electric-vehicle technology development. Converting to all electric vehicles, even conceding that their cost and comparable value proposition concerns could be overcome, would require massive increases in electric generation capacity. How would that electric generation be sourced? More renewables, nuclear, or natural gas? All of this would be influenced by commodity prices and the prevailing level of carbon taxes, absent any regulated mandates for specific sourcing options.

Nevertheless, at present, Alberta has established an eminently reasonable initial carbon pricing level, along with an appropriately conditioned escalator, for at least the short term. It should be adopted as the national pricing standard.

4. Conditionality

Canada, in contrast to the United States, has relatively little coal to eliminate from its energy mix. Many decades ago, Quebec, Manitoba, and British Columbia founded their electric grids on hydropower, and Ontario founded its on nuclear power. Ironically, Alberta uses a significant amount of coal to generate electricity. Canada came to its current targets based on no principle more profound than conforming to the U.S.'s Copenhagen commitments, which were in turn based on its original Kyoto commitments. Canada gave no apparent serious attention to assessing whether it could actually achieve those emission reductions within any economically reasonable cost, or to the global context in which it would have to achieve them — that is, whether other countries were living up to their emission reduction promises.

The cost of achieving Canadian carbon reduction goals will likely exceed $100/tonne of CO_2 — a price beyond what any pricing regime, whether cap-and-trade or carbon taxes, has achieved to date. In fact, global 2 °C containment requires much more than even removing coal from the fuel mix on a global basis, based on current IPCC assessments of the climate risk.[5] It will require transforming the transportation sector away from fossil fuels. Whether the world has the capacity to impose that cost on itself is unclear. Ultimately, rising carbon taxes must be democratically validated across the major emitting nations, confirming that current generations are prepared to impose costs on themselves in the short and medium term to mitigate future climate-change risk.

Applying carbon taxes uniformly across all relevant economies promises to deal with climate risk would be ideal. Economists such as Nordhaus and Stern have recognized and advocated for this since the issue of appropriate policy responses to the climate risk emerged in the 1990s. This notion is vitally important for Canada, because it means that any given global carbon tax level will determine the appropriate economic incentive resulting in the least costly emission reductions achieved first. As the carbon tax increases, it will eventually eliminate emissions that are more expensive to achieve. Certain emissions persist until the carbon tax reaches a point where avoiding it becomes cost effective. This schema means deferring the elimination of higher-cost emissions until the carbon tax reaches required levels, which implies that coal should be eliminated from the fuel mix before crude oil and natural gas.

A Canadian carbon tax design must be conditional on the carbon prices its major trading partners impose on themselves, explicitly or implicitly. Canada cannot afford to deviate from that principle. Canada's carbon policy should not exceed what those other countries are prepared to impose on themselves. Canada's current environmental minister, Catherine McKenna, characterized the nation's 2016 Paris commitment as a "floor, not a ceiling" — a baffling if not irresponsible comment for a Canadian Cabinet minister. Does she even know what the current commitment will cost to achieve? Or what implicit carbon price Canada's competitors have imposed on themselves? She talks in terms of carbon emission reduction targets, seemingly disconnected from the cost of achieving them. Canada's commitments in Paris do not compel absolute emission reductions; at most, the country has legally agreed to report its progress. Canada should clarify that its

Paris Intended Nationally Determined Contribution (INDC) is only an aspirational target. Prices, not targets, must define Canadian carbon policy. Ideally, all relevant economies would resort to carbon taxes, but, until then, Canada's government must assess the implicit prices other economies are imposing on themselves directly or indirectly. If the rest of the world has the will to impose carbon prices severe enough to meet the Paris agreement's nominal objective of 2 °C containment, then Canada must follow; however, if the world fails to impose such prices, then Canada cannot punish itself economically.

Roughly 30 percent of Canada's emissions are attributable to hydrocarbon production, and that level of emissions is roughly equal to the reduction levels it was asked to make at the 2016 Paris climate conference. But Canadian hydrocarbon production should be a function of commodity values, its own cost structure, and its capacity to absorb any relevant carbon taxes. Canadian hydrocarbons should internalize the average prevailing carbon price applicable in competitive countries that Canada materially trades with, whether that price is explicitly or implicitly prescribed. Until those competitors can impose such pricing levels that would materially constrain crude oil and natural gas supply and demand on a global basis, why would Canada?

5. **Relative Merits of Policy Instruments — Only Carbon Taxes**
Canada's carbon price must be achieved via taxes *only* — taxes framed as a legitimate compliance mechanism, equivalent to physical emission reductions. With a well-designed carbon tax, renewable and nuclear energy sources' inherent lack of emissions enjoy a built-in competitive advantage. Carbon-intensive coal, conversely, will face a higher tax burden. Regardless of some theoretical equivalence with cap and trade, carbon taxes are in practice transparent, equitable, and efficient — that is, fundamentally less costly to implement.

Cap and trade inevitably involves allocating permissible emissions, which means favouring some emitters over others. Emitters without sufficient allowances are required to bid on others' allowances, but this assumes that another emitter is actually selling. Otherwise, emitters must resort to acquiring other compliance mechanisms allowed within the cap-and-trade design, typically referred to as offsets. An offset is simply an emission that's allowed to exist. Any other rationale for them is simply sophistry. Some cap-and-trade designs have embedded "safety valves," which are, de facto, carbon prices that compliance devolves to. Add to this structural morass of "cap and trade" the prospect of "trading" allowances with the usual additional costs that intermediation and hedging imply. Offsets are by definition a shell game, often pure financial transfers to certain regions, industries, or countries. Experience tells us that economies always require more allowances than the initial cap prescribes, so either more allowances are granted, more offsets defined, or the safety valve is adjusted to some level that the overall economy can bear.

Carbon taxes should be Canada's pre-eminent policy instrument for dealing with the risk of climate change, regardless of how difficult that may be for some within the ENGO and climate denialist communities to accept.

If Canadians want more on the emission reduction front, they should democratically sanction higher carbon tax levels, even if they exceed what other relevant countries are imposing on themselves. But we must not mandate reductions in specific sectors or provide subsidies for specific technologies. The inherent gradualism and economic efficiency implicit to a carbon tax regime results in the "cheapest available reductions first for a given level of carbon tax." This should not be compromised. We must trust market responses for a given level of carbon tax. That level of tax can and should be validated by the political process, if it is to ever deviate from the conditionality principle that I espouse.

Within Canada, both Quebec and Ontario are currently committed to cap and trade.[6] To date, no evidence suggests these schemes approach the breadth or stringency of the Alberta carbon tax design.

6. Where Will the Proceeds Go?

The main point of a carbon tax is the incremental price signal it provides: forms of energy that emit carbon will cost more and so will using more hydrocarbon energy. But Canada must also determine what it will do with the tax's proceeds. As much as possible, Canada should keep its carbon taxes revenue neutral. That means governments would have no more total revenue after imposing carbon taxes than it would have had without them. Ideally, revenue neutrality would be achieved by reducing corporate and personal income taxes, as well as those other taxes that most negatively impact productivity and future investment. Carbon taxes could contribute meaningfully to tax reform — with emitters paying more, and the most productive Canadians paying less income and corporate taxes.

But the government could reasonably invest the proceeds in carbon mitigation and adaptation funding, for instance low-carbon technology development and infrastructure, to cope with the impacts of climate change itself. This option would deviate from strict revenue neutrality from carbon taxes, but would appeal to environmentalists, and would bolster Canada's international position as a positive actor in dealing with the climate-change risk. The public sector determines which mitigation, adaptation, and technology development projects to support. This option increases government spending, which is always problematic. Experience does not assure us that money would be spent reasonably. A more efficient alternative would see private-sector emitters spending their carbon-tax payable on approved carbon mitigation and adaptation projects. Rather than the government deciding how such spending should occur, the private sector would conform to acceptable guidelines to earn a tax offset, achieving more diverse decision-making and greater scope for innovation.

Lastly, carbon tax proceeds must at least in part offset the regressive impacts of Canada's carbon tax. The tax will impact all hydrocarbon consumers, regardless of income, at least in terms of heating and transportation. The marginal impact of any increase in energy costs will of course impact low-income consumers proportionately more than affluent ones. Rich and poor require about the same measure of space heating, for instance — certainly within Canada. Using some of the carbon tax proceeds in this manner is both inevitable and justifiable. Considering these options, Canada will need to strike an appropriate balance. My preference would see the carbon tax preferentially offset corporate taxes, the most economically destructive of existing taxes.

7. **Legitimate Self-Interest**

The U.N. climate process has always reduced itself to allocated emission reductions across developed countries, and facilitating economic transfers to developing economies. At the 2015 Paris conference, developed nations agreed to report on voluntary, unenforceable commitments, far from any fundamental reinvention of the U.N. process. Paris's outcome is grounded in an objective that requires massive transformation in global energy systems, at a cost the world cannot likely bear given current technology constraints.[7] For most countries, economic self-interest will prevail, tempering energy transformation; but sadly, the Trudeau government does not seem clear about how much the Canadian economy will have to bear. At worst, Canada could be pursuing policies that require constraining if not deconstructing its hydrocarbon sector, causing great damage to Canadian living standards.

Since the October 2015 election, the country is being led by the centre-left. Close to 70 percent of Canadians voted for Trudeau's Liberals and the New Democratic Party. Was that result a mandate for self-destructive carbon policy? Mandated carbon emission reductions are unwise policy. Alberta could become collateral damage, but in time, the whole country will feel the economic loss, with any lessons from KXL being lost. Before her election, Premier Notley advocated typical NDP positions on climate issues, but, remarkably, after a year at Alberta's helm, she advocated market access, with carbon taxes as the foundation of the province's new credibility on climate. To date, she has yet to achieve any breakthrough with the rest of Canada or the current federal government. A credible carbon tax, which the Alberta tax regime certainly is, should be sufficient to rationalize providing requisite market access to Alberta and the rest of Canada.

Late in October 2016, the Trudeau government did announce a national carbon pricing standard, with the expectation that provinces would conform to it by 2018. This standard was more stringent than currently applicable in Alberta. However, it contained none of the other conditions laid out above — most significantly no insistence on revenue neutrality to taxpayers' conditionality to pricing, like those in place in Canada's major trading partners, and no explicit quid pro quo on market access.[8]

CHAPTER TEN

RESTORING MARKET ACCESS

A credible carbon policy, as outlined in the prior chapter, should dispel any continuing invocations of inadequate "social licence" for Canadian hydrocarbon production, even if significant elements of the Canadian environmental movement do not hold to that view. Appropriate carbon pricing can rationalize hydrocarbon production.

But credible carbon policy is only a necessary, not a sufficient, condition to restore Canada's capacity to actually approve, construct, and operate required hydrocarbon infrastructure. Going forward, to maintain a private sector prepared to invest in Canada's hydrocarbons, it must have reasonable confidence to risk the necessary capital to pursue regulatory approval for required infrastructure. Five fundamental changes and clarifications of process and law are necessary to accomplish that objective.

1. **Fundamental Decision Criteria — Net National Benefits**
   First, Canada must reaffirm the fundamental decision criteria for any major hydrocarbon infrastructure project going forward; namely, whether it provides sufficient net national benefits. Inevitably, this principle creates the possibility that some elements within Canada may have to accept some physical risk, albeit mitigated according to

regulatory mandates, while some other elements gain a greater share of economic benefits from the product using the infrastructure. But surely, as a country with any serious regard for its economic interests, Canada must approve projects with national net benefits as the pre-eminent decision criteria. Resolving disputes, if any arise, on the distribution of economic rents can occur over time, but such disputes cannot disrupt seizing the basic economic opportunity at hand. Individual provinces do not have a veto on projects within federal jurisdiction. The costs and benefits to a specific province cannot determine approval; nor can some veto be extended to specific provinces simply because the infrastructure traverses its jurisdiction. A determination of net national benefit by the federal regulator must be sufficient for a project to proceed. The federal government must vigorously reaffirm this basic principle and in practice be prepared to enforce it. Ideally, all provinces should reaffirm their deference to this basic principle, foundational as it is to Canadian federalism.

Canadians must not allow any one province to set out its conditions before it is prepared to endorse a project under federal

Premier Rachel Notley and Prime Minister Justin Trudeau, circa spring 2016.

jurisdiction, as if it has a unique veto on the project, even before an adjudication of net national benefits has occurred. Individual provinces can vigorously participate in the federal regulatory process, bringing relevant evidence and setting out their expectations of appropriate mitigation; however, they must defer to the federal determination of net national benefits. Otherwise, for any applicant, what is the point of a federal application at all?

Deference to federal jurisdiction for national infrastructure projects should be obvious. But as we have seen with the disposition of Northern Gateway and TransMountain, provincial and municipal jurisdictions still contend that their opposition must be respected as a kind of binding constraint. National political leadership should have reaffirmed the primacy of a federal determination. More bluntly, access to tidewater must be a federal determination. The NEB, in its Northern Gateway decision, carried out its mandate and provided an affirmative recommendation,[1] but litigation and obstruction have since beset the decision and project. The federal government must reaffirm the fundamental standard of national net benefits.

Consider how the NEB itself describes the "public interest" as "inclusive of all Canadians.... A balance of economic, environmental, and social interests that changes as society's values and preferences evolve over time. The Board estimates the overall public good a project may create and its potential negative aspects, weighs its various impacts, and makes a decision."[2] A more explicit statement of net national benefits as the fundamental decision criteria should be considered as necessary to improve transparency and efficiency. As well, any finding of national net benefits by the regulator would satisfy, given any "social licence" considerations invoked by any interest group.

2. A New Regulatory Process

Throughout Harper's tenure as prime minister, the country's political left propagated the meme that Canadians had lost confidence and faith in the regulatory process, specifically in the National Energy Board. This loss of faith was supposedly most notably exemplified with respect to its decisions related to Northern Gateway and TransMountain. Rather than deferring to the basic integrity and professionalism of national regulators, various interest groups and politicians chose to resist its decision, based not on a critique of specific imposed conditions or the net benefits determination, but rather that any approval of hydrocarbon infrastructure was simply an anathema to them. Was the process flawed, or did it simply provide the "wrong answer" to opponents of hydrocarbon development? How much the Canadian public, beyond those unconditionally opposed to any hydrocarbon development, shared distrust in existing regulatory processes was never substantiated publicly.

Nevertheless, this "meme" became a major distinction between the Harper Conservatives and Canada's two left-of-centre political parties. This isn't surprising considering that since Trudeau's election, his government has taken various steps to make the Canadian regulatory process more obstruction friendly, not less. Obvious examples include the announced intention to reconsider many of the Harper reforms of 2012; imposing a moratorium on north coast B.C. crude oil tanker traffic, even after Northern Gateway received its federal certificate for its project; rescoping the environment assessment criteria for existing applications such as Energy East and Kinder TMP expansion to consider "upstream" carbon effects; and expressing uncertainty about current Canadian carbon emission reduction targets, stringency, and allocation. These positions and initiatives portend the prospects for an efficient and predictable regulatory and political process for major hydrocarbon infrastructure as ever more dubious.[3]

Applying for a major energy infrastructure project, especially a pipeline on the scale of Energy East or Northern Gateway, costs hundreds of millions of dollars, given the expected rigor and fulsomeness of the applications and then the related cost of the actual hearing process. To take that risk, developers must be confident in a predictable and fair regulatory process. Otherwise the risk becomes untenable. An inherently unreliable regulatory process is unsustainable, yet that is exactly what each of Canada's major pipeline projects have recently faced and seem destined to continue facing. A regulatory process used to continually relitigate the basic legitimacy of hydrocarbon development in Canada on a project-by-project basis is utterly dysfunctional. Similarly, failing to recognize the highly evolved technology of hydrocarbon pipelining and global marine transport of hydrocarbon, crude oil, and LNG, inclusive of appropriate mitigation, would be equally dysfunctional. Unless of course the intention of the regulatory process is to facilitate obstruction.

At the scale of the financial commitment now required to mount such applications, no prudent management or corporate governance could countenance the risk of a regulatory process so vulnerable to politicians "changing the rules" in process and so unprepared to defer to the regulator's professional determinations on what constitutes reasonable mitigation and determination of national net benefits. What was presumed of Canada back in 2010 to 2012 in terms of the reliability of the entire regulatory system no longer holds. If the political level cannot abide the possibility of a project proceeding, then it ought to declare that at the outset, not enable a fundamentally disingenuous process to play out.

An obvious solution is to split the federal regulatory process for major hydrocarbon infrastructure into two separate phases — a structure that could avoid much of the dysfunction associated with the various projects that we have described. A first public interest determination phase would validate the project's basic economic merits and identify any "showstoppers"; that is, environmental or safety impacts that cannot be appropriately mitigated within conventional industry standards. The most basic question of "go/no-go" would presumably be resolved in this initial phase, as expeditiously as possible. Is the project economic, involving credible credit-worthy counterparties? Does Canada accept hydrocarbon development? Is hydrocarbon development consistent with national carbon policy? Are reasonably mitigated risks from the relevant conventional technologies acceptable, whether those technologies are pipelines, marine tankers, or gas compression and liquefaction facilities? This structure would force the political level to make any definitive intervention against a project as early as possible, before significant dollars were expended in fixing specific conditions on the project. It would provide a practical alternative to outcomes such as Obama's KXL denial and Trudeau's crude tanker moratorium that effectively disabled the Northern Gateway project.

This first phase would culminate in a national net benefits analysis. If a project was deemed in the public interest, then a second phase would determine the specific conditions to govern the project. The determinations of the regulators in the second phase would not be subject to political intervention. The applicant would still need to meet the conditions set by the regulator, but the issue of public interest would have been resolved. This structure allows project developers to receive such public interest sanction after spending millions of dollars, rather than hundreds of millions. In the case of TransMountain, for example, the first phase would determine whether tanker traffic carrying dilbit in Burrard Inlet, using conventional technology, was acceptable, as a matter of fundamental public policy. Likewise, if Canada will not accept any crude oil pipeline that enables incremental oil sands production, in turn increasing carbon emissions, that would have to be declared in the first phase. Political intervention could occur only at the end of this first phase, not once the project moved on to the second phase. If a project passes the initial public interest test, the project would proceed subject to the specific conditions determined in the second phase, at which point the developer and regulator will file extensive routing, engineering, and operating plans. Participation in the second phase would be more rigorously limited to those directly impacted or who had evidence relevant to the fixing of specific operating and construction conditions.

The first phase would employ filings broadly consistent with existing NEB guidelines for the "preliminary information package," inclusive of the project's basic economic justification, technology description, route, and special issues. Moreover, the first phase determination should not take longer than a year after filing, and should cost no developer more than $100 million for a project on the scale of Energy East or KXL. Also, the developer would describe the technology the project would employ. Projects using unconventional technology or in special applications of conventional technology may devolve to the more extensive second phase examination before a national interest determination can be made. But that decision would be made in the first phase.[4]

No country should expect to treat capital disingenuously without consequences. Simply put, it should not take hundreds of millions of dollars to get to a basic public interest determination, based on a national net benefits test, and resolution of whether applicable conventional technologies and their attendant risks can be reasonably mitigated.

The existing process is unbalanced and inefficient, prioritizing inclusion for its own sake with insufficient regard for probative value or direct impact. Replacing most oral testimony, including cross-examination, with written filings and interrogatories would dramatically expedite the process. Oral hearings with cross-examination should be the exception, not the rule.

This regulatory reinvention would appropriately deny politicians who rely on procrastination to finesse denial rather than take responsibility for clarifying basic policy that would directly impact whether a project could proceed. The regulatory process for specific projects should not be the default forum for basic public policy decisions. KXL and Northern Gateway show, if anything, that we need climate and energy development policy to be determined externally to the regulatory process.

Either producing hydrocarbons is consistent with national policy or it isn't. A transparent and democratically sanctioned carbon tax should resolve that basic question: pay the tax, internalize the cost, and go forward or not, allowing infrastructure developers and hydrocarbon producers to respond accordingly. Canada cannot bear another KXL experience, where, after seven years of regulatory process, the United States declared its "climate credibility" could not withstand enabling oil sands production. Neither should we tolerate another situation such as the Trudeau government implementing a crude oil tanker moratorium for the B.C. north coast after the regulatory process's determination in Northern Gateway's favour, including marine conditions on marine operations and their spill contingencies. Rescoping to include upstream carbon effects in the cases of TransMountain and Energy East again misplaces carbon policy on projects after the fact, and for effects for which they are not directly responsible.

If Canada clarifies its policy, whether that is simply a carbon tax or regulated alternative, then infrastructure developers can conform to that policy reality. Obviously if Canada establishes a carbon tax accepted as the moral equivalent of an actual emission reduction, then carbon impacts will be rendered irrelevant to any project's approval. On the other hand, if an emissions cap applies to a particular hydrocarbon sector, then infrastructure developers must clarify upfront a specific project's attributed incremental emissions. Whatever the rules are, a project conforms to them.

Restoring efficiency in our regulatory process for major hydrocarbon infrastructure is essential for Canada to reasonably seize its economic opportunities in the hydrocarbon sector. That objective should not be controversial, but of course it will be. It is not my purpose here to set out extensive NEB guidelines for this two-phase filing structure. But I do contend that the level of detail contained in the NEB preliminary information guidelines is likely sufficient, with overall cost of the first phase to the proponent not to exceed $100 million or last longer than a year from initial filing. Why waste resources in a disingenuous process? Why not force politicians to clarify as soon as possible where they are prepared to abide hydrocarbon resource development and its related infrastructure? This structure would force them to that declaration irrevocably as early as possible.

3. **Make the National Interest Determination Meaningful — Three Clarifications of Canadian Law**

The Northern Gateway experience represents a nadir in the Canadian regulatory, legal, and political system's ability to realize a project already determined to be in the public interest. The project endured a lengthened process that indulged implacable opposition, all in the name of inclusion and sensitivity to "social licence." And though Enbridge received a positive determination, at last, from the NEB, confirmed by Harper's federal Cabinet in spring 2014, it did not move forward with the project during his remaining tenure as prime minister, in part because Enbridge lacked confidence that the Harper government would sufficiently support it while British Columbia and various Aboriginal entities opposed the project, played out in litigation if not also in physically obstruction of actual construction and operations. Subsequently, Prime Minister Trudeau has undercut any chance of the project proceeding with his crude oil tanker moratorium for the B.C. north coast. What does an approval mean if it cannot lead reasonably to actual construction?

First, the primacy of federal determinations of nation interest with respect to major hydrocarbon infrastructure must be re-affirmed. Simply put, if the federal Cabinet sanctions a determination of the national regulator, inclusive of required conditions, then all other governments and stakeholders must defer to that decision. Those governments and stakeholders may participate in the federal regulatory process, bringing their evidence for consideration — that is the forum for them to raise issues, express their interests, and argue for the considerations they believe appropriate. But subsequent to a national interest determination, disgruntled provinces or municipalities must not be allowed to obstruct the approved project, for example by withholding necessary provincial level permits or providing appropriate enforcement to frustrate the federal decision. The federal government must clarify, legally, that the federal determination trumps all other jurisdictions; otherwise, what is the point of federal jurisdiction in the first place? Individual provinces could then assert conditions for approval or outright absolute opposition, but must ultimately defer to the federal determination.[5]

Second, all Canadians are subject to certain legal remedies available to project proponents, to ensure that projects can be completed once determined in the national interests. This means all Canadians, including Aboriginal people, notwithstanding the fiduciary responsibility of the Canadian government in respect of their rights and interests. Regardless of whatever unique rights they may enjoy vis-à-vis other Canadians, Aboriginal people cannot be extended a veto on resource development and its associated infrastructure. If Aboriginal people acquire legal title to land, that title is still subject to Canadian law, just like any other Canadian landowner. Most importantly, any landowner can be forced to provide access to infrastructure deemed in the national interest, albeit with adequate compensation. Transferring an absolute veto to one class of Canadian is fundamentally undemocratic, as well as economically self-destructive.[6] The NEB Act seems to indicate no unique carve out for any class of landowners,[7] yet ambiguity on this basic point persists.

With respect to compensation for land access for land owned or claimed by Aboriginals, the same basic principles should apply as for any other Canadian. These principles have evolved over time to reflect the value of access, not the value of the goods that are using the transportation infrastructure. The view that Canadian Aboriginals are entitled to a more generous financial compensation in light of historical circumstances cannot be so open-ended and extreme as to undo fundamental economics of the project. Compensation is bounded between conventional land access payments for non-Aboriginal Canadian landowners and a payment more equivalent to municipal and provincial property taxes. The federal government should ensure that proponents can achieve land access within such predictable financial limits when consensual agreements with Aboriginal land owners, or even those that claim land ownership, cannot be reached.

Other conditions imposed on a project, such as extending procurement opportunities to proximate Aboriginals groups, should be reasonable to accommodate — and the operative word is *extending*, not *guaranteeing*. Various social infrastructure investments in Aboriginal communities proximate to the project should fall to the federal and provincial governments, and to the self-government structures within Aboriginal communities themselves. Projects may choose to provide social infrastructure investment or contribute ongoing operating costs, but should not be obliged to do so.

Whatever legitimate grievances and claims Aboriginal people have with the Canadian government, their resolution should not frustrate the realization of legitimate value for the country as a whole. If the law is ambiguous on that point, Canadian political leadership has an obligation to clarify it. If what constitutes "compelling national interest" is unclear, clarify it. Otherwise, no project can reasonably undertake the risk of either the regulatory process or attempting actual construction. One would hope that all Canadians identify with capturing value for the country as a whole, subject to regulatory processes that ensure appropriate mitigation and consistent Canadian law. What constitutes reasonable compensation for access should not be a function of ethnicity.

It is dysfunctional that Canada has no objective standards of what constitutes adequate consultation and reasonable offers of accommodation. Without clarity, any project manifestly in the public interest can be subject to a veto by those who claim after the fact that consultation, let alone accommodation, was inadequate. That judgment cannot be left to jurists. Canadian Parliament has to step up to provide clarification.

Third, the federal government must enforce free trade between the provinces, especially in the context of hydrocarbons produced in one province traversing other provinces. The federal government must ensure that one province does not impose "transit taxes" on hydrocarbons, or any other product for that matter, moving across their jurisdiction. The regulatory process ensures that specific operating and construction conditions as well as potential financial contingency funds to mitigate and deal with potential incidents that may occur from operations, such as spills or other disruptions of service, adequately bind project proponents. But "transit taxes" imposed after the fact are at odds with the original federal determination of national net benefits, and even more importantly could disrupt the inherent economics of the project itself. Such an "after the fact" tactic would disrupt the basic economic premises that had predicated the project's original approval, how producing provinces and the federal government share resource rents, and distort existing federal transfer programs. Transit taxes could take various forms, some more transparent than others, from extreme property tax assessments to denial of perfunctory permits or an explicit tax on goods moved through pipeline infrastructure.[8]

Revisiting the distribution of resource rents between provinces and the federal government is a separate process, not an exercise to be played out against specific infrastructure. Ironically, a debate about sharing resource rents seemingly only occurs if a project actually happens, generating incremental hydrocarbon production or cash flows — economic value. Complaints about unreasonable risks relative to realized benefits typically ignore the integrity of the regulatory process to impose reasonable conditions on operations and construction and to ensure reasonable mitigation of those risks and adequate financial set-asides. Even more astonishing is opponents' refusal to acknowledge hydrocarbon pipelining as an imminently reasonable transportation mode in terms of pipeline safety. They also ignore that marine transport of crude oil occurs across the world on a daily basis, with no significant resistance, thanks to its safety record.

Section 121 of Canada's Constitution Act, 1867, reads, "All Articles of the Growth, Produce, or Manufacture of any one of the Provinces shall, from and after the Union, be admitted free into each of the other Provinces."[9] Interprovincial trade is not to be encumbered by taxes or their equivalent. This fundamental tenet of how Canada was intended to work has to be reinforced, especially in the context of market access for Canada's hydrocarbons. Is Canada a real country or a loosely connected network of fiefdoms? If one province gains the most economic benefit and another is compelled to bear some mitigated risk, the national interest test has to prevail.

4. **Enforce the Rights of Proponents**

All the measures I suggest are, of course, rendered impotent unless Canada enforces the rights of proponents, in real time, in the face of obstructive civil disobedience. This requires the political will to deploy law enforcement, in all its dimensions, even against civil disobedience carried out by protestors who claim some higher moral purpose or special entitlement. A national interest determination can't be an academic exercise, divorced from the real world, and governments waste their time endorsing such determinations if they are not prepared to enforce them. What could be more disingenuous than that? Yet we have seen examples of governments simply unwilling to enable construction and even access necessary to complete environmental assessments. In northern British Columbia, such disruptions impacted TransCanada's pipeline to support LNG development at Kitimat. TransCanada had to work around the Unis'tot'en clan blockade of traditional lands, at additional cost, after extended efforts to find accommodation. The unwillingness of the B.C. government to enforce access even for environmental assessment simply diminishes a project proponent's capacity to accept the risk of development expenditures, even assuming all other regulatory and economic considerations fall into place. This will to enforce can't be legislated, but rather depends on the resolve of elected politicians.[10]

We might conclude that Canadian law already affirms these basic tenets, leaving no need for clarification. But forcing proponents to litigate in order to reaffirm that reality is an utterly unproductive process, lengthy and costly. All of which might nullify in the first instance any attempt to pursue otherwise economic projects. Political leadership should provide the required reaffirmation legislatively.

CONCLUSION

The first state dinner in nineteen years between Canada and the United States occurred on March 10, 2016. President Barack Obama and Prime Minister Justin Trudeau exuded warm human connection and beaming smiles, based on shared convictions and instincts about various public issues but especially climate policy, confident history would remember them on the right side.[1] One was nearing the end of his turn of "hope and change" — everything was now legacy. The other had just started governing, and basked in the afterglow of an unexpected mandate. Both doubtless shared great contempt and disdain for Stephen Harper. Neither had any connection to the North American energy industry, nor to the private sector substantively. How numerate either of them may be, by education or subsequent career resumé, is unclear. Their appreciation of concepts such as physical risk, as engineers would understand it, and the distribution and mitigation of that risk, let alone physical and economic implications of energy transformation on the scale implied by the 2 °C containment target, remains at best unclear as well.

For me, this image of President Obama and Prime Minister Trudeau at the state dinner was a dismal postscript to the demise of Keystone XL. Two beaming idealists of dubious economic acumen, unctuous and full of moral certitude. But worst, a Canadian prime minister unwilling to genuinely identify with Canada's economic interests, preferring to pander to a foreign politician who had willfully and capriciously imposed a great cost on Canada, and to bask in the glow of friendly reception from the American liberal intelligentsia.

A month later in Edmonton, at the national convention of the New Democratic Party, Canada's explicit socialist political alternative passed a resolution to consider the "Leap Manifesto" as official party policy for the next federal election. The document details radical restructuring of the Canadian economy, including a swift end to producing and using fossil fuels. The NDP passed its resolution despite the vigorous objections of Alberta's socialist premier. Although by spring 2016 the NDP's national popularity had sunk to slightly above 10 percent, I find it significant that one of Canada's three major federal political parties dedicated itself to the complete deconstruction of the Canadian hydrocarbon industry.[2]

I reflected that the zeitgeist within Canada had changed so much. Was the Canadian polity actually willing to impose on itself great cost, likely higher in relative terms than its trading partners would impose on themselves, for the sake of dealing with the climate-change risk? Was I part of a generation, region, and class so truly passé and at odds with a changed reality that the only logical response was to move on — to go quietly into that good night as the poet said? I console myself with the conviction that when these costs actually assert themselves, some greater rationality will emerge. Sadly, however, opportunities may be lost for Canada by that point.

The most disheartening thought that grips me in the aftermath of Keystone XL's lengthy demise is just how little Canada has learned — as I write, in the summer of 2016, the country's political leadership may be on course to replicate Obama's procrastination, duplicity, and ultimate rejection of pipeline projects fundamentally economic, environmentally acceptable, and, for Canada, manifestly in the national interest. Proponents of major hydrocarbon infrastructure in this country endure a lengthy, potentially disingenuous decision process, with outcomes that may not relate to the actual regulatory assessment of benefits and mitigated environmental risk. Instead, left-wing politicians rationalize denying genuine approvals, in order to placate the more extreme elements of their political base, and to ensure their alignment with what they believe will be the judgment of history. This is the epitome of dysfunction. TransCanada and Canada suffered a great injustice when Barack Obama denied the Keystone XL pipeline. Canadian political leadership has already replicated that result with Northern Gateway, and seems ever more likely to similarly frustrate Energy East. Will the TransMountain expansion, and the LNG-related pipelines traversing British Columbia, be any different?

A distinction between Canada and the United States is that the larger, wealthier, and more economically diverse United States can better afford bad decisions. Canada has no margin for error. This country cannot afford to forsake genuine economic opportunities. Nor can it afford excessive altruism, disproportionate to what its competitors are prepared to impose on themselves. It cannot afford to ignore that hydrocarbon pipelining is a well-established technology, unmatched for safety and efficiency, applied globally. Or that world demand for crude oil and natural gas are actually going to grow for most of the remainder of this century. Or that a significant component of the U.S. crude oil market is best served by Canadian dilbit.

Canada needs a regulatory, legal, and political system that can actually deliver essential major hydrocarbon infrastructure — infrastructure with sufficient predictability that private capital is prepared to accept that risk. No source of capital, foreign or domestic, can bear the risk of dealing with a jurisdiction so hostile, equivocal, or disingenuous to provide what should be reasonably predictable approvals.

One could only hope that more of what passes for presumably non-partisan elites within Canada would have rallied to the issue of restoring market access and rational carbon policy as national priorities. Sadly, that was not to be the case. From the most senior leadership of Canadian chartered banks to Canada's mainstream public policy think tanks and in academia, few, if any, were prepared to publicly exhort Canadian politicians to see the issue of market access as a pre-eminent national imperative. Instead, too many chose to avoid confrontation with the Canadian left and environmental movement, preferring to indulge in the most platitudinous of rhetoric, a mix of self-interest and risk aversion dominated. To prove that point, simply do a Google search on market access and Canadian academia, Canadian think tanks, or Canadian corporate elites. If Canada actually wishes to eschew its hydrocarbon potential then that has to be sanctioned by our political process, with real parties absolutely transparent about where they stand. If it is prepared to extend special vetoes to one class of Canadian citizens regardless of national benefit from hydrocarbon development and its required infrastructure, a similar explicit democratic sanction must apply. If Canada will tolerate no risk of marine oil spills or LNG eruptions to Canadian coastlines, ditto. Don't create a pretense of potential approvals after a long and extended process, with expenditures of hundreds of millions of dollars, if those proposals had from the start no genuine prospect of approval.

I have laid out the litany of the Keystone XL experience in detail. An outrageous and unfair outcome was imposed on Canada. It is one thing for a foreign government to treat Canada so disingenuously, but even more incredible that Canada does it to itself. Here's how Canada can take action to restore its hydrocarbon potential while rationalizing that development to a world seemingly committed to dealing with climate-change risk:

1. Restore the primacy of a national interest determination based on net benefits, not the specific allocation of benefits and mitigated risks between regions. Provinces and municipalities do not have rights to deny projects once a federal approval has been provided.
2. Extend no veto to one class of Canadians, regardless of geographical location or ethnicity. Canadians must defer to federal determinations of national interest, and then not resort to civil disobedience or purely obstructive litigation. All Canadians are subject to the same law in terms of being subject to potential expropriation but with appropriate financial compensation for land access. Objective standards of what constitutes adequate consultation and accommodation have to be established, not left ambiguous, otherwise a "de facto" veto will have been created.
3. Capital cannot be left to guess what risks it faces before it embarks on hydrocarbon development. Provide policy when it is needed. Don't abdicate to a disingenuous approval process. Identify absolute show-stoppers as early as possible.

4. Ensure efficiency in the regulatory processes. Do not mistake legitimate due process with facilitation of obstruction. Real evidence, not opinion and ideology, ensure appropriate mitigations. Directly impacted stakeholders deserve standing, and the capacity to have their issues adequately addressed. The participation of others should be determined by what quality of evidence and argument they actually bring to proceedings.

5. Ensure that approvals can be utilized on the ground. It is pointless if governments provide approvals and then give no assurance of their commitment to ensure that the rights of successful applicants will be enforced. That means a willingness to confront civil disobedience and criminality when it occurs and regardless of whom carries it out. And, if necessary, ensure that the national interest is served even if other Canadian institutions choose to stymie federal determinations of national interest.

6. Finally, carbon. If any legitimacy exists for the unique animus toward Canadian hydrocarbon development, it rests on the reality of the carbon intensity of the oil sands production, relative to other comparable heavy oil sources in the world. I contend there is only one way to rationalize the climate risk with Canadian hydrocarbon development, and that is by carbon pricing via carbon taxes. The necessary formulation for Canada is simple: impose a carbon tax equivalent to what the major trading partners are prepared, explicitly or implicitly, to impose on themselves. In that manner, Canada can internalize the climate-change risk economically without explicitly constraining its hydrocarbon potential via either disingenuous or implausible emission reduction targets. If the world has the will the impose carbon prices high enough to constrain Canadian hydrocarbon production, then so be it. Such a carbon price will send an appropriate economic signal across the Canadian economy that will impact literally all facets of energy consumption, capital for energy substitution, and relative fuel choices. Underscore "appropriately," exclusive of mandates, regulations, and subsidies. Canada will commit to do as much on carbon as other relevant economies are prepared to do, but via carbon pricing as the standard of comparable efforts.

Such an elegant rationalization of carbon policy and hydrocarbon development can become Canada's real contribution to how the developed world comes to terms with dealing with the risk of climate change over the remainder of this century.

And then Alberta. It has contributed much financially to the rest of Canada in various ways since the 1950s. But the province's prospects are especially difficult today in the wake of the Keystone XL demise and Canadian dysfunction with respect to providing market access. For close to seventy years, Alberta has been unique within Canada, set apart by its hydrocarbon endowment. Wealth was genuinely available to significant numbers of the Alberta polity for at least two or three generations — wealth that was not a consequence of government transfer or deference to central Canadian economic priorities and delusions, but derived from a hydrocarbon endowment sustainable economically and environmentally over time despite the vicissitudes of commodity prices.

But now Alberta faces the challenge of rationalizing its hydrocarbon production in relation to climate-change risk. I propose terms upon which that can be done. But Alberta still depends on Canada and the United States for market access. Its traditional contributions to the rest of the country are seemingly of little account in the current morass. Other provinces' resentment or misplaced moralizing manifests in economically "shaking down" Alberta for that access, beyond accepted mitigation conditions, or simply denying that access on the basis of some misguided moralistic stance on climate change. I see a perverse desire to impose on Alberta a kind of comeuppance, even while the rest of the country, whether it knows it or not, only reduces its own economic interest over time by frustrating hydrocarbon development.

One hopes Alberta is not reduced to hoping against improbable odds that some future U.S. president will reconsider Keystone XL — the only pipeline alternative that substantially avoids the rest of the country.

As always, this comes down to national leadership, which has typically been dominated by central Canada. How it may treat Alberta in respect of market access may serve only to reduce its own economic prospects. An obvious quid pro quo should apply. Alberta has taken a lead in the country on carbon taxes and, despite some significant imperfections, on revenue neutrality and illogical caps and mandates.

I recognize that for some Canadians, the issues of market access and carbon policy are matters of moral imperative rather than technocratic assessments of national net benefits, economic value, and proportionate contributions.

It is also a reality that Canada is part of a group of developed economies accountable for most of the currently accumulated GHG concentrations in the atmosphere, notwithstanding now being in the vanguard of trying to deal credibly with the risk of climate change. Some of these countries share an imperfect history of the treatment of aboriginal people in the Americas. But these same countries, historically at least, have been committed to establishing the value of economic resources and the distribution of that value primarily through market mechanisms, and a governance of resource development by regulatory systems that employ transparent technocratic assessment of risks and benefits consistent with evolved tolerances and standards.

Conceding all of that, I sincerely hope that over the remainder of 2016, Canada makes decisions that dispel my current pessimism. Approvals of the Petronas LNG and Kinder TMP expansion by the current federal government, on terms that would allow those projects to proceed, would be profoundly constructive. If at least these two projects were approved by the federal Cabinet led by Justin Trudeau, that would be an enormously positive development, even if there is much left to deal with into the future, with respect to perfecting for Canada appropriate carbon policy and approval processes for major hydrocarbon projects.

Of course, the converse would be a dreadful outcome. Two denials would impose a devastating economic impact, first on Alberta and then in time on Canada. Dysfunction indeed.

Late on November 8, 2016, the United States elected Donald Trump as president, which will certainly change how the United States, and likely the world, deals with the climate change risk over the remainder of the decade and beyond. It may even lead to a revival of the Keystone XL project. Canada will still face the same challenge described in this book — how to best rationalize its hydrocarbon potential to what the world can actually do to deal with the risk of climate change.

NOTES

Introduction

(1) John Kerry, "Keystone XL Pipeline Permit Determination," *U.S. Department of State*, November 6, 2015, www.state.gov/secretary/remarks/2015/11/249249.htm.

(2) Dennis McConaghy, "Denial of Keystone XL: An Opportunity Lost," *Niskanen Center*, November 6, 2015, https://niskanencenter.org/blog/denial-of-keystone-xl-an-opportunity-lost.

(3) "TransCanada Asks State Department to Pause Keystone XL Review," *TransCanada*, November 2, 2015, www.transcanada.com/announcements-article.html?id=1998318&t.

(4) Lauren Krugel, "Ex Pipeline Exec Urges Stronger Climate Action," *Global News*, October 23, 2015, http://globalnews.ca/news/2293283/ex-pipeline-exec-urges-stronger-climate-action.

(5) Larry Liebert and Justin Sink, "U.S. Rejects TransCanada Request to Suspend Keystone Review," *Globe and Mail*, November 4, 2015, www.theglobeandmail.com/report-on-business/industry-news/energy-and-resources/us-rejects-transcanada-request-to-suspend-keystone-review/article27107033/.

(6) Coral Davenport, "Citing Climate Change, Obama Rejects Construction of Keystone XL Oil Pipeline," *New York Times*, November 6, 2015, www.nytimes.com/2015/11/07/us/obama-expected-to-reject-construction-of-keystone-xl-oil-pipeline.html.

(7) "Keystone Pipeline to Expand to Serve the U.S. Gulf Coast," *TransCanada*, July 16, 2008, www.transcanada.com/3066.html.

(8) Kristine L. Delkus, "TransCanada Keystone Pipeline, L.P., Application for Presidential Permit," *TransCanada*, September 19, 2008, https://keystonepipeline-xl.state.gov/documents/organization/181769.pdf; "TransCanada Keystone, L.P. Keystone XL

Project: Preliminary Environmental Report," *TransCanada*, September 2008, https://keystonepipeline-xl.state.gov/documents/organization/181768.pdf; "Keystone XL Project" [route maps], *TransCanada*, September 10, 2008, https://keystonepipeline-xl.state.gov/documents/organization/181766.pdf.

(9) Genevieve Walker, ed., "Final Supplemental Environmental Impact Statement for the Keystone XL Project: Executive Summary," *U.S. Department of State*, January 2014, https://keystonepipeline-xl.state.gov/documents/organization/221135.pdf.

(10) "Canada's Oil Sands: Opportunities and Challenges to 2015: An Update," *National Energy Board (NEB)*, June 2006, www.neb-one.gc.ca/nrg/sttstc/crdlndptrlmprdct/rprt/archive/pprtntsndchllngs20152006/pprtntsndchllngs20152006-eng.pdf; "Facts and Statistics," *Alberta Energy*, accessed June 2016, www.energy.alberta.ca/oilsands/791.asp.

(11) Alberta Energy Regulator. "Oil Production," *Alberta Government*, accessed May 2016, http://economicdashboard.alberta.ca/OilProduction.

(12) "Greenhouse Gas Emissions by Economic Sector," *Environment and Climate Change Canada*, last modified April 14, 2016, www.ec.gc.ca/indicateurs-indicators/default.asp?lang=en&n=F60DB708-1.

(13) David Suzuki, "Paris Changed Everything, So Why Are We Still Talking Pipelines?" *Desmog Canada*, January 28, 2016, www.desmog.ca/2016/01/28/david-suzuki-paris-changed-everything-so-why-are-we-still-talking-pipelines.

(14) "Canada's Emissions Trends," *Environment Canada*, 2014, https://ec.gc.ca/ges-ghg/E0533893-A985-4640-B3A2-008D8083D17D/ETR_E%202014.pdf; "Greenhouse Gas Emissions," *Canadian Association of Petroleum Producers*, accessed June 2016, www.capp.ca/responsible-development/air-and-climate/greenhouse-gas-emissions.

(15) "International Energy Outlook 2016," *U.S. Energy Information Administration*, May 11, 2016, www.eia.gov/forecasts/ieo/world.cfm.

(16) "World Energy Outlook Special Report 2015: Energy and Climate Change," *International Energy Agency*, 2015, www.iea.org/media/news/WEO_INDC_Paper_Final_WEB.PDF.

Chapter One: Getting to Keystone XL

(1) "Leduc No. 1," *Wikipedia*, accessed June 2016, https://en.wikipedia.org/wiki/Leduc_No._1.

(2) "Resource Ownership," *Alberta Culture and Tourism*, accessed June 2016, www.history.alberta.ca/EnergyHeritage/sands/underground-developments/energy-wars/resource-ownership.aspx.

(3) Rasoul Sorkhabi, "The First Oil Shock," *GeoExPro*, June 2015, www.geoexpro.com/articles/2015/06/the-first-oil-shock.

(4) "Energy Wars," *Alberta Culture and Tourism*, accessed June 2016, www.history.alberta.ca/energyheritage/sands/underground-developments/energy-wars/default.aspx.

(5) Laurel Graefe, "Oil Shock of 1978–1979," *Federal Reserve History*, November 22, 2013, www.federalreservehistory.org/Events/DetailView/40.

(6) Allan J. MacEachen, "The Budget," *Department of Finance Canada*, October 28, 1980, www.budget.gc.ca/pdfarch/1980-plan-eng.pdf.

(7) "30th Anniversary of the Deregulation of Canada's Natural Gas Prices," *NEB*, November 16, 2015, www.neb-one.gc.ca/nrg/ntgrtd/mrkt/prcstrdrtcl/qrtrlprcpdts/ftrrtcl/11-01nnvrsrdrgltn-eng.html.

(8) "About Canada's Greenhouse Gas Inventory," *Environment and Climate Change Canada*, April 15, 2016, https://ec.gc.ca/ges-ghg/default.asp?lang=En&n=3E38F6D3-1.

(9) Philip Shabecoff, "Global Warming Has Begun, Expert Tells Senate," *New York Times*, June 24, 1988, www.nytimes.com/1988/06/24/us/global-warming-has-begun-expert-tells-senate.html.

(10) "UNFCC — 20 Years of Effort and Achievement: Key Milestones in the Evolution of International Climate Policy," *United Nations Framework Convention on Climate Change (UNFCC)*, accessed June 2016, http://unfccc.int/timeline.

(11) "Kyoto Protocol," *UNFCCC*, accessed June 2016, http://unfccc.int/kyoto_protocol/items/2830.php.

(12) Bill Doskoch, "Canada and the Kyoto Protocol — A Timeline," *CTV News*, December 5, 2011, www.ctvnews.ca/canada-and-the-kyoto-protocol-a-timeline-1.732766.

(13) "World Crude Oil Consumption by Year," *Index Mundi*, accessed June 2016, www.indexmundi.com/energy.aspx.

(14) Kenneth P. Green and Taylor Jackson, "Safety in the Transportation of Oil and Gas: Pipelines or Rail?" *Fraser Institute*, August 2015, www.fraserinstitute.org/sites/default/files/safety-in-the-transportation-of-oil-and-gas-pipelines-or-rail-rev2.pdf.

(15) "Pipeline Ruptures," *NEB*, last modified September 16, 2015, www.neb-one.gc.ca/sftnvrnmnt/sft/pplnrptr/index-eng.html; "List of Pipeline Accidents in the United States in the 21st Century," *Wikipedia*, accessed June 2016, https://en.wikipedia.org/wiki/List_of_pipeline_accidents_in_the_United_States_in_the_21st_century.

(16) "Pipelines Map," *TransCanada*, 2010, www.transcanada.com/investor/annual_reports/2010/mda/pipelines_map.

(17) *Surface Rights Board*, 2016, http://surfacerights.alberta.ca; "Frequently Asked Questions — Compensation of Lands Acquired or Damaged for Pipelines," *Natural Resources Canada*, accessed June 2016, www.nrcan.gc.ca/energy/infrastructure/natural-gas/pipeline-arbitration-secretariat/5915.

(18) "Canada's Oil Sands — Opportunities and Challenges to 2015: An Update — Questions and Answers," *NEB*, last modified September 25, 2015, www.neb-one.gc.ca/nrg/sttstc/crdlndptrlmprdct/rprt/archive/pprtntsndchllngs20152006/qapprtntsndchllngs20152006-eng.html.

(19) "What are Oil Sands?" *Canadian Association of Petroleum Producers*, accessed June 2016, www.capp.ca/canadian-oil-and-natural-gas/oil-sands/what-are-oil-sands.

(20) "Oil Sands Development," *Canadian Association of Petroleum Producers*, accessed June 2016, www.capp.ca/canadian-oil-and-natural-gas/oil-sands/oil-sands-development.

(21) "International Energy Statistics," *U.S. Energy Information Administration*, accessed June 2016, www.eia.gov/cfapps/ipdbproject/IEDIndex3.cfm?tid=5&pid=57&aid=6.

(22) "Facts and Statistics," *Alberta Energy*, accessed June 2016, www.energy.alberta.ca/oilsands/791.asp.

(23) "Crude Oil (Petroleum) Monthly Price — U.S. Dollars per Barrel," *Index Mundi*, accessed June 2016, www.indexmundi.com/commodities/?commodity=crude-oil&months=180.

(24) "Oil and Gas Fiscal Regimes of the Western Canadian Provinces and Territories," *Energy Alberta*, July 2011, www.energy.alberta.ca/Tenure/pdfs/FISREG.pdf.

(25) Canwest News Service, "Harper: Canada an 'Energy Superpower,'" *National Post*, July 15, 2006.

(26) "Canada's Oil Sands," *NEB*, accessed June 2016, www.neb-one.gc.ca/nrg/sttstc/crdlndptrlmprdct/rprt/archive/pprtntsndchllngs20152006/qapprtntsndchllngs20152006-eng.html.

(27) "TransCanada Proposes Keystone Oil Pipeline Project," *TransCanada*, February 9, 2005, www.transcanada.com/3174.html.

(28) "TransCanada Secures Long-Term Commitments for Keystone Oil Pipeline Project," *TransCanada*, January 31, 2006, www.transcanada.com/3135.html.

(29) "TransCanada Files Application to Construct Keystone Oil Pipeline," *TransCanada*, December 13, 2006, www.transcanada.com/3159.html.

(30) "Keystone Oil Pipeline Achieves Key Milestone in U.S. Final Federal Environmental Impact Assessment Issued," *TransCanada*, January 11, 2008, www.transcanada.com/3020.html.

(31) "Keystone Oil Pipeline Receives Presidential Permit — Construction to Begin in Second Quarter of 2008," *TransCanada*, March 14, 2008, www.transcanada.com/3036.html; TransCanada Corp., "State Dept. Grants Keystone Permit; Work to Start in Q2," *Downstream Today*, March 17, 2008, www.downstreamtoday.com/news/article.aspx?a_id=9385.

(32) "Reasons for Decision in the Matter of TransCanada Keystone Pipeline GP Ltd.," *NEB*, July 2008, http://publications.gc.ca/collection_2008/neb-one/NE22-1-2008-7E.pdf.

(33) Josh Lederman, "Keystone XL Review Drags on 5 Times Longer Than Average," *CTV News*, August 12, 2015, www.ctvnews.ca/business/keystone-xl-review-drags-on-5-times-longer-than-average-1.2513010.

(34) "TransCanada Markets Keystone Pipeline Expansion and Cushing Extension," *TransCanada*, January 30, 2007, www.transcanada.com/3087.html.

(35) "Understanding Crude Oil and Product Markets," *American Petroleum Institute*, 2014, www.api.org/~/media/files/oil-and-natural-gas/crude-oil-product-markets/crude-oil-primer/understanding-crude-oil-and-product-markets-primer-high.pdf.

(36) "TransCanada Advances Keystone Oil Pipeline Project Expects to Commence Construction in Spring 2008," *TransCanada*, October 30, 2007, www.transcanada.com/3118.

(37) "Sandhills (Nebraska)," *Wikipedia*, accessed June 2016, https://en.wikipedia.org/wiki/Sandhills_(Nebraska).

(38) "Keystone Pipeline to Expand to Serve the U.S. Gulf Coast," *TransCanada*, July 16, 2008, www.transcanada.com/3066.html.

(39) "Presidential Permit Application," *U.S. Department of State*, accessed June 2016, https://keystonepipeline-xl.state.gov/archive/proj_docs/presidentialpermit/index.htm.

(40) "Permit for Alberta Clipper Pipeline Issued," *U.S. Department of State*, August 20, 2009, www.state.gov/r/pa/prs/ps/2009/aug/128164.htm.

(41) "TransCanada to Become Sole Owner of the Keystone Pipeline System," *TransCanada*, June 16, 2009, www.transcanada.com/3473.html.

(42) "Annual Report 2009," *TransCanada*.

(43) "TransCanada Keystone Pipeline GP Ltd. — Keystone XL Pipeline — OH-1-2009,"
NEB, accessed September 2016, www.neb-one.gc.ca/pplctnflng/mjrpp/archive/kstnxl/
kstnxl-eng.html.

Chapter Two: 2009 to August 2011 —
Nebraska and the Department of State

(1) "Supplemental Filing," *U.S. Department of State*, July 6, 2009, https://keystonepipeline-xl.
state.gov/archive/proj_docs/supplemental2009; "Proposed Action and Alternatives,"
U.S. Department of State, July 6, 2009, https://keystonepipeline-xl.state.gov/
documents/organization/181803.pdf.

(2) "TransCanada Keystone, L.P. Keystone XL Project: Preliminary Environmental Report,"
U.S. Department of State, September 2008, https://keystonepipeline-xl.state.gov/
documents/organization/181768.pdf.

(3) "Scoping Summary for the Keystone XL Project Environmental Impact Statement"
U.S. Department of State, May 2009, https://keystonepipeline-xl.state.gov/documents/
organization/182418.pdf.

(4) "The Nebraska Sandhills," *Nebraska Extension*, accessed June 2016, http://extension.
unl.edu/statewide/westcentral/gudmundsen/sandhills.

(5) "Media Advisory — TransCanada Launches Ads Featuring Ogallala Aquifer Expert,"
TransCanada, September 26, 2011, www.transcanada.com/5862.html.

(6) Saul Elbein, "Jane Kleeb vs. the Keystone Pipeline," *New York Times*, May 16, 2014,
www.nytimes.com/2014/05/18/magazine/jane-kleeb-vs-the-keystone-pipeline.html.

(7) "Bold Nebraska," *Wikipedia*, accessed June 2016, https://en.wikipedia.org/wiki/Bold_
Nebraska.

(8) Steven Mufson, "Keystone XL Pipeline Is Issue of Property Rights for Some Ranchers,"
Washington Post, July 27, 2012, www.washingtonpost.com/keystone-xl-pipeline-is-issue-
of-property-rights-for-some-ranchers/2012/07/27/gJQAqlQgDX_story.html.

(9) Elizabeth McGowan, "Nebraska Senator Asks State Department to Reroute Oil Sands
Pipeline," *InsideClimate News*, October 18, 2010, http://insideclimatenews.org/
news/20101018/nebraska-senator-asks-state-department-reroute-oil-sands-pipeline.

(10) Deena Winter, "Nebraska Has Been a Keystone XL Obstacle, but Support Is Strong,"
Nebraska Watchdog, April 29, 2014, http://watchdog.org/141722/keystone-xl-2.

(11) "Draft Environmental Impact Statement (DEIS)," *U.S. Department of State*, accessed
June 2016, https://keystonepipeline-xl.state.gov/archive/dos_docs/deis/index.htm.

(12) "Keystone XL DEIS Public Comment Meeting Schedule," *U.S. State Department*,
accessed June 2016, https://keystonepipeline-xl.state.gov/documents/organization/
182330.pdf.

(13) Shawn McCarthy, "The Day the Oil-Sands Battle Went Global," *Globe and Mail*,
January 21, 2012, www.theglobeandmail.com/report-on-business/industry-news/
energy-and-resources/the-day-the-oil-sands-battle-went-global/article546574; "Tar
Sands Invasion: How Dirty and Expensive Oil from Canada Threatens America's New
Energy Economy," *Natural Resources Defense Counci*, May 2010, www.nrdc.org/sites/
default/files/TarSandsInvasion.pdf.

(14) Elizabeth Orlando, "Public Comments of the Sierra Club, Et Al., on the TransCanada Keystone XL Pipeline Draft Environmental Impact Statement," *Bold Nebraska*, July 2, 2010, www.boldnebraska.org/uploaded/pdf/NationalPartners_KXLDEISComments7.2.10.pdf.

(15) Susan Casey-Lefkowitz, "House Members Say Proposed Tar Sands Pipeline Will Undermine Clean Energy Future," *NRDC*, June 23, 2010, www.nrdc.org/experts/susan-casey-lefkowitz/house-members-say-proposed-tar-sands-pipeline-will-undermine-clean.

(16) Deb Weinstein, "Protesters, Waxman Urge Clinton to Vote No on Tar Sands Pipeline," *Truthout*, July 9, 2010, http://truth-out.org/archive/component/k2/item/90598:protesters-waxman-urge-clinton-to-vote-no-on-tar-sands-pipeline.

(17) Kennan Zhong, "Environmental Impact Analysis and the Keystone XL Pipeline Project," *Sabin Center for Climate Change Law*, June 21, 2011, http://blogs.law.columbia.edu/climatechange/2011/06/21/environmental-impact-analysis-and-the-keystone-xl-pipeline-project.

(18) "Macondo Prospect," *Wikipedia*, accessed June 2016, https://en.wikipedia.org/wiki/Macondo_Prospect.

(19) Transportation Research Board, "Effects of Diluted Bitumen on Crude Oil Transmission Pipelines," *Pipeline and Hazardous Materials Safety Administration*, 2013, www.phmsa.dot.gov/staticfiles/PHMSA/DownloadableFiles/Files/Pipeline/Dilbit_1_Transmittal_to_Congress.pdf. See also Committee on the Effects of Diluted Bitumen on the Environment, Board on Chemical Sciences and Technology, Division on Earth and Life Studies, and National Academies of Sciences, Engineering, and Medicine, *Spills of Diluted Bitumen from Pipelines: A Comparative Study of Environmental Fate, Effects, and Response* (Washington, D.C.: National Academies Press, 2016).

(20) "State Department Announces Next Steps in Keystone XL Pipeline Permit Process," *U.S. Department of State*, March 15, 2011, www.state.gov/r/pa/prs/ps/2011/03/158402.htm.

(21) Luiza Ch. Savage, "Podesta: 'Green Oil Sands' Like 'Error-Free Deepwater Drilling,'" *Maclean's*, June 22, 2010, www.macleans.ca/authors/luiza-ch-savage/podesta-green-oil-sands-like-error-free-deepwater-drilling.

(22) Savage, "Hillary Clinton: 'Inclined to' Okay Keystone XL Pipeline," *Maclean's*, October 20, 2010, www.macleans.ca/authors/luiza-ch-savage/hillary-clinton-inclined-to-okay-keystone-xl-pipeline.

(23) Kate Sheppard, "Johanns Challenges Clinton on Keystone Pipeline," *Mother Jones*, October 21, 2010, www.motherjones.com/blue-marble/2010/10/johanns-challenges-clinton-keystone-pipeline.

(24) Russell Girling, "Keystone XL Pipeline Project," *TransCanada*, November 3, 2010, http://plainsjustice.org/files/Keystone_XL/TC%20letter%20to%20State%2011-3-10.pdf.

(25) "Final PHMSA Recommended Conditions for Keystone XL State Dept. Presidential Permit," *U.S. Department of State*, February 10, 2011, https://keystonepipeline-xl.state.gov/documents/organization/182257.pdf.

(26) "Draft Supplementary Environmental Impact Statement (SEIS)," *U.S. Department of State*, accessed June 2016, https://keystonepipeline-xl.state.gov/draftseis.

(27) "TransCanada Received Confirmation of Keystone Environmental Review," *TransCanada*, April 15, 2011, www.transcanada.com/5708.html.

(28) "Keystone XL Tar Sands Pipeline Timeline," *NRDC*, accessed June 2016, www.nrdc.org/sites/default/files/ene_11110201a.pdf.

(29) United States Environmental Protection Agency, "Full Text of 'EPA Letter,'" *Internet Archive*, June 6, 2011, https://archive.org/stream/205133-epa-letter/205133-epa-letter_djvu.txt.

Chapter Three: The Environmental Movement Discovers Keystone XL

(1) "National Resources Defense Council," *Wikipedia*, accessed June 2016, https://en.wikipedia.org/wiki/Natural_Resources_Defense_Council; "Environmental Defense Fund," *Wikipedia*, accessed June 2016, https://en.wikipedia.org/wiki/Environmental_Defense_Fund.

(2) Steve Easterbrook, "Timeline of Climate Modeling," *Prezi*, February 9, 2015, https://prezi.com/pakaaiek3nol/timeline-of-climate-modeling.

(3) William Nordhaus, "Can We Control Carbon Dioxide?" *International Institute for Applied Systems Analysis*, June 1975, http://webarchive.iiasa.ac.at/Admin/PUB/Documents/WP-75-063.pdf.

(4) James Hansen. "Statement of Dr. James Hansen, Director, NASA Goddard Institute for Space Studies," *ProCon*, June 23, 1988, http://climatechange.procon.org/sourcefiles/1988_Hansen_Senate_Testimony.pdf; "Global Warming Has Begun, Expert Tells Senate," *New York Times*, June 24, 1988, www.nytimes.com/1988/06/24/us/global-warming-has-begun-expert-tells-senate.html.

(5) Hervé Le Treut et al., "Historical Overview of Climate Change Science," in *Climate Change 2007: The Physical Science Basis. Contribution of Working Group I to the Fourth Assessment Report of the Intergovernmental Panel on Climate Change*, eds. S. Solomon et al. (Cambridge: Cambridge University Press, 2007), 93–127.

(6) *Intergovernmental Panel on Climate Change (IPCC)*, accessed June 2016, www.ipcc.ch.

(7) J.T. Houghton, G.J. Jenkins, and J.J. Ephraums, eds. *Climate Change: The IPCC Scientific Assessment* (Cambridge: Cambridge University Press, 1990).

(8) "United Nations Framework Convention on Climate Change," *UNFCCC*, 1992, https://unfccc.int/resource/docs/convkp/conveng.pdf; "IPCC Second Assessment Report: Climate Change 1995," *IPCC*, 1995, www.ipcc.ch/pdf/climate-changes-1995/ipcc-2nd-assessment/2nd-assessment-en.pdf.

(9) "Two Degrees: The History of Climate Change's Speed Limit," *Carbon Brief*, August 12, 2014, www.carbonbrief.org/two-degrees-the-history-of-climate-changes-speed-limit.

(10) Brad Plumer, "Two Degrees: The World Set a Simple Goal for Climate Change. We're Likely to Miss It," *Vox*, April 22, 2014, www.vox.com/2014/4/22/5551004/two-degrees.

(11) "Kyoto Protocol," *Wikipedia*, accessed June 2016, https://en.wikipedia.org/wiki/Kyoto_Protocol.

(12) Daniel L. Albritton et al., "Summary for Policymakers: A Report of Working Group I of the Intergovernmental Panel on Climate Change," *IPCC*, accessed June 2016, https://www.ipcc.ch/ipccreports/tar/vol4/english/pdf/wg1spm.pdf.

(13) Nicholas Stern, "Stern Review Report on the Economics of Climate Change," *National Archives*, 2006, http://webarchive.nationalarchives.gov.uk/20100407172811/www.hm-treasury.gov.uk/stern_review_report.htm.

(14) Fiona Harvey and Jim Pickard, "Stern Takes Bleaker View on Warming," *Financial Times*, April 17, 2008, www.ft.com/cms/s/0/f8e1377a-0c15-11dd-9840-0000779fd2ac.html.

(15) Andrew Logan and David Grossman, "ExxonMobil's Corporate Governance on Climate Change," *Ceres*, May 2006, www.ceres.org/resources/reports/exxonmobils--governance-on-climate-change-2006.

(16) "Kyoto Protocol," *Wikipedia*, accessed June 2016, https://en.wikipedia.org/wiki/Kyoto_Protocol.

(17) "Waxman-Markey Climate Bill," *SourceWatch*, accessed June 2016, www.sourcewatch.org/index.php/Waxman-Markey_Climate_Bill.

(18) John M. Broder, "'Cap and Trade' Loses Its Standing as Energy Policy of Choice," *New York Times*, March 25, 2010, www.nytimes.com/2010/03/26/science/earth/26climate.html.

(19) "Copenhagen Accord," *Wikipedia*, accessed June 2016, https://en.wikipedia.org/wiki/Copenhagen_Accord.

(20) Naomi Klein, *This Changes Everything: Capitalism vs. the Climate* (Toronto: Knopf Canada, 2014).

(21) "Why Did Copenhagen Fail to Deliver a Climate Deal?" *BBC News*, December 22, 2009, http://news.bbc.co.uk/2/hi/8426835.stm.

(22) Ryan Lizza, "As the World Burns: How the Senate and the White House Missed Their Best Chance to Deal with Climate Change," *New Yorker*, October 11, 2010, www.newyorker.com/magazine/2010/10/11/as-the-world-burns.

Chapter Four: How Keystone XL Became an Icon

(1) Hansen, "Silence Is Deadly," *Columbia University*, June 3, 2011, www.columbia.edu/~jeh1/mailings/2011/20110603_SilenceIsDeadly.pdf.

(2) Andrew Leach, "On the Potential for Oilsands to Add 200ppm of CO2 to the Atmosphere," *Rescuing the Frog*, June 4, 2011, http://andrewleach.ca/oilsands/on-the-potential-for-oilsands-to-add-200ppm-of-co2-to-the-atmosphere.

(3) Robert Kunzig and Peter Essick, "The Canadian Oil Boom: Scraping Bottom," *National Geographic*, March 2009, http://ngm.nationalgeographic.com/2009/03/canadian-oil-sands/kunzig-text.

(4) Jane Mayer, "Taking it to the Streets," *New Yorker*, November 28, 2011, www.newyorker.com/magazine/2011/11/28/taking-it-to-the-streets.

(5) Naomi Klein et al., "Environmental Leaders Call for Civil Disobedience to Stop the Keystone XL Pipeline," *Common Dreams*, June 23, 2011, www.commondreams.org/views/2011/06/23/environmental-leaders-call-civil-disobedience-stop-keystone-xl-pipeline.

(6) Bill McKibben and L.D. Gussin, "Why Cleantech Should Join the Fight against Tar Sands," *GreenBiz*, August 5, 2011, www.greenbiz.com/blog/2011/08/05/why-cleantech-should-join-fight-against-tar-sands.

(7) Hansen et. al., "Letter from Scientific Experts to President Obama regarding Authorization of the Keystone XL Pipeline," *Tar Sands Action*, August 3, 2011, http://tarsandsaction.org/2011/08/03/scientists-keystone-xl-obama.

(8) "Nation's Largest Environmental Organizations Stand Together to Oppose Oil Pipeline," *Tar Sands Action*, August 24, 2011, http://tarsandsaction.org/2011/08/24/nations-largest-environmental-organizations-stand-together-to-oppose-oil-pipeline.

(9) Naureen Khan, "How Environmental Activists Turned a Pipeline into a Climate Movement," *Al Jazeera America*, February 9, 2015, http://america.aljazeera.com/articles/2015/2/9/how-climate-activists-turned-a-pipeline-into-a-green-movement.html.

(10) Jacobs Consultancy and Life Cycle Associates, "Life Cycle Assessment Comparison of North American and Imported Crudes," *Alberta Innovates – Energy and Environment Solutions*, July 2009, http://eipa.alberta.ca/media/39640/life%20cycle%20analysis%20jacobs%20final%20report.pdf.

(11) Nathan Vanderklippe, "Keystone XL: The Benefits and Costs of a Controversial Pipeline," *Globe and Mail*, March 16, 2013, www.theglobeandmail.com/report-on-business/industry-news/energy-and-resources/keystone-xl-the-benefits-and-costs-of-a-controversial-pipeline/article9843273.

(12) Shawn McCarthy, "Keystone Pipeline Approval 'Complete No-Brainer,' Harper Says," *Globe and Mail*, September 21, 2011, www.theglobeandmail.com/news/politics/keystone-pipeline-approval-complete-no-brainer-harper-says/article4203332.

(13) "The Keystone XL Pipeline," *U.S. Chamber of Commerce*, accessed June 2016, www.energyxxi.org/keystone-xl-pipeline; "Keystone Pipeline XL," *API*, accessed June 2016, www.api.org/news-policy-and-issues/keystone-pipeline-xl; "165 Business Leaders Support Keystone XL in Letter to President Obama," *Business Roundtable*, October 11, 2013, http://businessroundtable.org/resources/165-business-leaders-support-keystone-xl-in-letter-to-president-obama.

(14) Ben Adler, "The Inside Story of the Campaign that Killed Keystone XL," *Vox*, November 7, 2015, www.vox.com/2015/11/7/9684012/keystone-pipeline-won.

(15) "Environmental Organizations Stand Together," *Tar Sands Action*.

(16) "Final Environmental Impact Statement (FEIS)," *U.S. Department of State*, accessed June 2016, https://keystonepipeline-xl.state.gov/archive/dos_docs/feis/index.htm; "Final Environmental Impact Statement Re-Affirms Limited Environmental Impact from Keystone XL Pipeline," *TransCanada*, August 26, 2011, www.transcanada.com/5852.html.

(17) "60% Favor Building Keystone XL Pipeline," *Rasmussen Reports*, November 23, 2011, www.rasmussenreports.com/public_content/politics/general_politics/november_2011/60_favor_building_keystone_xl_pipeline.

(18) Art Hovey, "Heineman Wants President to Deny Pipeline Permit," *Lincoln Journal Star*, August 31, 2011, http://journalstar.com/news/local/heineman-wants-president-to-deny-pipeline-permit/article_49eeb3fd-b4f1-5e79-99ae-aea09c7757ab.html.

(19) Lucia Graves, "Keystone XL Pipeline Obama's 'Biggest Climate Test,' Green Groups Say," *Huffington Post*, October 24, 2011, www.huffingtonpost.com/2011/08/24/lead-environmental-organizations-endorse-tar-sands-protests_n_935312.html.

(20) Bill McKibben, "The Keystone Pipeline Revolt: Why Mass Arrests Are Just the Beginning," *Rolling Stone*, September 28, 2011, www.rollingstone.com/politics/news/the-keystone-pipeline-revolt-why-mass-arrests-are-just-the-beginning-20110928.

(21) "Keystone XL Route through Nebraska Safest Choice," *TransCanada*, September 9, 2011, www.transcanada.com/5859.html.

(22) JoAnne Young, "Heineman Calls Nov. 1 Special Session on Pipeline," *Lincoln Journal Star*, October 24, 2011, http://journalstar.com/news/local/govt-and-politics/heineman-calls-nov-special-session-on-pipeline/article_6470fff1-66cd-5321-abdf-67fce3af343a.html.

(23) "Ten Thousand Turn Up for Largest Yet Keystone XL Protest," *National Post*, November 6, 2011, http://news.nationalpost.com/news/ten-thousand-turn-up-for-largest-yet-keystone-xl-protest.

(24) "Keystone XL Pipeline Is the Wrong Target for Protesters," *Washington Post*, October 10, 2011, www.washingtonpost.com/opinions/keystone-xl-pipeline-is-the-wrong-target-for-protesters/2011/10/07/gIQA4se6aL_story.html; "Say No to the Keystone XL," *New York Times*, October 2, 2011, www.nytimes.com/2011/10/03/opinion/say-no-to-the-keystone-xl.html.

(25) John M. Broder and Dan Frosch, "U.S. Delays Decision on Pipeline Until After Election," *New York Times*, November 10, 2011, www.nytimes.com/2011/11/11/us/politics/administration-to-delay-pipeline-decision-past-12-election.html.

Chapter Five: 2012 and 2013

(1) "TransCanada to Work with Department of State on New Keystone XL Route Options," *TransCanada*, November 10, 2011, www.transcanada.com/5893.html.

(2) "TransCanada Set to Re-Apply for Keystone XL Permit Proceeding with Gulf Coast Project," *TransCanada*, February 27, 2012, www.transcanada.com/5966.html.

(3) Jennifer A. Dlouhy, "Republicans Unveil Plan to Force Obama to Decide on Keystone XL," *Fuel Fix*, November 30, 2011, http://fuelfix.com/blog/2011/11/30/republicans-unveil-plan-to-force-obama-to-decide-on-keystone-xl.

(4) John M. Broder and Dan Frosch, "Rejecting Pipeline Proposal, Obama Blames Congress," *New York Times*, January 18, 2012, www.nytimes.com/2012/01/19/us/state-dept-to-put-oil-pipeline-on-hold.html.

(5) "TransCanada Will Re-Apply for a Keystone XL Permit," *TransCanada*, January 18, 2012, www.transcanada.com/5928.html.

(6) Sheldon Alberts, "Obama Trumpets Keystone XL Pipeline Support in Face of Republicans," *National Post*, March 22, 2012, http://news.nationalpost.com/news/analysis-obama-trumpets-keystone-xl-pipeline-support-in-face-of-repulbicans; "President Obama Speaks on Expanding Oil and Gas Pipelines," *YouTube*, March 22, 2012, www.youtube.com/watch?v=YxkODM6lzUk.

(7) "TransCanada Welcomes Approval of Keystone XL Pipeline Route Through Nebraska," *TransCanada*, January 22, 2013, www.transcanada.com/6191.html.

(8) Alberts, "TransCanada's New Route for Keystone XL — Out of the Sand Hills in Nebraska?" *canada.com*, April 19 2012, http://o.canada.com/news/transcanadas-new-route-for-keystone-xl-out-of-the-sand-hills-in-nebraska.

(9) "TransCanada Applies for Keystone XL Presidential Permit," *TransCanada*, May 4, 2012, www.transcanada.com/6040.html.

(10) McKibben, "Global Warming's Terrifying New Math," *Rolling Stone*, July 19, 2012, www.rollingstone.com/politics/news/global-warmings-terrifying-new-math-20120719.

(11) "Robert Redford Supports Keystone Pipeline Rejection by Obama," *YouTube*, January 20, 2012, www.youtube.com/watch?v=aCHNoUcxRvY.

(12) "Myths & Facts," *TransCanada*, accessed June 2016, www.keystone-xl.com/facts/myths-facts.

(13) Mark Drajem, "Billionaire Steyer Highlights Exports in Anti-Keystone Ad," *Bloomberg*, September 8, 2013, www.bloomberg.com/news/articles/2013-09-08/billionaire-steyer-highlights-exports-in-anti-keystone-ad; Ryan Lizza, "The President and the Pipeline," *New Yorker*, September 16, 2013, www.newyorker.com/magazine/2013/09/16/the-president-and-the-pipeline.

(14) "Keystone XL Pipeline Draws Broad Support," *Pew Research Center*, April 2, 2013, www.people-press.org/2013/04/02/keystone-xl-pipeline-draws-broad-support.

(15) Michael A. Levi, "Five Myths about the Keystone XL Pipeline," *Council on Foreign Relations*, January 18, 2012, www.cfr.org/world/five-myths-keystone-xl-pipeline/p27099.

(16) "A Good Call on the Pipeline," *New York Times*, January 18, 2012, www.nytimes.com/2012/01/19/opinion/a-good-call-on-the-keystone-xl-oil-pipeline.html.

(17) "U.S. Pipeline Contractors Association and Unions Pledge Their Support for Keystone XL Project," *TransCanada*, September 14, 2010, www.transcanada.com/announcements-article.html?id=1318593.

(18) Steven Greenhouse, "A.F.L.-C.I.O. Backs Keystone Oil Pipeline, If Indirectly," *New York Times*, February 27, 2013, www.nytimes.com/2013/02/28/business/energy-environment/afl-cio-backs-keystone-oil-pipeline-if-indirectly.html.

(19) "TransCanada: Nebraska Evaluation Report on Keystone XL Re-Route Released," *TransCanada*, January 7, 2013, www.transcanada.com/announcements-article.html?id=1673336.

(20) "Draft SEIS," *U.S. Department of State*; "TransCanada: Keystone XL Draft Supplemental Impact Statement Released," *TransCanada*, March 1, 2013, www.transcanada.com/announcements-article.html?id=1693671.

(21) "Prestigious, Non-Partisan Scientific Organization Finds Diluted Bitumen No Riskier Than Other Crude Oils," *TransCanada*, June 27, 2013, www.transcanada.com/announcements-article.html?id=1736016.

(22) "2013 Alberta Floods," *Wikipedia*, accessed June 2016, https://en.wikipedia.org/wiki/2013_Alberta_floods.

(23) "Remarks by the President on Climate Change," *White House*, June 25, 2013, www.whitehouse.gov/the-press-office/2013/06/25/remarks-president-climate-change.

(24) Justin Sink, "Obama Surprises on Keystone in Second-Term Climate Speech," *Hill*, June 25, 2013, http://thehill.com/policy/energy-environment/307649-in-climate-speech-obama-sets-carbon-limits-on-keystone.

(25) "Obama's Keystone Pipeline Rejection Is Hard to Accept," *Washington Post*, January 18, 2012, www.washingtonpost.com/opinions/obamas-keystone-pipeline-rejection-is-hard-to-accept/2012/01/18/gIQAf9UG9P_story.html.

(26) John M. Broder, "Foes Suggest a Tradeoff If Pipeline Is Approved," *New York Times*, May 8, 2013, www.nytimes.com/2013/05/09/business/energy-environment/a-call-for-quid-pro-quo-on-keystone-pipeline-approval.html; James Cowan, "A Simple Way to Save Keystone XL," *Maclean's*, March 15, 2013, www.macleans.ca/economy/business/a-

simple-way-to-save-keystone-xl; Gary Lamphier, "Redford Seeking 'Quid Pro Quo' From U.S. on Carbon Tax," *Edmonton Journal*, November 2, 2013, http://edmontonjournal.com/business/local-business/redford-seeking-quid-pro-quo-from-u-s-on-carbon-tax.

(27) Lizza, "The President and the Pipeline."

(28) McKibben, "Obama and Climate Change: The Real Story," *Rolling Stone*, December 17, 2013, www.rollingstone.com/politics/news/obama-and-climate-change-the-real-story-20131217.

Chapter Six: The End of Keystone XL

(1) Greg Quinn and Erik Schatzker, "Harper Says U.S. Approval of Keystone Pipeline 'No Brainer,'" *Bloomberg*, September 21, 2011, www.bloomberg.com/news/articles/2011-09-21/harper-says-approval-by-u-s-of-transcanada-oil-pipeline-is-a-no-brainer.

(2) "Specified Gas Emitters Regulation," *Alberta Environment and Parks*, February 9, 2016, http://aep.alberta.ca/climate-change/guidelines-legislation/specified-gas-emitters-regulation/default.aspx.

(3) CTV News Staff, "Dion Introduces 'Green Shift' Carbon Tax Plan," *CTV News*, June 19, 2008, www.ctvnews.ca/dion-introduces-green-shift-carbon-tax-plan-1.303506.

(4) "Canadian Federal Election, 2008," *Wikipedia*, accessed June 2016, https://en.wikipedia.org/wiki/Canadian_federal_election,_2008.

(5) Les Whittington, "Carbon Pricing Just a Tax Grab, Stephen Harper Says," *Toronto Star*, April 23, 2015, www.thestar.com/news/canada/2015/04/23/carbon-pricing-just-a-tax-grab-stephen-harper-says.html.

(6) "Canada's Emissions Trends," *Environment Canada*, October 2013, www.ec.gc.ca/ges-ghg/985F05FB-4744-4269-8C1A-D443F8A86814/1001-Canada's%20Emissions%20Trends%202013_e.pdf; "Canada," *Climate Action Tracker*, May 20, 2015, http://climateactiontracker.org/countries/canada.html.

(7) Bruce Cheadle, "Redford Says $40 Per Tonne Carbon Penalty No 'Magic Number' for Her Government," *Canadian Business*, April 10, 2013, www.canadianbusiness.com/business-news/redford-says-40-per-tonne-carbon-penalty-no-magic-bullet-for-her-government; Lamphier, "Redford Seeking 'Quid Pro Quo.'"

(8) Ken Cohen, "ExxonMobil and the Carbon Tax," *Energy Factor*, December 2, 2015, https://energyfactor.exxonmobil.com/corporate-citizenship-sustainability/exxonmobil-and-the-carbon-tax; Elliott Negin, "Does ExxonMobil Really Support a Carbon Tax?" *Huffington Post*, February 17, 2016, www.huffingtonpost.com/elliott-negin/does-exxonmobil-really-su_b_9246950.html.

(9) Juliet Eilperin and Steven Mufson, "State Department Releases Keystone XL Final Environmental Impact Statement," *Washington Post*, January 31, 2014, www.washingtonpost.com/business/economy/state-to-release-keystones-final-environmental-impact-statement-friday/2014/01/31/3a9bb25c-8a83-11e3-a5bd-844629433ba3_story.html; Walker, ed., "Executive Summary"; "Final Environmental Review Demonstrates Keystone XL Should Be Approved," *TransCanada*, January 31, 2014, www.transcanada.com/announcements-article.html?id=1804094.

(10) Katie Brown, "Keystone XL Opponents' Scrambled Response to the State Department's FEIS," *Oil Sands Fact Check*, February 3, 2014, www.oilsandsfactcheck.

org/2014/02/03/keystone-xl-opponents-scrambled-response-to-the-state-departments-feis; Molly Redden, "Here's What People Are Saying about the Big Keystone XL Report," *Mother Jones*, January 31, 2014, www.motherjones.com/blue-marble/2014/01; "State Department KXL Report: Now Up to Obama Reject Pipeline," *Popular Resistance*, January 31, 2014, www.popularresistance.org/state-department-kxl-report-now-it-is-up-to-obama; Tom Steyer, "Tom Steyer's Response to the Keystone XL Final Environmental Impact Statement," *EcoWatch*, February 1, 2014, http://ecowatch.com/2014/02/01/tom-steyers-keystone-xl-eis.

(11) Patrick Rucker and Valerie Volcovici, "Nebraska Court Invalidates State's Keystone Pipeline Approval," *Reuters*, February 19, 2014, www.reuters.com/article/us-usa-keystone-court-idUSBREA1I24520140219.

(12) "TransCanada Disappointed and Frustrated with Keystone Delay," *TransCanada*, April 21, 2014, www.transcanada.com/announcements-article.html?id=1830549; Elizabeth Kolbert, "A Delay Worth Celebrating? Obama Prolongs Keystone XL Fight," *New Yorker*, April 25, 2014, www.newyorker.com/news/daily-comment/a-delay-worth-celebrating-obama-prolongs-keystone-xl-fight.

(13) Elperin and Mufson, "As House Approves Keystone Pipeline Bill, Obama Veto Grows More Likely," *Washington Post*, November 14, 2014, www.washingtonpost.com/politics/as-house-approves-keystone-pipeline-obama-veto-grows-more-likely/2014/11/14/6f6daffc-6c15-11e4-a31c-77759fc1eacc_story.html; Paul Koring, "Keystone Pipeline Good for Canada Not U.S., Obama Says," *Globe and Mail*, November 14, 2014, www.theglobeandmail.com/news/world/obama-unmoved-as-us-house-set-to-back-keystone-today/article21585797.

(14) Lauren Carroll, "Obama Says Keystone XL Is for Exporting Oil Outside the U.S., Experts Disagree," *Politifact*, November 20, 2014, www.politifact.com/truth-o-meter/statements/2014/nov/20/barack-obama/obama-says-keystone-xl-exporting-oil-experts-disag/.

(15) "Canada's INDC Submission to the UNFCCC," *UNFCCC*, accessed June 2016, www4.unfccc.int/submissions/INDC/Published%20Documents/Canada/1/INDC%20-%20Canada%20-%20English.pdf.

(16) Susan Cornwell, "Senate Fails to Override Obama's Veto of Keystone XL Approval," *Reuters*, March 4, 2015, www.reuters.com/article/us-usa-keystone-senate-idUSKBN0M02BT20150304; Patrick Hickey, "The Senate Failed to Override Obama's Veto of the Keystone Pipeline. Here's Why," *Washington Post*, March 5, 2015, www.washingtonpost.com/blogs/monkey-cage/wp/2015/03/05/the-senate-failed-to-override-obamas-veto-of-the-keystone-pipeline-heres-why; Paul Koring, "Congress to Send Keystone XL Bill to Obama on Tuesday," *Globe and Mail*, February 23, 2015, www.theglobeandmail.com/report-on-business/industry-news/energy-and-resources/obama-intends-to-quietly-kill-off-keystone-xl-bill-white-house-confirms/article23155500/. Paul Koring, "Obama Vetoes Proposed Keystone XL Pipeline Bill," *Globe and Mail*, February 24, 2015, www.theglobeandmail.com/news/world/obama-keystone-pipeline-decision/article23180005.

(17) Suzanne Goldenberg, "Nebraska Court Approves Controversial Keystone XL Pipeline Route," *Guardian*, January 9, 2015, www.theguardian.com/environment/2015/jan/09/keystone-xl-pipeline-nebraska-supreme-court.

(18) Sara Shor, "Tuesday: Reject Keystone XL Now!" *350*, January 12, 2015, http://350.org/tuesday-reject-keystone-xl-now.

(19) Girling, "Keystone XL Pipeline Project; EPA Comment Letter on Final Supplemental EIS," *TransCanada*, February 10, 2015, www.keystone-xl.com/wp-content/uploads/2015/02/response-to-epa-letter.pdf.

(20) "Fact Sheet: U.S. Reports its 2025 Emissions Target to the UNFCCC," *White House*, March 31, 2015, www.whitehouse.gov/the-press-office/2015/03/31/fact-sheet-us-reports-its-2025-emissions-target-unfccc.

(21) Joe Nocera, "Bloomberg Sees a Way on Keystone," February 28, 2015, www.nytimes.com/2015/02/28/opinion/joe-nocera-bloomberg-sees-a-way-on-keystone.html.

(22) Pope Francis, "Encyclical Letter Laudato Si' of the Holy Father Francis on Care for Our Common Home," *Vatican Press*, May 24, 2015, http://w2.vatican.va/content/francesco/en/encyclicals/documents/papa-francesco_20150524_enciclica-laudato-si.html.

(23) "Record of Decision and National Interest Determination: TransCanada Keystone Pipeline, L.P. Application for Presidential Permit," *U.S. Department of State*, accessed June 2016, https://keystonepipeline-xl.state.gov/nid/249254.htm; Amy Harder and Colleen McCain Nelson, "Obama Administration Rejects Keystone XL Pipeline, Citing Climate Concerns," *Wall Street Journal*, November 6, 2015, www.wsj.com/articles/obama-administration-to-reject-keystone-xl-pipeline-citing-climate-concerns-1446825732.

(24) CTV News, "Five Key Points That Fueled John Kerry's Rejection of Keystone XL," *CTV News*, November 6, 2015, www.ctvnews.ca/politics/five-key-points-that-fuelled-john-kerry-s-rejection-of-keystone-xl-1.2646162.

(25) Kathleen Harris, "Justin Trudeau 'Disappointed' with U.S. Rejection of Keystone XL," *CBC News*, November 6, 2016, www.cbc.ca/news/politics/canada-keystone-pipeline-trudeau-obama-1.3307458.

(26) "TransCanada Media Advisory: Keystone XL Permit Denial Compromises Environment, Economy, Jobs and Public Safety in the U.S. and Canada," *TransCanada*, November 6, 2015, www.transcanada.com/announcements-article.html?id=2000079.

(27) "U.S. Field Production of Crude Oil," *U.S. Energy Information Administration*, accessed June 2016, www.eia.gov/dnav/pet/hist/LeafHandler.ashx?n=PET&s=MCRFPUS1&f=M.

Chapter Seven: Keystone XL's Haunting Questions

(1) "Annual Report 2009," *TransCanada*, 2009, www.transcanada.com/investor/annual_reports/2009/mda/pipelines/opportunities_and_developments/index.html.

(2) "TransCanada Reports Fourth Quarter and Year-End 2015 Financial Result," *TransCanada*, February 11, 2016, www.transcanada.com/announcements-article.html?id=2024640.

(3) "State and Trends of Carbon Pricing," *World Bank Group*, September 2015, www.worldbank.org/content/dam/Worldbank/document/Climate/State-and-Trend-Report-2015.pdf.

(4) Don Braid, "Notley Pitches Pipeline to Full Federal Cabinet," *Calgary Herald*, April 25, 2016, www.calgaryherald.com/news/politics/braid-notley-pitches-pipeline-approvals-to-full-federal-cabinet.

(5) Andrew Leach et al., "Climate Leadership: Report to the Minister," *Alberta Government*, November 20, 2015, www.alberta.ca/documents/climate/climate-leadership-report-to-minister.pdf

Chapter Eight: Canada Post-XL

(1) Jonathan Chait, "The Keystone Fight Is a Huge Environmentalist Mistake," *New York Magazine*, October 30, 2013, http://nymag.com/daily/intelligencer/2013/10/keystone-fight-a-huge-environmentalist-mistake.html; Levi, "Five Myths about the Keystone XL Pipeline"; Joe Nocera, "The Keystone XL Illusion," *New York Times*, January 16, 2015, www.nytimes.com/2015/01/17/opinion/joe-nocera-the-keystone-xl-illusion.html; Lisa Riordan Seville, "What Happens If the Keystone XL Pipeline Isn't Built?" *CNBC*, March 24, 2014, www.cnbc.com/2014/03/24/what-happens-if-the-keystone-xl-pipeline-isnt-built.html.

(2) "One of the Largest Private Infrastructure Projects in B.C. History," *Northern Gateway*, accessed June 2016, www.gatewayfacts.ca/Benefits/Jobs-And-Training.aspx.

(3) "Northern Gateway Project," *Enbridge*, accessed June 2016, www.enbridge.com/NorthernGatewayProject.aspx.

(4) "Volume 1: Overview and General Information of Enbridge Northern Gateway Project," Canadian Environmental Assessment Agency, May 2010, http://ceaa.gc.ca/050/documents_staticpost/cearref_21799/43499/Volume_1_-_Overview_and_General_Information.pdf.

(5) "The Joint Review Panel," *NEB*, accessed June 2016, http://gatewaypanel.review-examen.gc.ca/clf-nsi/bts/jntrvwpnl-eng.html.

(6) "Yinka Dene Alliance," *Wikipedia*, accessed June 2016, https://en.wikipedia.org/wiki/Yinka_Dene_Alliance.

(7) "Volume 2: Project Overview, Economics and General Information of Trans Mountain Expansion Project," *Kinder Morgan*, December 2013, http://transmountain.s3.amazonaws.com/application14/V2_PROJ_OVERVIEW/index.html.

(8) "Proposed Expansion," *Kinder Morgan*, accessed June 2016, www.transmountain.com/proposed-expansion.

(9) Harsha Walia, "Burnaby Mountain: Latest Wall of Opposition against Tar Sands," *Rabble*, November 4, 2014, http://rabble.ca/columnists/2014/11/burnaby-mountain-latest-wall-opposition-against-tar-sands.

(10) Jillian Bell, "Energy East Pipeline: What You Need to Know," *CBC*, January 26, 2016, www.cbc.ca/news/canada/energy-east-pipeline-explained-1.3420595; "Updated Study Confirms Real and Lasting Benefits for Canada," *TransCanada*, December 17, 2015, www.energyeastpipeline.com/updated-study-confirms-real-and-lasting-benefits-for-canada.

(12) "Energy East and Eastern Mainline Projects," *NEB*, accessed June 2016, www.one-neb.gc.ca/pplctnflng/mjrpp/nrgyst/index-eng.html.

(13) Natural Resources Canada, "National Energy Board Deems Energy East Pipeline Project Application Complete," *Government of Canada*, June 16, 2016, http://news.gc.ca/web/article-en.do?nid=1085749.

(14) Jean-Denis Fréchette, Parliamentary Budget Officer, "Canada's Greenhouse Gas Emissions: Developments, Prospects and Reductions," *Office of the Parliamentary Budget Officer*, April 21, 2016, www.pbo-dpb.gc.ca/web/default/files/Documents/Reports/2016/ClimateChange/PBO_Climate_Change_EN.pdf.

(15) Grant Bishop and Benjamin Dachis, "The National Energy Board's Limits in Assessing Upstream Greenhouse Gas Emissions," *Parliament of Canada*, accessed June 2016, www.parl.gc.ca/content/sen/committee/421/TRCM/Briefs/TRCM_2016-04-19_BrieffromBenjaminDachis_e.pdf.

(16) "Frequently Asked Questions about Aboriginal Peoples," *Indigenous and Northern Affairs Canada*, accessed June 2016, www.aadnc-aandc.gc.ca/eng/1100100013800/1100100013801.

(17) Mary C. Hurley, "The Crown's Fiduciary Relationship with Aboriginal Peoples," *Parliament of Canada*, December 18, 2002, www.lop.parl.gc.ca/content/lop/research-publications/prb0009-e.htm; "Aboriginal Consultation and Accommodation — Updated Guidelines for Federal Officials to Fulfill the Duty to Consult," *INAC*, March 2011, www.aadnc-aandc.gc.ca/eng/1100100014664/1100100014675.

(18) CBC News, "Tsilhqot'in First Nation Granted B.C. Title Claim in Supreme Court Ruling," *CBC News*, June 26, 2014, www.cbc.ca/news/politics/tsilhqot-in-first-nation-granted-b-c-title-claim-in-supreme-court-ruling-1.2688332; "Tsilhqot'in Nation v British Columbia," *Wikipedia*, accessed June 2016, https://en.wikipedia.org/wiki/Tsilhqot%27in_Nation_v_British_Columbia.

(19) Jonathan Fowlie, "Christy Clark Projects $100 Billion LNG Windfall for B.C. in Throne Speech," *Vancouver Sun*, February 11, 2013, www.vancouversun.com/news/Christy+Clark+projects+billion+windfall+throne+speech/7953712/story.html.

(20) "B.C.'s Five Conditions for Heavy-Oil Pipelines Reiterated at UBCM," *BC Gov News*, September 26, 2012, https://news.gov.bc.ca/stories/bcs-five-conditions-for-heavy-oil-pipelines-reiterated-at-ubcm; "BC Government Reaffirms All Five Conditions Must Be Met Before Support for Northern Gateway Pipeline Will Be Considered," *BC Gov News*, December 20, 2013, https://news.gov.bc.ca/stories/bc-government-reaffirms-all-five-conditions-must-be-met-before-support-for-northern-gateway-pipeline-1.

(21) Ian Bailey and Brent Jang, "Clark, Redford Have Framework for Pipeline Deal," *Globe and Mail*, November 6, 2013, www.theglobeandmail.com/news/national/clark-redford-reach-deal-on-pipelines/article15260483.

(22) Chris Varcoe, "Lack of Market Access for Oil Costing Province $3B Annually, Prentice Says," *Calgary Herald*, October 7, 2014, www.calgaryherald.com/business/Lack+market+access+costing+province+ annually+ Prentice+ says/10268084/story.html.

(23) "Report of the Joint Review Panel for the Enbridge Northern Gateway Project," *Government of Canada*, accessed June 2016, http://gatewaypanel.review-examen.gc.ca/clf-nsi/dcmnt/rcmndtnsrprt/rcmndtnsrprt-eng.html; CBC News, "Northern Gateway Pipeline Recommended for Federal Approval, with Conditions," *CBC News*, December 19, 2013, www.cbc.ca/news/canada/calgary/northern-gateway-pipeline-recommended-for-federal-approval-with-conditions-1.2470465.

(24) "Decision Statement Issued Under Section 54 of the *Canadian Environmental Assessment Act*, 2012 and Paragraph 104 (4) (b) of the *Jobs, Growth and Long-Term Prosperity Act*," *Government of Canada*, June 17, 2014, http://gatewaypanel.review-examen.gc.ca/clf-nsi/dcmnt/dcsnsttmnt-eng.html; Laura Payton and Susana Mas, "Northern Gateway Pipeline Approved with 209 Conditions," *CBC News*, June 17, 2014, www.cbc.ca/news/politics/northern-gateway-pipeline-approved-with-209-conditions-1.2678285.

(25) "B.C.'s Northern Gateway Pipeline," *Canadian Press*, 2013, http://cponline.thecanadianpress.com/graphics/2013/northern-gateway-timeline.

(26) "Enbridge Northern Gateway Project Joint Review Panel," *Government of Canada*, accessed June 2016, http://gatewaypanel.review-examen.gc.ca/clf-nsi/hm-eng.html.

(27) "Legal Backgrounder: What Are the Northern Gateway Court Challenges About?" *West Coast Environmental Law,* July 2015, http://wcel.org/sites/default/files/2015-07-16%20Backgrounder%20on%20Applicant%20arguments%20in%20Enbridge%20JR%20(final).pdf.

(28) David Bursey et al., "Northern Gateway: BC Supreme Court Rules That British Columbia Must Issue Its Own EA Decision and Consult First Nations," *Bennett Jones,* February 9, 2016, www.bennettjones.com/Publications/Updates/Northern_Gateway__BC_Supreme_Court_Rules_that_British_Columbia_Must_Issue_its_Own_EA_Decision_and_Consult_First_Nations; Krugel, "B.C. Supreme Court Hands Another Setback to Northern Gateway Pipeline," *CTV News,* January 13, 2016, www.ctvnews.ca/business/b-c-supreme-court-hands-another-setback-to-northern-gateway-pipeline-1.2736653.

(29) Sander Duncanson and Shawn Denstedt, "Federal Government Releases Draft Legislation to Reform Federal Regulatory System," *Osler,* April 27, 2012, www.osler.com/en/resources/regulations/2012/federal-government-releases-draft-legislation-to-r; James Munson, "The New National Energy Board: A User's Guide," *iPolitics,* May 3, 2012, http://ipolitics.ca/2012/05/03/the-new-national-energy-board-a-users-guide.

(30) Joe Oliver, "An Open Letter from Natural Resources Minister Joe Oliver," *Globe and Mail,* January 9, 2012, www.theglobeandmail.com/news/politics/an-open-letter-from-natural-resources-minister-joe-oliver/article4085663.

(31) "Government of Canada Accepts Recommendation to Impose 209 Conditions on Northern Gateway Proposal," *Natural Resources Canada,* accessed June 2016, http://news.gc.ca/web/article-en.do?nid=858469.

(32) Tracy Johnson, "Is Northern Gateway Quietly Being Shelved?" *CBC,* February 20, 2015, www.cbc.ca/news/business/is-northern-gateway-quietly-being-shelved 1.2965355.

(33) Brian Morton, "Trudeau Bans Oil Tankers on B.C.'s North Coast, Threatening Pipeline Plan," *Vancouver Sun,* November 14, 2015, www.vancouversun.com/business/trudeau+bans+tankers+north+coast+threatening+pipeline+plan/11515875/story.html.

(34) "13-05-23 Trans Mountain Pipeline ULC — Project Description for the Trans Mountain Expansion Project (A51996)," *NEB,* December 26, 2013, https://docs.neb-one.gc.ca/ll-eng/llisapi.dll?func=ll&objId=956916&objAction=browse.

(35) "Key Milestones for Trans Mountain Expansion Project Review," *NEB,* accessed June 2016, www.neb-one.gc.ca/pplctnflng/mjrpp/trnsmntnxpnsn/mlstns-eng.html.

(36) Chris Hall, "Trudeau Government Names Trans Mountain Environmental Review Panel," *CBC,* May 17, 2016, www.cbc.ca/news/politics/trans-mountain-kinder-morgan-pipeline-review-panel-1.3585154.

(37) "Trans Mountain Pipeline ULC — Trans Mountain Expansion," *NEB,* accessed June 2016, www.neb-one.gc.ca/pplctnflng/mjrpp/trnsmntnxpnsn/index-eng.html.

(38) "Energy East Pipeline Project," *TransCanada,* accessed June 2016, www.transcanada.com/energy-east-pipeline.html.

(39) Rebecca Penty and Andrew Mayeda, "Keystone Pipeline Alternative Faces $1-Billion Gas Feud That Could Kill Energy East Project," *Financial Post,* October 21, 2014, http://business.financialpost.com/news/energy/keystone-pipeline-alternative-faces-1-billion-gas-feud-that-could-kill-energy-east-project.

(40) Bell, "Energy East Pipeline: What You Need to Know."

(41) "Energy East Project Amended to Reflect Landowner, Environmental, Community and Customer Input," *TransCanada*, December 17, 2015, www.transcanada.com/announcements-article.html?id=2011835.

(42) CBC News, "Montreal Mayor Denis Coderre Says Energy East Pipeline Too Risky," *CBC News*, January 21, 2016, www.cbc.ca/news/canada/montreal/montreal-mayor-denis-coderre-energy-east-opposition-1.3413117; Geoffrey Morgan, "TransCanada's Energy East Application Needs to Be Simper, NEB Says," *Financial Post*, February 3, 2016, http://business.financialpost.com/news/energy/transcanada-energy-east-pipeline-project-to-create-120-jobs-in-quebec.

(43) Krugel, "Energy East Application Too Hard to Understand: National Energy Board," *CTV News*, February 3, 2016, www.ctvnews.ca/business/energy-east-application-too-hard-to-understand-national-energy-board-1.2763683.

(44) Bloomberg News, "TransCanada Submits Energy East to Deeper Review," *Calgary Herald*, April 23, 2016, http://calgaryherald.com/business/energy/transcanada-submits-energy-east-to-deeper-review.

(45) Natural Resources Canada, "National Energy Board Deems Energy East Pipeline Project Application Complete," *Government of Canada*, June 16, 2016, http://news.gc.ca/web/article-en.do?nid=1085749.

(46) Jeff Lewis, "Energy East Costs Jump to $15.7 Billion on Route Changes," *Globe and Mail*, December 17, 2015, www.theglobeandmail.com/report-on-business/industry-news/energy-and-resources/transcanada-files-new-energy-east-pipeline-plan-puts-cost-at-157-billion/article27800142.

(47) Jane Taber, "Premiers Reach 'Aspirational' Deal on National Energy Strategy," *BNN*, July 17, 2015.

(48) CBC News, "B.C., Alberta Premiers Agree on Pipeline Framework," *CBC News*, November 5, 2013, www.cbc.ca/news/canada/british-columbia/b-c-alberta-premiers-agree-on-pipeline-framework-1.2404544.

(49) Max Fawcett, "The Interview: Alberta Premier Jim Prentice on Pipelines, First Nations, and Why He Didn't Run for Prime Minister," *Alberta Oil*, January 5, 2015, www.albertaoilmagazine.com/2015/01/interview-jim-prentice.

(50) CBC News, "Alberta Election 2015 Results: NDP Wave Sweeps Across Province in Historic Win," *CBC News*, May 5, 2015, www.cbc.ca/news/elections/alberta-votes/alberta- election-2015-results-ndp-wave-sweeps-across-province-in-historic-win-1.3062605.

(51) Darcy Henton, "Notley Issues Fiery Stance on Pipeline Position in First NDP Period," *Calgary Herald*, June 16, 2015, http://calgaryherald.com/news/politics/notley-issues-fiery-stance-on-pipeline-position-in-first-ndp-question-period.

(52) Chris Fournier, Aoyon Ashraf, and Jeremy van Loon, "Alberta's Notley Says She Supports Trans Mountain, Energy East Pipelines," *Financial Post*, September 30, 2015, http://business.financialpost.com/news/energy/albertas-notley-says-she-supports-trans-mountain-energy-east-pipelines.

(53) Leach et al., "Climate Leadership: Report to Minister."

(54) Kristy Kirkup, "NDP Agrees to Debate Radical 'Leap Manifesto' That Calls to Wean Country Quickly Off Fossil Fuels," *National Post*, April 10, 2016, http://news.

nationalpost.com/news/canada/canadian-politics/ndp-agrees-to-debate-radical-leap-manifesto-that-calls-to-wean-country-quickly-off-fossil-fuels.

(55) Aaron Wherry, "Justin Trudeau Distances Himself from Harper at World Economic Forum in Davos," *CBC News*, January 20, 2016, www.cbc.ca/news/politics/justin-trudeau-arrives-davos-world-economic-forum-1.3411041.

(56) Bruce Campion-Smith, "Liberal Leader Justin Trudeau Talks Pipeline Politics," *Toronto Star*, September 10, 2015, www.thestar.com/news/canada/2015/09/10/liberal-leader-justin-trudeau-talks-pipeline-politics.html.

(57) "Trudeau Hopes for 'Fresh Start' with Obama After Keystone Rejection," *Sputnik*, November 6, 2015, http://sputniknews.com/politics/20151106/1029725626/trudeau-fresh-start-with-obama.html.

(58) CBC News, "Crude Oil Tanker Ban for B.C.'s North Coast Ordered by Trudeau," *CBC News*, November 13, 2015, www.cbc.ca/news/canada/british-columbia/crude-oil-tanker-traffic-moratorium-bc-north-coast-1.3318086.

(59) Graham Slaughter, "Pipeline Reviews to Include Environmental Regulations, First Nations Consultations," *CTV News*, January 27, 2016, www.ctvnews.ca/politics/pipeline-reviews-to-include-environmental-regulations-first-nations-consultations-1.2754062.

(60) James Fitz-Morris, "Justin Trudeau Promises 'Canadian Approach' to Climate Change," *CBC News*, November 23, 2015, www.cbc.ca/news/politics/trudeau-first-ministers-meet-climate-change-1.3331290.

(61) Cheadle, "Catherine McKenna Says Canada Won't Set Emissions Target, Tory Targets will be 'Floor,'" *CBC News*, November 9, 2015, www.cbc.ca/news/politics/catherine-mckenna-paris-talks-tory-target-1.3311482.

(62) Justin Trudeau, "Minister of Natural Resources Mandate Letter," *Office of the Prime Minister*, accessed June 2016, www.pm.gc.ca/eng/minister-natural-resources-mandate letter.

(63) NRC, "Governmental of Canada Moves to Restore Trust in Environmental Assessment," *Government of Canada*, January 27, 2016, http://news.gc.ca/web/article-en.do?nid=1029999.

(64) John Ivison, "Trudeau Convinced That Pipeline Strategy Must Be Top Priority," *National Post*, April 11, 2016, http://news.nationalpost.com/full-comment/john-ivison-trudeau-convinced-that-pipeline-strategy-must-be-top-priority.

(65) Shawn McCarthy and Jeff Lewis, "Court Overturns Ottawa's Approval of Northern Gateway Pipeline," *Globe and Mail*, June 30, 2016, www.theglobeandmail.com/report-on-business/industry-news/energy-and-resources/federal-court-overturns-ottawas-approval-of-northern-gateway-pipeline/article30703563.

Chapter Nine: A Credible and Proportionate Canadian Carbon Tax

(1) "Pricing Carbon Emissions," *David Suzuki Foundation*, accessed June 2016, http://davidsuzuki.org/issues/climate-change/science/climate-solutions/carbon-pricing.

(2) Adrian Morrow and Greg Keenan, "Ontario to Spend $7-Billion on Sweeping Climate Change Plan," *Globe and Mail*, May 16, 2016, www.theglobeandmail.com/news/national/ontario-to-spend-7-billion-in-sweeping-climate-change-plan/article30029081.

(3) "State and Trends of Carbon Pricing," *World Bank Group*.

(4) "Greenhouse Gas Abatement Cost Curves," *McKinsey & Company*, accessed June 2016, www.mckinsey.com/business-functions/sustainability-and-resource-productivity/our-insights/greenhouse-gas-abatement-cost-curves.

(5) See *Intergovernmental Panel on Climate Change*.

(6) Jason Kroft and Jay Kellerman, "Six Months and Counting for Ontario Cap-and-Trade — Are You Ready?" *Canadian Energy Law*, June 3, 2016, www.canadianenergylaw.com /2016/06/articles/climate-change/six-months-and-counting-for-ontario-capandtrade-are-you-ready.

(7) Romain Weikmans and Timmons Roberts, "Climate Finance: Time to Know Who Gives What," *Climate Strategies and Climate Policy Journal Blog*, May 16, 2016, https://climatestrategies.wordpress.com/category/paris-agreement.

(8) Shawn McCarthy, Daniel LeBlanc, "Liberal Government's Carbon Tax Plan Provokes Anger from Provinces," *Globe and Mail*, October 3, 2016, www.theglobeandmail.com/news/politics/liberals-to-set-carbon-price-at-10-a-tonne-in-2018-rising-to-50-by-2022/article32206937.

Chapter Ten: Restoring Market Access

(1) "Determining the Canadian Public Interest," *Government of Canada*, accessed June 2016, http://gatewaypanel.review-examen.gc.ca/clf-nsi/dcmnt/rcmndtnsrprt/rcmndtnsrprtvlm2chp2-eng.html.

(2) "What Does 'In the Public Interest' Mean?" *NEB*, accessed June 2016, www.neb-one.gc.ca/prtcptn/lndwnrgd/lndwnrgdch1-eng.html#q1.

(3) "National Energy Board Hearing Process Handbook," *NEB*, accessed June 2016, www.neb-one.gc.ca/prtcptn/hrng/hndbk/index-eng.html.

(4) "Pre-Application Project Descriptions," *NEB*, accessed June 2016, www.neb-one.gc.ca/bts/ctrg/gnnb/prpplctnprjctdscr-eng.html.

(5) "Paramountcy (Canada)," *Wikipedia*, accessed June 2016, https://en.wikipedia.org/wiki/Paramountcy_(Canada).

(6) Julie Gordon, "Canada's Aboriginals Tell Trudeau They Can Block Pipelines," May 20, 2016, http://ca.reuters.com/article/domesticNews/idCAKCN0YB2R7.

(7) "National Energy Board Act," *Justice Laws Website*, accessed June 2016, http://laws-lois.justice.gc.ca/eng/acts/N-7/page-1.html.

(8) Kevin Libin, "B.C., Alberta Pipeline Bartering Is Nothing More than Shoddy Protectionism," *Financial Post*, March 7, 2016, http://business.financialpost.com/fp-comment/kevin-libin-provinces-barter-piffle-for-pipelines.

(9) "Constitutions Acts, 1867 to 1982: Table of Contents," *Justice Laws Website*, accessed June 2016, http://laws-lois.justice.gc.ca/eng/const.

(10) Elizabeth McSheffrey, "What You Need to Know About the Unist'ot'en-Pipeline Standoff," *Vacouver Observer*, August 31, 2015, www.vancouverobserver.com/news/what-you-need-know-about-unistoten-pipeline-standoff.

Conclusion

(1) Robin Levinson King, "Trudeau, Obama like Best Buds During Lively State Dinner," *Toronto Star*, March 10, 2016, www.thestar.com/news/canada/2016/03/10/washington-gears-up-for-glamour-as-justin-trudeau-attends-state-dinner.html.

(2) Canadian Press, "Leap Manifesto: NDP Agrees to Explore Staunch Stance on Fossil Fuels," *CBC News*, April 10, 2016, www.cbc.ca/news/politics/ndp-to-debate-leap-manifesto-1.3529570.

FURTHER READING

I fully recommend the following list of books, reference materials, and opinion pieces to the reader for further exploration of the issues raised and arguments made in this book. Several relate to the actual regulatory record of the various projects discussed. Others more fully elaborate on various policy options for dealing the climate-change risk. Others deal with the economics of certain low-carbon options and projections of future energy utilization. I have also included Bill McKibben's seminal 2012 *Rolling Stone* article, "Global Warming's Terrifying New Math," as an eloquent articulation of the convictions of many who resisted the Keystone XL pipeline.

BP. "2016 Energy Outlook." www.bp.com/content/dam/bp/pdf/energy-economics/energy-outlook-2016/bp-energy-outlook-2016.pdf.

Chait, Jonathan. "The Keystone Fight Is a Huge Environmentalist Mistake." *New York*, October 30, 2013. http://nymag.com/daily/intelligencer/2013/10/keystone-fight-a-huge-environmentalist-mistake.html.

Climateactiontracker.org. http://climateactiontracker.org/countries/canada.html.

CoP21. *COP 21 — Final Agreement — Paris 2015: 2015 Paris United Nations Climate Change Conference.* CreateSpace Independent Publishing Platform (December 14, 2015).

Covert, Thomas, Michael Greenstone, and Christopher R. Knittel. "Will We Ever Stop Using Fossil Fuels?" *Journal of Economic Perspectives* 30, no. 1 (Winter 2016): http://pubs.aeaweb.org/doi/pdfplus/10.1257/jep.30.1.117.

Darwall, Rupert. *Age of Global Warming: A History.* London: Quartet Books Ltd., 2013.

Environment Canada. "Canada's Second Biennial Report on Climate Change." www.ec.gc.ca/GES-GHG/default.asp?lang=En&n=02D095CB-1#BR-Sec5-1.

Environment Canada. "Greenhouse Gas Emissions by Economic Sector." www. ec.gc.ca/indicateurs-indicators/F60DB708-6243-4A71-896B-6C7FB5CC7D01/ GHGEmissions_EN.pdf.

Environmental Protection Agency. "Estimates of the Social Cost of Carbon." www3.epa. gov/climatechange/EPAactivities/economics/scc.html.

Epstein, Alex. *The Moral Case for Fossil Fuels.* New York: Portfolio/Penguin, 2014.

ExxonMobil. "ExxonMobil's Perspectives on Climate Change." http://corporate. exxonmobil.com/en/current-issues/climate-policy/climate-perspectives/ engagement-to-address-climate-change.

ExxonMobil. "2016 Outlook for Energy." http://cdn.exxonmobil.com/~/media/global/ files/outlook-for-energy/2016/2016-outlook-for-energy.pdf

Girling, Russell. Letter to Amos Hochstein and Judith G. Garber re: Keystone XL Pipeline Project; EPA Comment Letter on Final Supplemental EIS. "TransCanada Rebuttal to the Environmental Protection Agency." February 10, 2015. www.globalwarming. org/wp-content/uploads/2015/02/TransCanada-Letter-to-State-Rebutting-EPA-GHG-Analysis-Feb-10-2015.pdf.

Henson, Robert. *The Thinking Person's Guide to Climate Change.* Revised edition. Chicago: University of Chicago Press, 2014.

Hsu, Shi-Ling. *The Case for a Carbon Tax: Getting Past Our Hang-ups to Effective Climate Policy.* 2nd ed. Washington, D.C.: Island Press, 2011.

Intergovernmental Panel on Climate Change. *Climate Change 2014: Mitigation of Climate Change: Working Group III Contribution to the IPCC Fifth Assessment Report.* Cambridge, U.K.: Cambridge University Press, 2015.

International Emissions Trading Association. www.ieta.org/The-Worlds-Carbon-Markets.

Leach Report to the Alberta Government on Climate Policy. November 2015. www.alberta. ca/documents/climate/climate-leadership-report-to-minister.pdf.

Levi, Michael. "Five Myths About the Keystone XL Pipeline." *Council on Foreign Relations.* January 18, 2012. www.cfr.org/world/five-myths-keystone-xl-pipeline/p27099.

Massachusetts Institute of Technology. "The Future of Natural Gas." 2011 http://energy. mit.edu/wp-content/uploads/2011/06/MITEI-The-Future-of-Natural-Gas.pdf.

———. "The Future of Solar Energy." 2015. http://energy.mit.edu/wp-content/ uploads/2015/05/MITEI-The-Future-of-Solar-Energy.pdf.

———. "On the Road Toward 2050: Potential for Substantial Reductions in Light-Duty Vehicle Energy Use and Greenhouse Gas Emissions." November 2015. http://energy. mit.edu/wp-content/uploads/2015/12/MITEI-RP-2015-001.pdf.

McKibben, Bill. "Global Warming's Terrifying New Math." *Rolling Stone,* July 19, 2012. www. rollingstone.com/politics/news/global-warmings-terrifying-new-math-20120719.

McKinsey & Company. "Greenhouse Gas Abatement Cost Curves." Last modified December 19, 2013. www.mckinsey.com/business-functions/sustainability-and-resource-productivity/ our-insights/greenhouse-gas-abatement-cost-curves.

National Energy Board. "Recommendations for Approval of Northern Gateway Project."

Last modified December 19, 2013. http://gatewaypanel.review-examen.gc.ca/clf-nsi/dcmnt/rcmndtnsrprt/rcmndtnsrprt-eng.html.

———. "Recommendations for Approval of TransMountain Pipeline Expansion." Last modified May 16, 2016. www.neb-one.gc.ca/pplctnflng/mjrpp/trnsmntnxpnsn/smmrrcmmndtn-eng.html.

Nordhaus, William D. *Climate Casino*. New Haven, CT: Yale University Press, 2015.

Oliver, Joe. "An Open Letter from Natural Resources Minister Joe Oliver." *Globe and Mail*, January 9, 2012. www.theglobeandmail.com/news/politics/an-open-letter-from-natural-resources-minister-joe-oliver/article4085663.

Pielke, Roger, Jr. *The Rightful Place of Science: Disasters and Climate Change*. Tempe, AZ: Consortium for Science, Policy, & Outcomes, 2014.

Stern, Nicholas. *The Economics of Climate Change: The Stern Review*. Cambridge, U.K.: Cambridge University Press, 2007.

Taylor, Jerry. "The Conservative Case for a Carbon Tax." Niskanen Center. March 23, 2015. http://niskanencenter.org/wp-content/uploads/2015/03/The-Conservative-Case-for-a-Carbon-Tax1.pdf.

Tol, Richard S.J. *Climate Economics: Economic Analysis of Climate, Climate Change and Climate Policy*. Cheltenham, U.K.: Edward Elgar Publishing, 2014.

The United States Government. "Keystone XL Project Executive Summary: Final Supplemental Environmental Impact Statement." InterWorld Publishing Inc., 2014.

ACKNOWLEDGEMENTS

My thanks to Naomi Lewis, who contributed so much over the process of converting my recollections and insights into a compelling manuscript. A wonderful colleague.

Special thanks to the entire team at Dundurn Press for supporting this project, with particular recognition for Dominic Farrell and Kirk Howard for their contributions. Thanks also to Carrie Gleason, Kathryn Lane, Cheryl Hawley, Courtney Horner, and Jennifer Gallinger. And thanks to Kendra Martin. I very much appreciated them.

To my wife, Maureen, who always provided me with both the support and challenge to undertake and complete this project.

To my former professional colleagues, Bill Langford, Don Whishart, and Peter Krushelnicki, special thanks for their help with this project, their recollections, and corrections and support.

Thanks to Jim Prentice, Jack Mintz, Andrew Leach, and Joe Oliver for their review and endorsement of the book.

Thanks to TransCanada, Enbridge, and TransMountain for their generous provision of maps for inclusion in the book.

IMAGE CREDITS

INDEX

dundurn.com   dundurnpress

@dundurnpress   dundurnpress

dundurnpress   info@dundurn.com

FIND US ON NETGALLEY & GOODREADS TOO!

DUNDURN